SCHOLASTIC

PHONICS

A COMPLETE SYNTHETIC PROGRAMME

WENDY JOLLIFFE

FOR AGES 4+

Author
Wendy Jolliffe

Illustrations
Gaynor Berry

Editor
Victoria Lee

Series Designer
Anna Oliwa

Assistant Editor
Rachel Mackinnon

Designer
Erik Ivens

With thanks to Carol Ogden for her expertise and advice

Acknowledgements
The publishers gratefully acknowledge permission to reproduce the following copyright material:
Mallinson Rendel for the use of an extract and illustration from *Hairy Maclary from Donaldson's Dairy* by Lynley Dodd © 1983, Lynley Dodd (1983, Mallinson Rendel Publishers Ltd., Wellington, New Zealand).
Walker Books for the use of an extract from *Sound City* by Sarah Hayes, illustrated by Margaret Chamberlain © 1998, Sarah Hayes (1998, Walker Books).
Celia Warren is the author of the following poems 'Let's tap out a pattern song' © 2006, Celia Warren; the poem 'Humpty Dumpties' © 2006, Celia Warren; the puppet play 'Listen to me' © 2006, Celia Warren (all previously unpublished) and the poem 'Lots of socks' © 2005, Celia Warren, first published in *Bouncing with the budgie* by Celia Warren (2005, QED) and the seven phonic related stories *Minibooks 1–7* © 2006, Celia Warren (previously unpublished).
Every effort has been made to trace copyright holders for the works reproduced in this book, and the publishers apologise for any inadvertent omissions.

Text © 2006 Wendy Jolliffe
© 2006 Scholastic Ltd

Designed using Adobe InDesign

Published by Scholastic Ltd
Villiers House
Clarendon Avenue
Leamington Spa
Warwickshire CV32 5PR

www.scholastic.co.uk

Printed by Bell and Bain Ltd.

1 2 3 4 5 6 7 8 9   6 7 8 9 0 1 2 3 4 5

British Library Cataloguing-in-Publication Data
A catalogue record for this book is available from the British Library.

ISBN 0-439-94496-1
ISBN 978-0439-4496-0

The right of Wendy Jolliffe to be identified as the author of this work has been asserted by her in accordance with the Copyright, Designs and Patents Act 1988.

Extracts from The National Literacy Strategy © Crown copyright. Reproduced under the terms of HMSO Guidance Note 8.

Due to the nature of the web, we cannot guarantee the content or links of any site mentioned. We strongly recommend that teachers check websites before using them in the classroom.

PHONICS:
CONTENTS

PHONICS
INTRODUCTION

WHY PHONICS?
Phonics has recently been the subject of much debate, research and media coverage. So what do we now know that is important for teaching reading and spelling?

■ Phonics is a key strategy in learning to read as has been shown by a range of research over the last 20 years.

■ A systematic phonics programme, taught fast and early, as shown by the study in Clackmannanshire, Scotland, and other studies showed that children taught using systematic phonics made better progress in reading and spelling.

■ The Rose Review of the teaching of early reading (March, 2006) has concluded that the case for systematic phonic work is overwhelming and much strengthened by a synthetic approach.

WHY HAS SYSTEMATIC PHONICS NOT BEEN TAUGHT MORE WIDELY BEFORE?
While many teachers have been teaching phonics, some very successfully using multi-sensory approaches, the following are reasons for a general lack of coherent and systematic teaching.

Lack of subject knowledge
English is complex – we have approximately 44 phonemes (sounds) represented by 26 letters. Therefore it requires extensive knowledge by teachers in order to teach it successfully. The complexity of English is shown by the fact that English-speaking children take two, to two and a half times as long to reach the same level of competence with reading as other European languages, with Finnish having the simplest structure. Other European countries have long relied on phonics as the main method of teaching reading.

Irregular words
There are a number of words in English that do not appear to be phonetically regular. For many teachers and parents the simple fact that words such as '/w/a/s/' spelled phonetically will never blend into the word 'was' (at least on the surface), shows that English cannot be taught phonetically. Yet estimates show that the English spelling system is about '75 per cent regular'.

Previous teaching methods were unhelpful
Approaches to phonics instruction that teach sounds that match a letter are confusing because of the possible correspondences involved. For example, the sound /f/ can be written with the letter 'f', but also commonly with 'ph' as in 'phone' or 'ff' as in 'coffee'. The most effective phonics instruction teaches children to identify phonemes in spoken language first, then to understand how these are represented by letters and letter combinations (graphemes). In addition, it is important to make clear that it is not just one letter that can make a phoneme, it can be two, as in /Ph/i/l/ or three as in /l/igh/t/.

APPROACHES TO TEACHING PHONICS
Synthetic phonics
The term 'synthetic phonics' has become widely used since the report on the Clackmannanshire study.

Synthetic phonics is an approach where the sounds and the corresponding letters are learned first, pronounced in isolation, and then children are taught to blend the sounds together (for example: /c/a/t/ makes 'cat') to make words. They also learn to segment words into phonemes (for example: 'pen' – /p/e/n/).

Analytic phonics
This is where sounds are taught in connection with words and not in isolation. So that children learn, for example, that a number of words share the same initial sound, as in 'bat', 'bus', 'beg' and 'bill'. Children therefore learn phonics by deduction from texts and the teacher draws attention to letter sounds as they occur. There is often an emphasis on learning to blend sounds by analogy, so if they read 'hand' they can read 'sand', and so on.

Key differences
One of the key differences between the two approaches is the emphasis that is placed on phonics in the teaching of reading. With the synthetic method, children focus on learning the sounds

and corresponding letters and initially read only phonetically regular reading books. With analytic phonics children learn about sounds through words and combine learning phonics with the use of other reading strategies, such as learning whole words or using the context or grammatical structure of the sentence to read a word (such as, 'He.........his bike fast.'). These have been referred to in the National Literacy Strategy as 'searchlights', although the recommendation of the Rose Review of the teaching of early reading is that this concept should be restructured to reflect the importance of word recognition and comprehension.

KEY ISSUES FOR THE SUCCESSFUL TEACHING OF PHONICS
Fast and early and systematic

Children can learn phonics quickly, that is, by the end of Reception (depending on the maturity of the child) and there are substantial benefits in early reading and writing as it releases mental capacity for comprehension and composition. The Clackmannanshire study shows a much faster pace than has previously been recommended by the National Literacy Strategy.

This has been backed up by other research in the United States. Learning phonics early provides children with the tools to decode and can

significantly impact on their progress with spelling.

It is, however, important to bear in mind that children develop at different rates. For some children, progress will need to be slower with frequent practice and over-learning. This is particularly true with children who have dyslexia. Accurate assessment of progress is therefore a vital feature of the successful teaching and learning of phonics.

Blending and segmenting

As soon as children have mastered a few phonemes, it is important that blending and segmenting are specifically taught (see Stage 2). To do this it is important that some vowel phonemes are introduced early. This programme, therefore, teaches some short vowel phonemes by Lesson 10 and incorporates blending, initially with CVC words (for example, 'cat').

It is important to begin blending and segmenting as soon as possible so that children can apply the skills they are learning. Both of these can be taught successfully to young children using 'robot talk' as described in Stage 2 on pages 36 and 37.

Accurate assessment of progress

Teaching needs to be pitched appropriately to children's ability and, for this purpose, assessments are a key aspect of the programme. This consists of the ability to identify sounds correctly, then not only to learn the phonemes and match them to graphemes, but also to blend the sounds together for reading and segment them for spelling. Accurate assessment of children's progress needs to be made regularly before continuing with each stage of the programme, ensuring that it is tailored to children's needs. It is important to provide support for those children who are not progressing well, as early intervention and support can be vital to later success.

Sight vocabulary

The National Literacy Strategy introduces 45 words by the end of Reception and a further 150 words between Year 1 and Year 2 to be learned as high frequency words. Many of these words can be decoded phonetically, and it is therefore only necessary to teach a small number as high frequency or 'sight' words. A list of these words is included in the Revision Lesson (39/40) for Stage 3 on page 120.

Teaching methods

It is also important that young children are not expected to sit for lengthy sessions listening to the teacher, or to complete inappropriate pencil and paper activities. Phonics should be predominately oral, however it is important to make links between hearing, reading and writing the phonemes. This should not mean worksheets! The teaching methods described here are multi-sensory, to support young children's learning. The importance of play and informal learning for young children is well documented, but the short focused sessions described here can take place within a play-rich curriculum. Group focused tasks together with some larger group/class games and songs are part of an effective Foundation Stage provision, which is how many of these activities can be carried out. All of this work should be alongside introducing children to the wealth of children's literature to support a love of reading.

Understanding the phoneme-grapheme correspondence

Teachers need a clear understanding of the phoneme-grapheme correspondence (that is: how the sounds are represented by letters) of the English language. This consists of 44 phonemes, although this number varies slightly, according to different phonetic interpretations. However the International Phonetic Alphabet agrees on 44 and this forms the basis of this programme (and indeed many others). The chart below denotes these, together with the most common graphemes (spellings).

Phoneme-grapheme chart

Consonant phonemes and short vowel phonemes			
Phoneme	Common spellings	Phoneme	Common spellings
/s/	sun, mouse, city, mess, science, mice	/f/	fish, photo, coffee
/a/	apple	/l/	leg, spell
/t/	tap, better	/h/	hat
/p/	paper, hippo	/sh/	ship, mission, chef
/i/	ink, bucket	/z/	zebra, please, is, fizzy, sneeze
/n/	noise, knife, gnat	/w/	water, wheel, queen
/e/	egg, bread	/ch/	chip, watch
/d/	dog, puddle	/j/	jug, judge, giant, barge
/m/	man, hammer, comb	/v/	van, drive
/g/	game, egg	/y/	yes
/o/	octopus, want	/th/	thin
/c/ /k/	cat, Chris, king, luck, queen	/th/	then
/u/	umbrella, love,	/ng/	ring, sink
/r/	rabbit, wrong, berry	/zh/	treasure
/b/	baby, cabbage		

Long vowel phonemes			
Phoneme	Common spellings	Phoneme	Common spellings
/ae/	play, take, snail, baby	/ur/	burn, girl, term, heard, work
/ee/	feel, heat, me	/au/	sauce, horn, door, warn, claw, ball
/ie/	tie, fight, my, bike, tiger	/ar/	car
/oe/	float, slow, stone, nose	/air/	hair, bear, share
/u/	book, could, put	/ear/	ear, here, deer
/ue/	moon, clue, grew, tune	/ure/	sure, tour
/ow/	cow, shout	/er/	teacher, collar, doctor
/oi/	coin, boy		

One letter does not always make one sound

One of the key causes of confusion in teaching phonics in English is that one letter can make more than one sound. So, for example, the letter 's' usually makes the sound /s/ as in the word 'sun', but can make the sound /zh/ as in 'treasure'. The Phoneme-grapheme charts here and on pages 41 and 105 should be used a constant reference guide and this with constant practice will enable familiarity.

Rules and exceptions

As children progress you may find it helpful to teach some rules in order to help them make the correct spelling choice. One example of a rule is for 'ck': words of one syllable ending in the phoneme /k/ with a short vowel and no other consonant letter before the last /k/ sound, take 'ck', as in 'clock', 'duck', 'back' and so on. There are a range of such rules to support spelling and many will need to be taught as part of a systematic spelling programme once children have a basic understanding of the 44 phonemes. Such rules are therefore not covered in depth in this book.

One exception that can cause difficulty is the phonemes /q/u/, where the /u/ makes a /w/ sound as in 'square'. These two phonemes are always found together in English and represent a blend.

It should also be noted that the letter 'x' is not specifically taught as it is a blend of two phonemes /k/ and /s/.

Consonant blends

Another cause of confusion is that some consonant letters placed at the beginning and end of words are blended together, however they consist of separate phonemes. They do not need to be taught separately as it is possible to demonstrate how the phonemes are blended together. Practice at reading consonant blends does help reading fluency and the same applies to vowel rimes, for example 'ot' as in 'lot', 'hot',

'rot', and so on. The list below contains examples of common blends. The slashes indicate the division between phonemes.

sp (/s/p/oo/n/)	st (/s/t/ar/)
sc (/s/c/ar/f/)	sm (/s/m/u/g/)
sn (/s/n/a/ck/)	sl (/s/l/i/p/)
grain (/g/r/ai/n/)	frog (/f/r/o/g/)
plum (/p/l/u/m/)	squash (/s/q/u/a/sh/)
splash (/s/p/l/a/sh/)	string (/s/t/r/i/ng/)

Letter names and letter sounds

Another common cause of confusion is the use of letter names alongside the phonemes. It now commonly recognised that it is important that children learn both early. They will see frequent example of letter names and this need not cause any difficulties while learning the phonemes. The best way to address this is to say that a letter has a name and a sound, so that the letter 'B' has the name 'B' and makes the sound /b/. The use of the 'Alphabet rhyme' on page 25 early, alongside phonological awareness training, can soon help children to learn the letter names (see Stage 1 for more details).

Correct pronunciation

It is very important to model the correct pronunciation of phonemes when teaching. The most common error is to add an 'uh' sound to phonemes (as in 'r' often pronounced 'ruh'). While it is difficult to say some phonemes purely, every effort should be made to do so. One way that might help is to appreciate that some phonemes are 'sustained' or 'stretched' phonemes and can be pronounced purely, as listed below.

Sustained sounds: all vowel phonemes + /f /l / /m /n /r /s /v /z /th /ng /

A pronunciation chart is provided in Stage 2 on page 40 to highlight in detail how each phoneme is pronounced, as it is so important to say the sounds purely. As Stage 3 covers long vowel phonemes and these include more than one phoneme sound, a pronunciation chart for this section is not required.

Unsustained sounds

The other phonemes should be pronounced as purely as possible. For voiced sounds (where the voice vibrates) children can put fingers on their throats to feel the vibration and for unvoiced sounds (/t/, /p/, /k/, /f/, /h/, /th/), they can whisper them which helps keep the sound pure. For further guidance on teaching correct pronunciation to children, see the pronunciation chart on page 40.

Partner work

Throughout this programme, you will see references to partner work. This can be developed with very young children with support and encouragement. Partner work can support their learning through encouraging talk. It also ensures that *all* children participate rather than one or two who respond to a question or instruction. You may like to develop regular partnerships or allow them to alternate.

STRUCTURE OF THIS BOOK

This book is divided into the following sections:

Stage 1: Identifying sounds
Stage 2: Consonants and short vowels
Stage 3: Long vowel sounds

See the charts on pages 8–10 for full details of the teaching order.

Assessments are provided at the end of each section. Activities last approximately 15 to 20 minutes and can be reinforced by a range of suggested games for each stage. At Stages 2 and 3 a new phoneme is introduced every day and review and revision activities are provided.

Terminology

A full glossary of terms is included in the Appendix on page 192.

STAGE 1: IDENTIFYING SOUNDS

Step	Activities	Objectives	Suggested Activities
Listening (page13)	*A good listener*	To listen attentively	Read the Listen to me story (page 20)
	Environmental sounds	To identify environmental sounds	Use everyday objects to identify different sounds
	Speech sounds	To identify speech sounds	Sing the traditional rhyme Tommy Thumb
Rhyme (page15)	*Hearing rhymes*	To hear examples of rhymes	Read the rhyming extract from *Hairy McLary* (page 21)
	Identifying rhymes	To identify rhymes	Identify rhyming pictures (page 22)
	Generating rhymes	To generate rhymes	Read alternative versions of familiar nursery rhymes (page 23)
Words (page16)	*Hearing words*	To identify individual words	Count the repeated word using counters (page 24)
Syllables (page17)	*Identifing syllables*	To identify syllables	Play clapping games
	Maintaining syllable patterns	To maintain a syllable pattern	Make patterns using musical instruments
Phonemes (page18)	*Learning the alphabet*	To learn the alphabet	Sing the Alphabet rhyme (page 25)
	Identifying lower- and upper-case letters	To identify lower- and upper-case letters	Match upper- and lower-case cards on a washing line
	Identifying initial letter sounds	To identify initial letter sounds	Point out initial letter sounds using silly sentences (page 29).

STAGE 2: CONSONANTS & SHORT VOWELS

	Lesson	Phoneme	Common spellings	List of other words with same spelling
Week 1 (pages 54–58)	1	/s/	**s**un	mou**se**, **c**ity, me**ss**, **sc**ience, mi**ce**
	2	/a/	**a**pple	
	3	/t/	**t**ap	be**tt**er
	4	/p/	**p**aper	hi**pp**o
	5	reinforce and practice		
Week 2 (pages 59–62)	6	/i/	**i**nk	buck**e**t
	7	/n/	**n**oise	**kn**ife, **gn**at
	8	/e/	**e**gg	br**ea**d
	9	/d/	**d**og	pud**dl**e
	10	reinforce and practice		
Week 3 (pages 63–66)	11	/m/	**m**an	ha**mm**er, co**mb**
	12	/g/	**g**ame	e**gg**
	13	/o/	**o**ctopus	w**a**nt
	14	/c/ /k/	lu**ck**	**c**at, **Ch**ris, **k**ing, **q**ueen
	15	reinforce and practice		
Week 4 (pages 67–70)	16	/u/	**u**mbrella	l**o**ve,
	17	/r/	**r**abbit	**wr**ong, be**rr**y
	18	/b/	**b**aby	ca**bb**age
	19	/f/	**f**ish	**ph**oto, cof**f**ee
	20	reinforce and practice		
Week 5 (pages 71–74)	21	/l/	**l**eg	spe**ll**
	22	/h/	**h**at	

	Lesson	Phoneme	Common spellings	List of other words with same spelling
Week 5 (cont) (pages 71–74)	23	/sh/	**sh**ip	mi**ss**ion, **ch**ef
	24	/z/	**z**ebra	plea**se**, **is**, fi**zz**y, snee**ze**
	25	reinforce and practice		
Week 6 (pages 75–78)	26	/w/	**w**ater	**wh**eel, q**u**een
	27	/ch/	**ch**ip	wa**tch**
	28	/j/	**j**ug	ju**dge**, **g**iant, bar**ge**
	29	/v/	**v**an	slee**ve**
	30	reinforce and practice		
Week 7 (pages 79–83)	31	/y/	**y**es	
	32	/th/	**th**in	
	33	/th/	**th**en	
	34	/ng/	ri**ng**	si**nk**
	35	/zh/	trea**s**ure	
Week 8 (page 83)	Reinforce, practice and overall assessment			

STAGE 3: LONG VOWEL SOUNDS

	Lessons	Phoneme	Grapheme	Common Spellings	List of other words with same spelling
Week 9 (pages 117–120)	36	/ae/	ay	d**ay**	may say, play, tray
	37		ai	t**ai**l	sail, mail, fail, rail, aid
	38		a	**a**corn	able, acre, baby, apron
	39 & 40	reinforcement and practice			
Week 10 (pages 121–124)	41	/ee/	ee	s**ee**	tree, agree, deep, fee, sleep
	42		ea	b**ea**ch	teach, bead, cheap, east
	43		e	m**e**	he, she, we, be
	44		y	pon**y**	bony, mummy, stony
	45	reinforcement and practice			
Week 11 (pages 125–128)	46	/ie/	ie	t**ie**	lie, pie, cried, die
	47		igh	l**igh**t	might, sight, right
	48		y	m**y**	shy, fly, cry, dry
	49		i	t**i**ger	cider, hi, idea, lilac
	50	reinforcement and practice			
Week 12 (pages 129–131)	51	/oe/	oa	b**oa**t	float, coat, foal, goat, groan
	52		ow	sn**ow**	flow, row, bowl, know
	53		o	c**o**ld	sold, ago, only, over
	54 & 55	reinforcement and practice			
Week 13 (pages 132–134)	56	/u/	oo	b**oo**k	rook, cook, hood
	57		ou	w**ou**ld	could, should
	58		u	p**u**t	
	59 & 60	reinforcement and practice			
Week 14 (pages 135–137)	61	/ue/	oo	m**oo**n	soon, hoop, roof, school
	62		ue	cl**ue**	true, fuel, glue, cue
	63		ew	gr**ew**	drew, few, dew, new, screw
	64 & 65	reinforcement and practice			

STAGE 3: LONG VOWEL SOUNDS continued

	Lessons	Phoneme	Grapheme	Common Spellings	List of other words with same spelling
Week 15 (pages 138–141)	66	/ae/	a–e	m**a**k**e**	cake, wake, fake, take, hate
	67	/ie/	i–e	t**i**m**e**	crime, fine, file, mice, hive
	68	/oe/	o–e	b**o**n**e**	lone, phone, code, mode
	69	/ue/	u–e	t**u**n**e**	duke, fuse, dune, cube
	70		reinforcement and practice		
Week 16 (pages 142–145)	71	/ow/	ow	c**ow**	now, row, vow, sow
	72		ou	sh**ou**t	house, mouse, doubt
	73	/oi/	oi	c**oi**n	join, coil, foil, oil, toil
	74		oy	b**oy**	toy, joy, ploy
	75		reinforcement and practice		
Week 17 (pages 146–150)	76	/ur/	ur	b**ur**n	turn, curl, fur, hurl
	77		ir	g**ir**l	shirt, fir
	78		er	t**er**m	fern, herb, jerk
	79		ear	h**ear**d	early, earth, search
	80		or	w**or**k	worm, word, worse, worth
	81		reinforcement and practice		
Week 18 (pages 151–154)	82	/au/	au	h**au**l	sauce, maul, August, autumn
	83		or	h**or**n	fork, born, corn, horse
	84		oor	d**oor**	moor, floor
	85		ar	w**ar**n	war, ward, wart
	86		reinforcement and practice		
Week 19 (pages 155–157)	87	/au/ (cont)	aw	cl**aw**	draw, paw, dawn, flaw, lawn
	88		a	b**a**ll	bald, call, fall
	89	/ar/	ar	c**ar**	far, tar, dark, park, ark, farm
	90 & 91		reinforcement and practice		
Week 20 (pages 158–160)	92	/air/	air	h**air**	fair, lair, chair, stair, pair
	93		ear	b**ear**	pear, wear, tear
	94		are	sh**are**	square, dare, fare
	95 & 96		reinforcement and practice		
Week 21 (pages 161–163)	97	/ear/	ear	f**ear**	ear, tear, rear, dear
	98		ere	h**ere**	sphere, mere
	99		eer	d**eer**	cheer, steer, peer, jeer
	100 & 101		reinforcement and practice		
Week 22 (pages164–166)	102	/ure/	ure	s**ure**	lure, pure, cure
	103		our	t**our**	detour, velour
	104	/er/	er	sist**er**	teacher, cover, preacher
				alternatives:	
				coll**ar**	dollar
				wood**en**	garden
				circ**us**	fungus
				doct**or**	inspector
	105 & 106		reinforcement and practice		

STAGE ONE
IDENTIFYING SOUNDS

STAGE ONE:
SUBJECT KNOWLEDGE

As a first step before learning phonics, children must be able to accurately hear and discriminate sounds (known as phonological awareness). Failure to develop this adequately can have a significant impact on later reading success. These important skills can be developed through carefully planned teaching. Children find it easier to begin with the larger units (words and rhymes) and then begin to break these into smaller units (syllables and phonemes).

STEPS IN DEVELOPING PHONOLOGICAL AWARENESS

Phonological awareness also consists of different steps. These can be thought of as ranging from larger to smaller units:

■ word awareness (understanding that sentences consist of individual words)
■ rhyme awareness (being able to identify words that have identical final sound segments)
■ syllable awareness (being able to hear segments of phonemes that comprise the rhythm of the word)
■ phonemic awareness (being able to identify, and manipulate the sounds that are representative of graphemes in the English language).

A STEP-BY-STEP PROGRAMME

The activities in this section take the children through the following stages to develop their phonological awareness.

Listening

The first step is to develop children's listening skills to allow them to discriminate fine differences in sounds. Children also need to develop their ability to remember a sequence of sounds (auditory recall).

Rhyming

Next rhyming work needs to be taught in steps, from rhyme exposure (opportunities to hear rhymes); rhyme detection (same or different) and rhyme generation (children making up their own rhymes).

Identifying words

The next step is for children to be able to identify individual words from the continuous stream of speech that they hear. Seeing nursery rhymes written down and noting individual words will help their discrimination skills.

Syllables

It is important to ensure that children can begin the process of breaking down words, first into syllables. There are many fun games involving clapping and tapping that can help this.

Phonemes

Children must be able to identify individual phonemes, before teaching them to map the 44 phonemes to graphemes in English. Work on the alphabet, and knowing letter names and their most common sounds begins here, before the systematic teaching in the next stage of the programme.

TEACHING PROGRAMME

The activities in this section provide support for each step in building phonological awareness along with suggestions for further activities. The emphasis is on providing fun activities combined with songs, rhymes and opportunities for play. The grid on page 8 shows the order of teaching and any accompanying photocopiables for Stage 1.

VISUAL PERCEPTION

Developing children's visual perception and discrimination skills will also support their later reading success. Activities to support this can be jigsaws, matching activities or copying a sequence such as coloured beads or bricks.

ASSESSMENT

It is important to be able to track the children's progress as often as possible to ensure that no one is falling behind. Assessment activities are provided on pages 30–34 and will need to be undertaken in small groups or individually. Ensure that children have achieved full phonological awareness before proceeding to the next stage.

STAGE ONE:
ACTIVITIES

LISTENING

Teaching children to develop good listening skills is not only a vital step in the future success of learning phonics, it is also crucial for developing good learning dispositions. This can be sub-divided into:
■ specific skills training
■ listening to sounds in the environment
■ identifying speech sounds.

A GOOD LISTENER

Objective
To be able to listen attentively.

What you need
'Listen to me' photocopiable page 20; two puppets; easel.

What to do
■ With a small group of children or the whole class read the story of 'Listen to me' on photocopiable page 20, using the puppets to role play the good and bad listener.
■ Talk about the different characters and ask the children why it is important to be a good listener.
■ Encourage the children to re-enact the story in role play. You may like to set up a role play specifically, for the children.
■ Later, or on another day, recap on the story. Ask the children to turn to their partner and decide on one thing that we need to remember when we are listening.

■ Take the children's responses and write the main points on the easel. Include a small drawing to represent each, similar to the example at the bottom of the page.
■ Use this as a poster to remind the children of the main aspects of good listening.
■ As a follow-up, use the puppets to identify good listeners, or play a game of 'Who is Rag looking at?' Follow instructions given by the puppet, for example: to stand up, sit down, walk to the door and so on. Ask children to recall the sequence of instructions by choosing different children to either tell the others the order they carried out the instructions, or to re-enact them.

Further activities
■ Play a game of 'Simon says'.
■ Play 'Follow-my-leader'. Ask the children to copy either the teacher or another child with a range of actions (holding up left arm or shaking right leg) as they move around the room.
■ Play *Look hear* (available from LDA Learning, ISBN 0-742-42372-7). The idea is to give the children a gameboard with pictures that represent sounds. They listen to a tape and put a counter on the corresponding sound.
■ Play 'I went to market and I bought...' Model the game first. Say to the class: 'I went to market and I bought a loaf of bread, a pint of milk and a piece of cheese.' Ask the children to take turns to repeat the items and then add another one of their own.
■ Play 'Hum the tune'. Hum a nursery rhyme or familiar tune and ask children to guess what it is.
■ Sing a range of songs with the children that require them to listen carefully and repeat.

| Good listening Look at the speaker | Be quiet | Keep still |

ENVIRONMENTAL SOUNDS

Objective
To identify sounds all around us.

What you need
Screen; range of everyday objects that can be used to make a noise (for example: rubber band, tinfoil, jug of water and container to pour into, tissue paper, bubble wrap, polystyrene, crunchy cereal in a small bag).

What to do
■ Explain to the children that many things around us make noises and they are going to play a guessing game to see which thing make a certain noise.
■ Show the children the objects and demonstrate the noises they each make.
■ Now hide the objects behind the screen and ask the children to listen carefully as you make a noise with each one.
■ Each time you make a noise with an object, ask the children to agree with a partner which object they are listening to.
■ Carefully assess the children's ability to discriminate noises as you choose pairs to tell you which object they have heard.

Further activities
■ As a follow-on (at a later time), use a pre-recorded tape of sounds around the home (washing machine spinning, microwave bleeping, telephone ringing, alarm clock, car starting, door bell and so on). Play the taped sounds and ask the children to guess the noises they can hear. You could leave this in the role-play area for children to incorporate into their imaginative play.

■ Ask the children to help you tape sounds around the school, or in the local environment, and then play the tape for other children to guess what they are.
■ Set up a water tray with a range of objects and talk to the children while they explore the objects and the noises they can make.
■ Have fun singing songs that require the children to make different noises, for example: 'Old MacDonald Had a Farm'.

SPEECH SOUNDS

Objective
To identify different speech sounds.

What to do
■ Sing the traditional rhyme 'Tommy Thumb, Tommy Thumb' to the children. You may need to teach it to them if it is unfamiliar.
■ Now have fun substituting names for children in the class with 'Tommy Thumb' and sing the rhyme together.

Further activities
■ Provide a range of different types of telephones in the role-play area. Model using the telephone and encourage the children to 'make calls' in the context of play, for example: 'Quick! Phone for the ambulance!'
■ Read *Polar Bear, Polar Bear What Do You Hear?* by Bill Martin Jr and Eric Carle (Puffin Books, ISBN 0-140-54519-0) and talk about the different sounds mentioned in the story.
■ Play a whispering game. Whisper something to the child next to you and ask them to repeat what they hear round the circle. See what the final message is.

RHYME ACTIVITIES

Children who can hear and generate rhyme find it easier to hear and discriminate sounds. Teaching rhyme should be taught in stages as follows:

■ rhyme exposure (lots of opportunities to hear rhymes)

■ rhyme detection (same or different)

■ rhyme generation (children coming up with their own rhymes).

HEARING RHYMES

Objective
To hear examples of rhymes.

What you need
Enlarged copy of 'Hairy Maclary from Donaldson's Dairy' photocopiable page 21; copy of *Hairy Maclary From Donaldson's Dairy* by Lynley Dodd (Puffin Books, ISBN 0-141-38189-2).

What to do
■ With a small group or the whole class show the children the rhyming book *Hairy Maclary From Donaldson's Dairy*. Take time to talk about the rhyming title and pictures, and ask for predictions of what it might be about.

■ Now read the book to the children in a lively fun way, enjoying the rhyming words together. Look carefully at the illustrations.

■ Using the extract on the photocopiable sheet, read the text again and point at the words as you do. Emphasise the rhyming words each time and highlight them with a coloured pen.

■ Have fun together saying the rhyming words.

■ Next, invite the children to make up their own rhymes based on the extract. Encourage the class to suggest different rhyming words for each character.

■ When they are happy with their new rhyming sentences, read the extended version of the extract together.

■ Leave the book and extract clearly displayed for the children to look at during independent work.

Further activities
■ Have a regular time for enjoying a range of nursery rhymes and extend with role play.

■ Read rhyming books to the class, such as *Cat in the Hat* by Dr Seuss (HarperCollins Children's Books, ISBN 0-007-17957-X).

IDENTIFYING RHYMES

Objective
To be able to identify same or different rhymes.

What you need
Enlarged copy of 'Rhyming pictures' photocopiable page 22, laminated and cut up.

What to do
■ Show the children the pictures and ensure that they know what each one is.

■ Next mix them up and randomly hold up two pictures, saying what they are each time, for example, 'moon' and 'hat'. Tell the children to quickly hold up their hands if they rhyme.

■ Have fun in this way and then leave the cards available, if possible on a magnetic board, for children to explore during independent work.

■ At a later stage, use the cards to play 'Rhyme pairs'. Organise for a pair of children to play this together. Tell them to place all the cards face down and to take turns turning over two cards. If the cards rhyme they can keep them. The child with the most pairs at the end is the winner.

Further activities
■ Recite a range of nursery rhymes with the children but make deliberate mistakes for the children to spot. For example: 'Little Jack Horner sat in a chair', 'Little Bo Peep has lost her shoes', 'Jack and Jill went up the field' and so on.

STAGE ONE: ACTIVITIES

GENERATING RHYMES

Objective
To be able to supply a rhyming word.

What you need
Easel and pen; copies of 'Humpty Dumpties' photocopiable page 23.

What to do
■ Begin by saying the familiar nursery rhyme 'Humpty Dumpty' ensuring the children are familiar with it.
■ Read the alternative versions on photocopiable page 23 and have plenty of fun with them. You may be aware of other versions to share.
■ Next tell the children they are going to help you think of more versions.
■ Devise some rhyming couplets with the children, for example:

> Humpty Dumpty sat on a box
> Humpty Dumpty saw a fox.
> Humpty Dumpty sat on a log
> Humpty Dumpty saw a dog.

■ For further practice, ask the children to help you make up some more rhyming sentences by fitting rhyming words into the following:

> Mr Chor went to the ....
> Mrs Lat was very ....
> Mr Pin was very ....
> Mrs Ring liked to ....
> Mr Ball was very ....

Further activities
■ Sing a range of familiar songs and have fun substituting alternatives rhymes, for example: 'Row, row, row your boat gently down the sea. Merrily, merrily, merrily, merrily, it's fun for you and me.' Encourage the children to make up their own rhymes.
■ Recite further rhymes to which you can encourage the children to add simple rhyming words, for example: Mr Lynn is very thin. Mr Cort is very... (short). Mrs Hall is very... (tall). Write the children's examples on the board and encourage them to read the sentences back to you.

IDENTIFYING WORDS
This section supports children's understanding of individual words and being able to discriminate them from the continuous flow of speech. It is a further important part of developing fine discrimination skills to support phonological awareness.

HEARING WORDS

Objective
To identify individual words.

What you need
Copies of 'Lots of socks' photocopiable page 24.

What to do
■ Explain to the children that you are going to read a poem that contains the same word lots of times. The word is 'socks'. Ask the children to put their hand up every time they hear the word 'socks'.
■ Now read the poem with lots of expression and have lots of fun with the repetition of the same word.
■ You may like to show the children an enlarged copy of the poem and highlight the word each time it appears.
■ Leave the poem on display for the children to look at while they play. You may wish to follow up with other poems that repeat the same word many times.

Further activities
■ Invite the children to count the words using coloured counters. Read a sentence to the children while they track each word on a printed copy and encourage them to move a counter to correspond with each word.
■ Using a Big Book and a pointer, ask one child to point to the words and track them as you read to the rest of the children. Select different children for each page.
■ Sing traditional songs that emphasise individual words, for example: 'POP goes the weasel!' You can ask the children to do an action every time they hear a specific word, such as starting the song by crouching on the floor, and then jumping up into a star shape when they hear the word 'POP!'.

IDENTIFYING SYLLABLES

In this section, the programme begins the process of identifying smaller units within words. You need to choose multi-syllabic words and help the children to tap or clap the number of syllables.

IDENTIFYING SYLLABLES

Objective
To know how many syllables in a word.

What you need
Range of objects from around the classroom on a tray (for example: pencil, paper, telephone, register).

What to do
■ With the children sitting in a circle, begin by clapping names, modelling your own name first (for example, /Miss/Harr/i/son/) and one or two others in the class (/Na/tash/a/, /San/jit/ and so on).

■ Go round the circle clapping names in this way, supporting the children where needed, initially clapping the child's name first for them to copy.

■ Now explain that you are going to clap the correct number of syllables in different objects' names. Have a range of items on a tray in the middle of the circle and ask children to choose an object. Clap the number of syllables in the object's name, for example, a 'telephone' would have three claps.

■ Finally choose an object without telling the class and clap the number of syllables. The rest of the group have to guess which it is.

Further activities
■ Play clapping games by saying a range of multi-syllabic words for the children to clap the syllables.

■ Play 'Tap your name': children tap with fingers on their body, or with a stick on a drum, the number of syllables in their names.

■ Place objects in a feely bag. Invite children to choose one and clap the correct number of syllables.

■ Ask children to sort objects according to beats/syllables. Have a few objects displayed alongside enlarged numbers (1, 2 and 3). Children take turns to come and choose an object, clap the number of syllables and then place the object next to the correct number.

MAINTAINING SYLLABLE PATTERNS

Objective
To maintain a syllable pattern.

What you need
Range of musical instruments, sufficient for one between two in a large group or one each for a small group.

What to do
■ Introduce the song below, sung to the tune of 'The Wheels on the Bus':

> Let's tap out a pattern on our lap;
> On our lap: tap, tap, tap.
> Let's tap out a pattern on our lap,
> As we sing.
> Let's clap out a pattern with our hands;
> With our hands: clap, clap, clap.
> Let's clap out a pattern with our hands;
> One, two, three.

STAGE ONE: ACTIVITIES

■ Now give out sticks or instruments and sing it again with the children tapping the syllables.
■ Repeat the activity with different instruments.

Further activities

■ Provide a range of instruments and ask the children to copy a pattern demonstrated and to continue it for as long as possible.
■ Play the 'Clap, clap game'. This is a game with a rhythmic beat, interspersed by movement. After you say a body part, clap according to the number of syllables. Start by clapping a rhythmic beat. For example:

> [Clap, clap]
> [Clap, clap]
> [Clap, clap]
> Pat your knee
> [Clap]
> Touch your nose
> [Clap]
> Touch your toes
> [Clap]
> Rub your tummy
> [Clap, clap].

PHONEMES

This section supports the children's discrimination of sounds further by helping the process of identifying individual phonemes. Work on the alphabet through songs and rhymes are useful here, alongside recognition of letters, both upper- and lower-case. Plenty of examples of alliteration all support initial letter sound recognition.

LEARNING THE ALPHABET

> **Objective**
> To know the letters of the alphabet.

What you need

'Alphabet rhyme' photocopiable page 25 and picture cards from 'Alphabet rhyme picture cards' photocopiable pages 26, 27, 28 for each letter of the alphabet, laminated and cut up so they can form a frieze.

What to do

■ Introduce the 'Alphabet rhyme' and over a period of days teach the children sections of the rhyme. Create and teach some simple actions to match each letter (for example, for the letter 'D', pretend to open a door). You can use the actions that are suggested on the 'Alphabet rhyme' photocopiable sheet, or alternatively, ask the children to suggest their own actions to help them remember the letters.
■ Show the children the matching 'Alphabet rhyme picture cards' as you teach each section. These can form a frieze around the classroom, which the children can help to put together.
■ Gradually build up the rhyme until the children can remember it all and repeat it together clearly without too much prompting.
■ Practise every day and continue to practise througout the entire of Stage 2. It should be fun and lively with plenty of actions to support their learning.

Further activities

■ Using further copies of the alphabet rhyme picture cards, provide some or all of the cards and ask a group or pairs of children to try and put them in order, using the frieze for help.

IDENTIFYING LOWER- AND UPPER-CASE LETTERS

Objective
To be able to match lower- and upper-case letters.

What you need
Large letter cards for every letter of the alphabet (upper- and lower-case); washing line and small pegs; large paper clips; name cards for the children.

What to do
■ Explain to the children that sometimes we use big, or upper-case, letters for important things like people's names. Hold up one or two of the children's name cards to illustrate this. Tell them that letters have a name, just as they have a name, and the letter also makes a sound. Explain that you are learning the names (not the sounds).

■ Next say that you are playing a matching game. Hand out some lower- and upper-case letters that correspond (select about six pairs each day).
■ Ask one of the children with a letter to come and peg it on the washing line.
■ Now ask if anyone thinks they have the small or lower-case letter to match. Ask the children to hold it underneath. You can then clip it together using large paper clips.
■ Repeat until all the cards for that day are on the washing line.
■ Continue in this way with a number of letters each day until the washing line is complete.

Further activities
■ Using examples of print, from leaflets and magazines, ask the children to highlight all the capital letters.
■ Using magnetic letters – mixed upper- and lower-case – ask the children to put all the capitals on one side of a magnetic board and all the lower-case letters on the other side.

IDENTIFYING INITIAL LETTER SOUNDS

Objective
To be able to spot the same sounds.

What you need
'Silly sentences (1)' photocopiable page 29.

What to do
■ Explain that you have some very silly sentences to share with the children and you want them to listen very carefully.
■ Read out the sentences from the photocopiable sheet, for example, 'Bats and balls bring big blue balloons.'
■ Ask the children to say which sound they can hear repeated.
■ Continue reading all the sentences on the photocopiable sheet.
■ Now try and devise some 'silly sentences' with the children. Have fun in this way.

Further activities
■ Repeat songs and rhymes that illustrate hearing initial letter sounds: for example: 'To market, to market to buy a fat pig. Home again, home again jiggety jig.' Next, substitute 'pig' for 'wig', 'dig', 'fig' and so on.
■ Play 'I spy' games, saying the letter sound.
■ Devise a range of alliterative sentences, for example: 'Wayne wears wellies' and alliterative names (Big Brian, Tall Thomas).

Assessment
Ensure that you carry out the assessment on pages 30–31 before proceeding to Stage 2. Provide revision and reinforcement lessons for children who are not secure with their phonological awareness learned in Stage 1. This knowledge is required for progression.

STAGE ONE: ACTIVITIES

Listen to me

Meet Rag (holding up first puppet) and Muffin (holding up second puppet). They are best friends. Only sometimes they fall out. It is usually when Muffin won't listen.

Rag: *(Playing the first three notes of 'Three Blind Mice')* Listen, Muffin. Can you tell what tune I'm playing?

Muffin: Is it 'Humpty Dumpty'? *(Starts to sing 'Humpty Dumpty' loudly.)*

Rag: No, Muffin. Listen again. *(Plays the three notes twice more while Muffin carries on singing 'Humpty Dumpty'.)*

Rag: *(Louder)* MUFFIN! Stop singing and listen to my tune.

Muffin: Let me play. I bet you can't tell what this tune is… *(Muffin snatches stick from Rag and plays a jumble of tuneless notes.)*

Rag: That's not a proper tune. Let me show you how to play 'Three Blind Mice'.

Muffin: I bet you don't know how.

Rag: Yes I do. That's the tune I was playing just now.

Muffin: *(handing the stick back to Rag)* Go on, then.

Rag: Look, Muffin. See you hit the third note first. *(Points to the third note and then plays the first three notes again – Muffin isn't looking or listening.)*

Rag: *(Holding out the stick)* You have a go.

Muffin: Which note do you start on?

Rag: I told you. The third note.

Muffin: The first note… *(Plays the first three notes in reverse order.)* Ha! That is not 'Three Blind Mice'! – nothing like it!

Rag: But, Muffin, you played the wrong notes.

Muffin: I played the notes you said.

Rag: But not in the right order…! Don't you want to hear me play the tune? *(Starts to play correctly. Muffin sings again.)*

Rag: *(Picks up xylophone)* I'm going home. My mum will listen even if you won't!

by Celia Warren

PHONICS: A COMPLETE SYNTHETIC PROGRAMME FOR AGES 4+

Hairy Maclary From Donaldson's Dairy

Schnitzel von Krumm
with a very low tum,
Bitzer Maloney
all skinny and bony,
Muffin McLay
like a bundle of hay,
Bottomley Potts
covered in spots,
Hercules Morse
as big as a horse
and Hairy Maclary
from Donaldson's Dairy.

by Lynley Dodd

Text from *Hairy Maclary From Donaldson's Dairy* by Lynley Dodd (1983, Mallinson Rendel, New Zealand); illustration © 1983, Lynley Dodd

STAGE ONE: PHOTOCOPIABLES

Rhyming pictures

bell	shell	hat
cat	moon	spoon
box	fox	mouse
house	snake	cake

PHONICS: A COMPLETE SYNTHETIC PROGRAMME FOR AGES 4+

Humpty Dumpties

Humpty Dumpty sat on a brick
Humpty Dumpty felt a bit sick
All the king's horses and all the king's men
Couldn't make Humpty feel better again.

Humpty Dumpty sat on the rocks
Humpty Dumpty lost both his socks
All the king's horses and all the king's men
Had to let Humpty go barefoot again.

Humpty Dumpty ran down a hill
Humpty Dumpty had a bad spill
All the king's horses and all the king's men
Couldn't put Humpty together again.

Humpty Dumpty sat on the hedge
Humpty Dumpty fell off the edge
All the king's horses and all the king's men
Couldn't put Humpty together again.

by Celia Warren

STAGE ONE: PHOTOCOPIABLES

Lots of socks

I've got lots of socks:
long socks, short socks,
school socks, sport socks,

socks with stripes,
socks with spots,
socks all tangled up in knots,

white socks, grey socks,
everyday socks,
blue socks, red socks,
fluffy bed-socks,

socks **too big**,
socks too small,
socks I never wear at all,

socks on my feet,
socks in the drawer,
one odd sock
on the bedroom floor,

that's the sock I'm looking for!

Celia Warren
[first published in *Bouncing with the Budgie*, by Celia
Warren, QED, 2005]

Alphabet rhyme

A is for ants as well as for juicy apples
B is for balloon that shines and dapples
C is for cat, camel, cup and cake
D is for door, dog and drake
E is for elephant, egg and éclair
F is for flower, fish and fair
G is for giggle, goat and gear
H is for hat, hand and hear
I is for insect, Indian and ill
J is for jam and Jack and Jill
K is for kettle, kitten and kite
L is for lemon and light shining bright
M is for monkey, man and moon
N is for nest, net and noon
O is for octopus, orange, ox and odd
P is for paper, pen and pea pod
Q is for queen, quiet and quick
R is for robot, rabbit, rat and Rick
S is for sun, sand and slithery snakes
T is for Thomas, tap, tent and takes
U is for uncle, us and umbrella
V is for vinegar, vet and vulture
W is for water, wheels and writer
X is for x-ray, in box and fox too
Y is for yacht, yoghurt and you
Z is for zebra, zip, and zoo

Can you find words in this alphabet rhyme too?

Actions

A pretend to bite an apple
B pretend to hold a balloon on a string
C children meow and pretend to lick paws
D pretend to open a door and bark like a dog
E hold arm in front and pretend to sway like an elephant's trunk
F hold arms out with palms of hands together and move like a fish swimming
G make a giggling or goat noise
H pretend to put a hat on your head
I stick your tongue out and look ill
J pretend to lick a spoon of jam
K pretend to fill the kettle
L squeeze a lemon and taste: pull a face!
M bend and swing arms like a monkey
N pretend to hold a net and catch things
O bend and wave arms around like an octopus
P pretend to write with a pen
Q put a crown on your head and look important
R move stiffly like a robot
S move arm like a snake
T tap your neighbour
U put an umbrella up
V flap arms like a giant bird
W move arms round like a water wheel
X pretend to take a photo
Y pretend to eat some yoghurt
Z pretend to zip up your coat

STAGE ONE: PHOTOCOPIABLES

Alphabet rhyme picture cards (1)

SCHOLASTIC
www.scholastic.co.uk

PHONICS: A COMPLETE SYNTHETIC PROGRAMME FOR AGES 4+

Alphabet rhyme picture cards (2)

Alphabet rhyme picture cards (3)

SCHOLASTIC
www.scholastic.co.uk

PHONICS: A COMPLETE SYNTHETIC PROGRAMME FOR AGES 4+

Silly sentences (1)

Annie Ant and Andy Ape ask for apples.

Bats and balls bring big blue balloons.

Caterpillars climb crazy cliffs catching caps.

Dinosaurs do dizzy dips behind dopey doors.

Elephants, earwigs and eagles eat eggs.

Fish and feathers fly past flowers and flags.

STAGE ONE: PHOTOCOPIABLES

STAGE ONE:
ASSESSMENT

These assessments are part of overall observations of children's progress. The majority of this information will be gained from your observations of the children generally.

ASSESSMENT 1

A ATTENTIVE LISTENING
What to do

■ Read a short story to a child. Note if they can sit still and concentrate while you are reading. Invite the child to tell you what happened first and at the end of the story. Ask a question related to the story and when finished, to put the book in a certain place.

B DISCRIMINATION OF ENVIRONMENTAL SOUNDS
What to do

■ Make a tape of common sounds (for example: a vacuum cleaner, chairs scraping, car engines and so on). Play the tape to the child in an area with extraneous noise and note the child's ability to concentrate and discriminate the sounds.

C DISCRIMINATION OF SPEECH SOUNDS
What to do

■ Read the following list of words to the child and ask him/her to tell you the odd one out:

> **Practice:** happy, hop, Harry, huge, fish, heavy, hat
> **Assessment:** boy, big, ball, giraffe, bag, bang, bell

■ Say the following words to the child and ask them to repeat the sequence:

> desk, chair, door, book, pen

> Record the child's progress for each section on Assessment 1 photocopiable page 32.

ASSESSMENT 2

A RHYME AWARENESS
What to do

■ Read the following nursery rhymes to the child and ask them to supply the missing words:

> Baa, baa black sheep have you any...
>
> Old Mother Hubbard went to the cupboard to fetch her poor dog a...
>
> Mary, Mary quite contrary, how does your...
>
> Pussy cat, pussy cat where have you been? I've been to...

B RHYME IDENTIFICATION
What to do

■ Ask the child to tell you which three words rhyme each time out of the following:

> man, van, mix, fan
> sock, bring, lock, rock
> moon, spoon, farm, tune
> hat, mat, mouse, rat

C RHYME GENERATION
What to do

■ Ask the child to tell you another word that rhymes with the following:

> sun, pun _____   bat, hat _____
> ten, pen _____   bell, dell _____

> Record the child's progress for each section on Assessment 2 photocopiable page 33.

ASSESSMENT 3

A WORD AWARENESS
What to do
■ For this assessment, children need to listen to a sentence and then repeat it with you placing a counter down for each word. Ensure you do the practice sentence together first.

Practice:	Sam loves ham.
Sentence 1:	Look here!
Sentence 2:	The red car.
Sentence 3:	The rain pours down.

B SYLLABLE AWARENESS
What to do
■ First say a word, for example: 'rabbit'; then ask the child to repeat it. Then clap the syllables and ask the child to do the same. Once the child clearly understands the task (repeat with more words if necessary), ask him/her to clap the syllables in the following words:

elephant (3)	tiger (2)
dinosaur (3)	television (4)

C MAINTAINING A SYLLABLE PATTERN
What to do
■ Say the following rhyme and tap the pattern; then ask the child to repeat and continue the pattern:

Pat-a-cake, pat-a-cake
Baker's man
Bake me a cake,
As fast as you can
Pat it and prick it
And mark it with 'B'
And put it in the oven
For Baby and me.

Record the child's progress for each section on Assessment 3 photocopiable page 34.

ASSESSMENT 4

A ALPHABET KNOWLEDGE
What to do
■ Using the set of alphabet cards from photocopiable pages 26, 27, and 28, ask the child to choose three and tell you which letter they represent. Do this again with three more cards to show overall alphabet knowledge.

B IDENTIFICATION OF LOWER- AND UPPER-CASE LETTERS
What to do
■ Copy the two grids below onto the whiteboard, and point to the letters at random. Ask the child to tell you the letter name. Ensure that the child can identify both upper- and lower-case letters.

J	X	O	D	Y	T	L
H	Q	A	K	G	W	N
C	P	I	R	Z	F	U
V	M	B	E	S		

j	x	o	d	y	t	l
h	q	a	k	g	w	n
c	p	i	r	z	f	u
v	m	b	e	s		

C IDENTIFICATION OF INITIAL LETTER SOUNDS
What to do
■ Say the following alliterative lines and ask the child to tell you the sound they hear lots of times.

Lucy loves licking lollies.
Billy buys blue badges.
Wendy's wobbly walks.
John's jolly jumps.

Record the child's progress for each section on Assessment 4 photocopiable page 34.

STAGE ONE: ASSESSMENT

Child's name:	Date:

ASSESSMENT 1

Focus	Objective	Comments
A Attentive listening	Ability to maintain concentration for short periods	
	Ability to sit still and focus on the speaker	
	Ability to wait to speak without interrupting the speaker	
	Recall of main facts	
	Recall of instructions	
	Appropriate response to questions	
B Discrimination of environmental sounds	Not distracted by extraneous noises	
	Good alertness to sounds	
	Ability to differentiate noises	
	Ability to describe noises correctly	
C Discrimination of speech sounds	Ability to discriminate a range of speech sounds	
	Ability to hear and copy speech sounds accurately	

Overall comments:

Areas for development:
NB Children need to show proficiency in each of these areas before progressing further.

Child's name:	Date:

ASSESSMENT 2

Focus	Objective	Comments/No. of correct answers
A Rhyme awareness	To know a range of nursery rhymes	
B Rhyme identification	To identify two rhyming words	
C Rhyme generation	To be able to generate own rhymes	

Overall comments:

Areas for development:

NB Children need to be secure in each of these areas before progressing further.

Child's name:	Date:

ASSESSMENT 3

Focus	Objective	Comments/No. of correct answers
A Word awareness	Children's ability to identify individual words	
B Syllable awareness	To identify syllables	
C Maintaining a syllable pattern	To maintain a syllable pattern	

Overall comments:

Areas for development:

NB Children need to show proficiency in each of these areas before progressing further.

ASSESSMENT 4

Focus	Objective	Comments/No. of correct answers
A Alphabet knowledge	To have overall awareness of letters of the alphabet	
B Identification of lower- and upper-case letters	To know letter names for all 26 letters, upper and lower case	
C Identification of initial letter sounds	To be able to identify a letter sound when repeated	

Overall comments:

Areas for development:

NB Children need to show proficiency in each of these areas before progressing further.

STAGE TWO
CONSONANTS AND SHORT VOWELS

STAGE TWO:
SUBJECT KNOWLEDGE

TEACHING ORDER AND PACE

Once children have developed the ability to hear distinctly and differentiate sounds, then the next step is to begin to teach the correspondence between phonemes and graphemes (the sounds and letters that represent them). It is easiest to begin with consonant phonemes and the short vowel phonemes. These can then be combined together (or blended) to support quick progress in reading. The programme is divided as follows:

> **Lessons 1-10:** introducing initial, medial and final phonemes using consonant-vowel-consonant (CVC) words
> **Lessons 11-20:** further phonemes and including consonant blends – consonant-consonant-vowel-consonant (CCVC), as in 'clap' and consonant-vowel-consonant-consonant (CVCC) words), as in 'vest'
> **Lessons 21-35:** further phonemes including digraphs and trigraphs as in 'chef' and 'watch'.

TEACHING ORDER GRID

The grid on page 9 shows the order of teaching one phoneme a day with the fifth day consisting of revision of phonemes taught that week (that is: four phonemes a week). This will need to be amended where there are fewer than five days in school in a week.

Not all children will be able to progress at this pace, particularly those who have an identified learning difficulty. However, the continual revision and over-learning within the lessons will help many children grasp this at a fast pace. You will find it useful to carry out the assessment activities regularly to monitor the children's progress and pick up any problems early on.

THE LESSONS

All the lessons follow the same format and link the phoneme to the grapheme and include blending and segmenting. Lessons have been provided for all phonemes, although once you become familiar with the structure, you may wish to adapt the lessons to suit your needs. The teaching order provides for four phonemes per week with revision of phonemes on the fifth day (typically a Friday). However, you will want to base the content of the lesson on the progress of your children. It is important to keep each lesson fast and pacy and they should last no longer than 20 minutes, ideally around 15 minutes.

AIDS FOR LEARNING

To help the children remember each phonic sound, the 'Phoneme cards' on photocopiable pages 42–45 provide a visual element to help their learning. Each card contains the phoneme, the alliterative phrase and an illustration to help children commit the sounds to memory. This information is also provided in more detail on the 'Phoneme–grapheme chart' on photocopiable page 41, which includes a list of all the phonemes and alliterative phrases, plus it includes details of fun actions and movements to use while teaching each phoneme and a list of common spellings for each sound. These are all used in the lesson plans for Stage 2.

The 'Phoneme pronunciation chart' on photocopiable page 40 gives detailed advice on how to pronounce each phoneme in the lesson plans for Stage 2. As the most common error is to add an 'uh' sound to phonemes (as in 'r' often pronounced 'ruh'), it is vital to ensure that each sound is pronounced correctly.

BLENDING AND SEGMENTING: USING 'ROBOT TALK'
Segmentation and blending

Segmentation means hearing the individual phonemes within a word; for instance the word 'crash' comprises four phonemes – /c/r/a/sh/. In order to spell, a child must segment a word into its component phonemes and choose a letter or letter combination (for example, 'sh') to represent each phoneme.

You might like to test your phonic knowledge by filling in the following chart on the page opposite. Answers can be found in the appendix at the back of this book, page 192.

Word	Number of phonemes	Split the word into phonemes
that		
ship		
thing		
splash		
day		
train		
spoon		
girl		
burn		
three		
sound		
spoil		
dress		
scrap		
flop		
stand		
make		
green		
smoke		
grass		
join		
bear		
horse		
know		

Blending is the process of combining phonemes together to pronounce a word. In order to read an unfamiliar word phonemically, a child must attribute a phoneme to each letter or letter combination in the word and then merge the phonemes together to pronounce the word (for example, /f/ /a/ /t/ = 'fat').

Robot talk

One way to introduce blending and segmenting to children is by using the analogy of 'robot talk'. Ask if any of the children have seen the Daleks in *Dr Who* on television. Ask for a volunteer to do an impersonation of a Dalek speaking. Use this as a springboard to explain how talking like a Dalek will help them learn to read. Introduce Robbie the Robot, using the picture on photocopiable page 39, which

you can enlarge on the photocopier and laminate. You may like to fix it to a small stick so you can hold it like a puppet.

> **Introducing Robbie the Robot:**
> 'This is Robbie and because he is a robot he talks in a strange way – a bit like a Dalek. Let's here him talk:
>   "/p/e/n/" (hold up the picture of the robot and pretend it is talking)
>   What do you think he said? Can you repeat it?
>   Yes "/p/e/n/". What does he mean? Well done! Yes he says "pen".
>   Now he does not understand you unless you talk like a robot. You need to say the sounds, remember we call them phonemes, separately. Shall we have a go? Let's try with pan. Good it's /p/a/n/. Can you say that to Robbie? Let's see if he says it back to you.
>   "/p/a/n/".
>   Well done! Remember when we talk to Robbie we must remember to talk in phonemes.'

Letter cards

It will be very useful to make a set of letter cards for all 26 letters (these should be large: approximately A4 size) and printed in a plain font. They should be laminated for constant use. You may like to make smaller (A5 size) cards for display also. Alternatively, photocopy and cut out the 'Phoneme cards' on photocopiable pages 42–45 to use as letter cards as well as phoneme cards, during each lesson for Stage 2.

Games and activities

Games are a great way to practise phonics skills. Phonics should consist of mainly oral activities mixed with some writing practice of graphemes and words. The use of games is particularly important for this age in order to make the activities fun, oral and interactive. A range of games is provided on pages 46 to 49. See also the range of games provided in the titles *Playing with Sounds* and *Progression in Phonics* (both available from the DfES, visit www.dfes.gov.uk). Suggestions are made within the lesson plans for when to use these games.

Assessment

It is important to accurately assess the children's

progress as you go along and to provide reinforcement as soon as children show signs of falling behind. Much of this can be done as you teach by observing the children closely and looking particularly at when they tell you how many phonemes are in a word or when they write a word for you to see on their whiteboards. The review lesson (every 5 days) is an ideal opportunity to check on progress by asking children to write words using the learned phonemes. If some children cause concern, provide extra support with individual or small group work. The assessment activity on photocopiable page 99 is planned to be used at the end of Stage 2, after all the consonant and short vowel sounds have been taught. You may wish to use the activities as a basis for creating more frequent assessments.

Reading practice and links with home

Links with home and encouraging parents to support children when they begin to learn to read are widespread. However, many parents are unsure how to help. The 'Minibooks' from photocopiable pages 84–98 for Stage 2 and photocopiable pages 169–186 for Stage 3 can be used to strengthen links with home, encouraging parents to support children when they begin to learn to read. Where possible, provide parents with guidance on using phonics to support early reading. Key elements to emphasise are the correct pronunciation of the phonemes and supporting children to read the words by blending the phonemes. Provide parents with a copy of the 'Phoneme pronunciation chart' on photocopiable page 40 to ensure the correct sounds are being made at home and school.

MINIBOOKS

The minibooks provide context for and revision of the phonemes. The grid below shows how the words used in the minibooks link to the phonemes taught. The minibooks should provide practice for children in blending the phonemes they have learned in order to read the words. There are a few words, however, (mainly high frequency words) which are recommended to be taught as sight vocabulary (see the list of sight words on page 120) that children will

need support with. These are clearly shown on the back page of each book.

Corresponding lessons	Book	New Words	Words children will need support with
1–10 New phonemes: /s/, /a/, /t/, /p/, /i/, /n/, /e/, /d/	1	in, sat, Ned, tap, a, an, Nat, din, at, tip, ant, sad, tent, it's, and, nip	never, camp, with, the
11–20 New phonemes: /m/, /g/, /o/, /c/ /k/, /u/, /r/, /b/, /f/	2	fog, rock, go, rub, gap, mend, must, stop, clap, duck, luck, strap, dub, big, or, can, get, no	good, we, the
21–35 New phonemes: /l/, /h/, /sh/, /z/, /w/, /ch/, /j/, /v/, /y/, /th/, /th/, /ng/, /zh/	3	lock, left, flat, help, land, hen, went, jump, van, yes, then, king, ring, string, till, fell, cluck, rug, the, his, had, with, top	when, there, sheep, sleep, treasure, watch, he, she, of

How to make the minibooks

Initially you might want to prepare the books before the lesson; however, later on the children might be eager to make their own books.

1. Photocopy the book pages onto A4 paper.

2. Fold the front and back cover sheet in half. Keep the fold line to the left-hand side.

3. Fold the inner pages in half. This time the fold line will be on the right-hand side.

4. Place the inner pages inside the cover.

5. Either staple or sew along the spine.

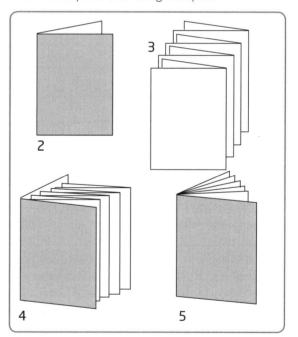

Robbie the Robot

SCHOLASTIC
www.scholastic.co.uk

PHONEME PRONUNCIATION CHART

Phoneme	Pronunciation guide for children
/s/	When we say /ssss/ the mouth is slightly open and the tongue is flat behind your teeth. Air comes out between your teeth. You can stretch the sound /s/s/s/s/.
/a/	Open your mouth wide and make a loud sound, as if something is nipping you /a/a/a/. You can stretch the sound.
/t/	When you say /t/ your mouth is open and your tongue is behind your teeth. It starts at the top of your mouth and goes down, feel the air come out of your mouth as you do it. Make it a very short sound and whisper it /t/t/t/.
/p/	When you say /p/ your lips touch together quickly. Imagine you are blowing a candle out on a cake and make it a very short sound and whisper it /p/p/p/.
/i/	When you say /i/ your mouth is open a tiny bit. The corners of your mouth pull back. You can stretch the sound /i/i/i/i/.
/n/	When you say /n/ the tip of your tongue goes behind your top teeth and your tongue does not move. You can stretch the sound /n/n/n/n/.
/e/	When you say /e/ your mouth is open a little and your teeth are apart. It looks like you are smiling.
/d/	When you say /d/ you put the tip of your tongue behind your top teeth and your tongue moves down. It's a bit like /t/ but only a little air comes out of your mouth.
/m/	When you say /m/ your lips are together and it sounds like humming. You can stretch the sound /m/m/m/.
/g/	When you say /g/ you can feel the sound right at the back of your mouth. If you put your fingers on your throat you can feel the sound /g/g/g/.
/o/	When you say /o/, your mouth is open and your chin drops down a little. You can stretch the sound /o/o/o/.
/c/ /k/	When you make the sound /k/ you can feel the sound in the back of your mouth. It sounds a bit like /g/, but when you say /k/ you can feel air coming out from your mouth and whisper it /k/k/k/.
/u/	When you say /u/ your mouth is open just a little. You need to push some air out as you do it /u/u/u/.
/r/	When you make the /r/ sound your tongue lifts up in the back of your mouth. It sounds like a car going fast. You can stretch the sound /r/r/r/.
/b/	When you make this sound your lips go together and pop open when you say /b/. It is like /p/ but no air comes out /b/b/b/.
/f/	When you say /f/ your teeth touch your bottom lip. You make the /f/ sound by pushing air between your teeth. You can stretch the sound and whisper it /f/f/f/.
/l/	When you say /l/ your tongue moves to the top of your mouth. It stays there as you make the sound in the back of your mouth. You can stretch the sound /l/l/l/.
/h/	When you make the sound /h/ your mouth is open a little. You push air out of your mouth to whisper it /h/h/h/. You can stretch the sound.
/sh/	When you make the sound /sh/ your teeth are together and you push air out of your mouth. It is the sound you make when you want someone to be quiet. You can stretch the sound /sh/sh/sh/.
/z/	When you make the sound /z/ your teeth are together and your tongue is near the front of your mouth and behind your teeth. You push air through your teeth and it makes a buzzing noise. You can stretch the sound /z/z/z/.
/w/	When you say the sound /w/ your lips are close together in a little circle, then they open up /w/w/w/.
/ch/	When you say /ch/ your lips stick out a little. Your teeth are together at first and then they open up. It sounds like a steam train /ch/ch/ch/.
/j/	When you say the sound /j/ your lips stick out a little. Your tongue is near the top of your mouth and it moves when you open your mouth /j/j/j/.
/v/	When you say /v/ your teeth touch your bottom lip. You make the /v/ sound by pushing air between your teeth. You can stretch the sound /v/v/v/.
/y/	When you make the /y/ sound your mouth is open a little and your tongue is near the top of your mouth. Your tongue touches the sides of your teeth. Your mouth is open a little more at the end of the sound /y/y/y/.
/th/	When you make the sound /th/ as in 'thin', you put your tongue between your teeth and stick it out. You push air between your tongue and teeth. You can stretch the sound and whisper it /th/th/th/.
/th/	When you make this sound as in 'this' your tongue touches the top of your mouth and it vibrates. Your can feel the sound in your throat. You can stretch the sound /th/th/th/.
/ng/	When you make this sound it is like a humming sound at the back of your throat but you make it with your mouth open. You can stretch the sound /ng/ng/ng/.
/zh/	When you make this sound your lips are open in a little circle and you blow air through your mouth. Your mouth opens wider at the end of the sound. /zh/zh/zh/.

PHONEME-GRAPHEME CHART

Phonemes in teaching order	Alliterative phrase	Action	Common spellings	List of other words for most common spelling
/s/	Snakes on slippery sand	Move hand like a snake	**s**un, mou**se**, **c**ity, me**ss**, **sc**ience, mi**ce**	sat, sad, saw, sand, see, snake, sit, son
/a/	Ants and apples	Fingers crawl up to mouth and then pretend to munch an apple	**a**pple	age, ant, and, ask, add, at, angry, rat, pan, wag, man
/t/	Ten tall towers	Stand on tiptoe and hold ten fingers up straight	**t**ap, be**tt**er	ten, tea, take, table, tank, tape, tell, tent, tin, top, tower
/p/	Pet in the park	Pretend to stroke a pet	**p**aper, hi**pp**o	pen, pin, pat, pant, park, peg, pet, pig, pip, pot
/i/	Imps and itchy insects	Jump up and down and pretend to scratch	**i**nk, buck**e**t	Indian, inch, imp, it, insect, tin, sit
/n/	Nests and nets catch nuts	Pretend to throw a nut and catch in a net	**n**oise, **kn**ife, **gn**at	net, nut, nest, neck, nap, new, nose, nut
/e/	Elephants eat eleven eggs	Pretend to be an elephant with one arm dangling like a trunk	**e**gg, br**ea**d	elephant, elf, end, edge, echo, eleven, ten
/d/	Dogs and ducks dig dens	Pretend to dig with two hands like a dog with paws	**d**og, pu**dd**le	dig, drill, doll, desk, dish, duck, dinosaur
/m/	Monkeys march up mountains	Do a funny march	**m**an, ha**mm**er, co**mb**	monkey, my, mad, me, mountain, moon,
/g/	Girls giggle with goats	Giggle and point to a girl	**g**ame, e**gg**	goose, girl, gurgle, giggle, goat
/o/	Octopuses on oranges	Wave arms around and try and balance on one leg	**o**ctopus, w**a**nt	ox, on, orange, dot, top, pot, log
/c/ /k/	Camels kick cakes	Bend and hunch your back and then kick one leg	**c**at, **Ch**ris, **k**ing, lu**ck**, **q**ueen	caterpillar, cake, camel, cap, kitten, kite, kettle, kick
/u/	Umbrellas and uncles jump	Pretend to hold an umbrella and jump	**u**mbrella, l**o**ve,	under, uncle, up, us, plug, sun, jump
/r/	Rabbits run and rest	Pretend to be a rabbit whichs hops then suddenly stops	**r**abbit, **wr**ong, be**rr**y	rain, ran, rat, read, rest, rag
/b/	Boys and bells on the bus	Pretend to sit on a bus and jump up and ring the bell	**b**aby, ca**bb**age	bat, ball, belt, bug, bus, book
/f/	Five floppy fish flap	Flap arms like a fish	**f**ish, **ph**oto, co**ff**ee	fun, flat, flower, fall, feet, fire, five
/l/	Lick the lemon lolly	Lick a lolly	**l**eg, spe**ll**	log, lock, leaf, lid, lamb, lolly, leaf, lemon, lick
/h/	Hopping happy hens	Hop and squawk	**h**at	hand, he, hear, heel, hen, here, hit, hop, hot, hug
/sh/	Sharks and shells on the shore	Open your mouth and show your teeth and with arms outstretched and hands together, move arms	**sh**ip, mi**ss**ion, **ch**ef	shoe, shark, she, shop, shy, shell, dish, crash, shore
/z/	Zebras buzz in zoos	Gallop round and make buzzing noise	**z**ebra, plea**se**, i**s**, fi**zz**y, snee**ze**	zip, zoo, zigzag, buzz
/w/	Water wheels went whoosh	Circle arms round and say 'whoosh'	**w**ater, **wh**eel, q**u**een	was, web, wave, wish, wag, went
/ch/	Chop chips and cheese	Pretend to chop with a knife	**ch**ip, wa**tch**	cheese, choose, church, chop, chick, chair
/j/	Jelly jiggles in the jug	Pretend to hold a jug which wobbles	**j**ug, ju**dge**, **g**iant, bar**ge**	jam, jeep, jet, jump, jelly
/v/	Vinegar on the van and vest	Try and wipe off split vinegar	**v**an, slee**ve**	voice, vest, vet, very, vinegar, verb, vulture
/y/	Yell for yummy yoghurt	Shout 'yum, yum' and rub your tummy	**y**es	yawn, young, you, yell, yo-yo, yoghurt
/th/	Thimble on a thumb	Point to a pretend thimble on your thumb	**th**in	thumb, thick, thunder, moth
/th/	Feather with this	Pretend to tickle with a soft feather	**th**en	that, this, feather, with
/ng/	King with a ring	Pretend to put a crown on your head and a ring on your finger	ri**ng**, si**n**k	pong, song, string, bang, king, hang, fang
/zh/	Pleasure to find treasure	Pretend to open a box and find treasure and say, 'Wow!'	trea**s**ure	measure, leisure, pleasure

Phoneme cards

/s/	/a/
Snakes on slippery sand	Ants and apples
/t/	/p/
Ten tall towers	Pet in the park
/i/	/n/
Imps and itchy insects	Nests and nets catch nuts
/e/	/d/
Elephants eat eleven eggs	Dogs and ducks dig dens

STAGE TWO: PHOTOCOPIABLES

PHONICS: A COMPLETE SYNTHETIC PROGRAMME FOR AGES 4+

Phoneme cards

/m/ Monkeys march up mountains

/g/ Girls giggle with goats

/o/ Octopuses on oranges

/c/ /k/ Camels kick cakes

/u/ Umbrellas and uncles jump

/r/ Rabbits run and rest

/b/ Boys and bells on the bus

/f/ Five floppy fish flap

STAGE TWO: PHOTOCOPIABLES

Phoneme cards

/l/ Lick the lemon lolly

/h/ Hopping happy hens

/sh/ Sharks and shells on the shore

/z/ Zebras buzz in zoos

/w/ Water wheels went whoosh

/ch/ Chop chips and cheese

/j/ Jelly jiggles in the jug

/v/ Vinegar on the van and vest

PHONICS: A COMPLETE SYNTHETIC PROGRAMME FOR AGES 4+

Phoneme cards

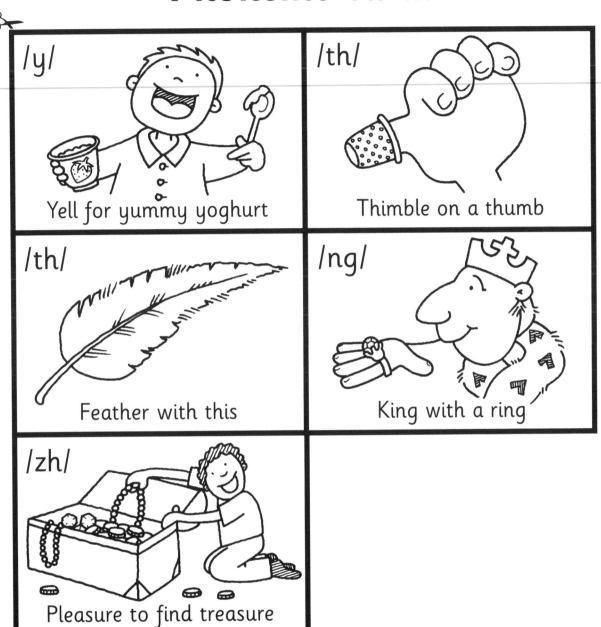

/y/	/th/
Yell for yummy yoghurt	Thimble on a thumb
/th/	/ng/
Feather with this	King with a ring
/zh/	
Pleasure to find treasure	

STAGE TWO:
PHONIC GAMES

These games can be used in a variety of ways and are aimed at practice, particularly for the revision lessons.

YES/NO GAME

Use this game
When teaching lessons 1–20 for practice in discriminating sounds.

What you need
Two large pieces of card.

What to do
■ Write the words 'yes' and 'no' on large pieces of card and fix them in clear positions on the wall in two corners of the room.

■ Ask a group or class of children to sit on the carpet, quickly revise the phonemes taught during the week by showing the corresponding phoneme cards (see photocopiable pages 42–45) and saying the alliterative phrases.

■ Now read from the following list of words, mixing words that do, or do not, begin with phonemes taught. Explain that if it begins with a phoneme they have been learning this week, they should point to the 'yes' word and if not to the 'no' word.

■ Ensure the game is fast, fun and lively.

Week	Words beginning with taught phonemes	Words NOT beginning with taught phonemes
1	sat, sad, saw, sand, see, snake ant, apple, ask, at, ask tap, ten, tea, table, tank, top pen, pin, pat, peg, pig, pot	dog, egg, ink, cat, baby fish, hat, van, game rat, mad, bus, fun hot, yawn, wish, jump
2	inch, imp, it, insect, ink nest, net, nut, neck, nap, new egg, elephant, eat, elf, echo dog, dig, drill, doll, duck	sun, tea, pin, top, sit hand, octopus, berry girl, kite, leaf, hot fat, man, ant, leg
3	man, monkey, master, mouse game, goose, girl, goat orange, ox, octopus, odd cat, cake, caterpillar, kite, kitten	neck, eat, duck, tea apple, elephant, table fish, dish, elf, eleven nut, hot, zip, cheese
4	umbrella, uncle, up, us, under rat, run, rain, read, rag baby, bent, bat, ball, book flower, fish, fun, fire, five	girl, cake, sand, ten Indian, nest, egg happy, dinosaur, game log, moon, ox, tower

GRAPHEME PAIRS

Use this game
When teaching lessons 1–20 for practice reading graphemes for initial letter sounds.

What you need
Copies of 'Graphemes pairs' photocopiable page 50 cut up into cards.

What to do
■ Copy, laminate and cut up the cards. The name of the object and the picture should be separate.

■ Play a game of 'Pairs'. Provide a group of children with the cards spread out face down over a table. Ask the children to take turns to turn over two cards. If they turn over a word that corresponds to the picture, they are allowed to keep the pairs.

■ The winner is the child who has the most pairs at the end of the game.

MAGNETIC LETTERS

Use this game
When teaching any lessons from 1–35 for practice in manipulating graphemes and blending phonemes.

What you need
A large pack of magnetic letters and several small magnetic boards (one between two pupils) for use with a small group, or one large magnetic board for demonstration.

What to do
■ With a small group or the whole class, display the graphemes taught recently on the magnetic board and ask the children what sounds they make.

■ Next explain that you want to try and make some words with the letters and ask the children to help you. You may need to demonstrate one or two first, but encourage children to suggest and make words themselves.

■ If they come up with 'non-words', such as 'pon', praise their efforts as this shows a clear ability to blend phonemes but point out that this is not a real word.

■ Where possible, provide small magnetic boards for the children to use for further practice.

POLLY PUPPET

Use this game
When teaching any lessons from 1–35 for practice in discriminating, blending and segmenting sounds. It is useful for the revision lessons.

What you need
A puppet.

What to do
■ The aim is that the puppet will either always pronounce phonemes wrongly, or make other mistakes such as miscounting the number of phonemes. Alternatively the puppet can be used in the same way as 'Robbie the Robot' who only talks in phonemes.

■ Hold up the puppet and the phoneme card for one of the phonemes you are revising (see pages 42–45

for phoneme cards). In the voice of the puppet, say the phoneme wrongly and ask the children to correct her. Ensure the correct pronunciation is emphasised.

■ As a follow-up, display some words created from the phonemes you wish to practise. In the voice of the puppet, say the phonemes and then say the word. Again ask the children to help when the puppet gets it wrong.

READ WITH YOUR PARTNER

Use this game
When teaching any lessons from 1–35 for practice in blending phonemes.

What you need
Word cards from 'Grapheme pairs' photocopiable page 50; sand timer; minibooks at the appropriate stage for the children.

What to do
■ This game can be played in two ways.

■ First, ask the children to work in pairs and provide each pair with a set of words cards. Tell the children to take turns reading the cards to each other, sounding out the phonemes and blending them

together to make the word. Challenge them to read as many words as they can in one minute. Can their partner beat their score?

■ Later, pair up children by ability and give each pair one of the minibooks suitable for their level. Ask the children to take turns to read a page of the book to their partner (helping each other as necessary). Tell them to swap readers for each page until the book is completed.

WHICH GRAPHEME?

Use this game
When teaching lessons 1–35 for practice in making grapheme choices.

What you need
'Which grapheme?' photocopiable page 51 cut up into cards and laminated – you will need one set per pair of children.

What to do
■ Organise the children into pairs.
■ Say a word from the list below, emphasising the phoneme highlighted in bold.

■ Ask the children to consult with their partner and then hold up the correct grapheme for the part of the word you emphasise.

sun	**c**ity	**t**ap
be**tt**er	**p**aper	hi**pp**o
nut	**kn**ife	**e**lephant
br**ea**d	**m**an	ha**mm**er
game	e**gg**	**r**at
be**rr**y	**f**ish	**ph**oto
leg	spe**ll**	**sh**ip
chef	**z**ebra	plea**se**
wig	**qu**een	**ch**ip
wa**tch**	**j**ug	**g**iant

SILLY SENTENCES

Use this game
When teaching lessons 21–35 for practice in blending phonemes.

What you need
'Silly sentences (2)' photocopiable page 52 cut up into individual sentence cards and laminated – you will need one set per pair of children.

What to do
■ In a small group or with the whole class, organise the children to work in pairs. Hold up the sentences and ask the children to work with their partner to blend the phonemes to read the words. Pick children to tell you the sentence.
■ Alternatively give one sentence to each pair and ask them to help each other to read the sentence, ensuring they blend the phonemes together.

HOW MANY PHONEMES?

Use this game
When teaching lessons 21–35 for practice in blending phonemes.

What you need
List of words below:

sand (4)	trip (4)	strip (5)	rich (3)	flick (4)
hunch (4)	shell (3)	thick (3)	string (5)	she (2)

STAGE TWO: PHONIC GAMES

CONSONANTS AND SHORT VOWELS

What to do

■ Say the words from the list above as clearly as possible. Ask the children to quickly work out how many phonemes in the word and hold up the corresponding number of fingers.

■ Keep the activity short and fast paced and fun.

FIND THE SOUND IN THE RHYME

Use this game
When teaching lessons 21–35 for practice in making grapheme choices.

What you need
An enlarged copy of 'The Lodge' photocopiable page 53.

What to do

■ Read the poem on photocopiable page 53 to the children, without showing it to them.

■ Re-read it, instructing the children to listen carefully and to put their hand up every time they hear the phoneme /j/.

■ Afterwards show the poem to the children and talk about the different graphemes for the phoneme /j/.

SPELL IT!

Use this game
When teaching lessons 11–35 for practice in segmenting and spelling words.

What you need
List of words below; whiteboards.

man	king	kick	photo	rest	lemon
hand	shop	shell	zip	chick	jam
van	yell	thick	with	ring	bang

What to do

■ The aim of this game is for children to hear words and then segment them into phonemes to help spell the word.

■ Working with a small group or the whole class, read from the list of words above to the children.

■ Read each word slowly, asking the children to write the word on their whiteboard. Repeat each word as necessary and give children time to write the word. You may like to ask children to work in pairs to support each other with this.

STAGE TWO: PHONIC GAMES

Grapheme pairs

snake	ant	tower	pet
insect	nest	elephant	dog
monkey	girls	octopus	camel
umbrella	rabbit	bells	fish

SCHOLASTIC
www.scholastic.co.uk

PHONICS: A COMPLETE SYNTHETIC PROGRAMME FOR AGES 4+

Which grapheme?

s	c	t	tt	p
pp	n	kn	e	ea
m	mm	g	gg	r
rr	f	ph	l	ll
sh	ch	z	se	w
u	ch	tch	j	g

■SCHOLASTIC
www.scholastic.co.uk

Silly sentences (2)

The queen ran with the rabbit and the rat.

Eggs and fridges watch big wheels.

Caterpillars lick lollies in the mist.

Treasure chests and ships sink.

Under the sun sits a duck, ox and kitten.

It is fish, coffee and cabbage for dinner.

Ants and apples catch shells.

Kings and queens sit at desks and hop.

STAGE TWO: PHOTOCOPIABLES

PHONICS: A COMPLETE SYNTHETIC PROGRAMME FOR AGES 4+

The Lodge

Cousin Reg
Got stuck on a ledge.
Uncle Dodge
Dislodged him.
But Cousin Reg
Went over the edge
And landed on
Auntie ... Bridget!

Dad's got the plunger,
Mum's got the sponge,
Who filled the sink
With galactic gunge?

by Sarah Hayes

From *Sound City* by Sarah Hayes (1998, Walker Books)

STAGE TWO: PHOTOCOPIABLES

STAGE TWO:
LESSON PLANS

LESSON 1 /s/

1 ALPHABET FUN *(2-3 mins)*
■ Begin by reciting in a lively way the 'Alphabet rhyme' (on photocopiable page 25) which has been taught at Stage 1.
■ Encourage the children to do the actions for each letter (for example: 'A' is for apple – pretend to bite an apple) and ensure that the children understand that these are the names of the letters.

2 NEW LETTER SOUND /s/ *(6-8 mins)*
Hear it
■ Show the phoneme picture card of the phoneme /s/ on photocopiable page 42. Ask the children what they can see on the picture. Describe the picture emphasising the initial sounds of 'sssssnake' and 'ssssand'.
■ Read the alliterative phrase 'Snakes on slippery sand' emphasising the initial sounds. Ask the children to repeat it and tell their partner what sound they can hear.
■ Teach the corresponding action as you say the phrase (move hand like a snake).

> **Now or later**
> ■ Play a game such as the 'Tray game' found in *Progression in Phonics* (see page 37) for reinforcement.

Say it
■ Ask the children to repeat the phoneme /s/ /s/ /s/ to their partner. Reinforce correct pronunciation and explain that when we say /ssss/ our mouths are slightly open and the tongue is flat behind our teeth. Air comes out between our teeth. Model how you can stretch the sound /s/s/s/s/ and ask the children to repeat it.
■ Encourage the children to talk in 'robot talk' by using 'Robbie Robot' (see guidance on pages 36–37). Say a word beginning with 's', for example, 'sun' in 'robot talk': /s/u/n/, and ask the children to guess

what word it is. Explain that they will be learning more robot talk in the future.

Read it
■ Hold up a letter card for the lower-case letter 's' (or alternatively use the 'Phoneme cards' on pages 42–45). Quickly show the children the 's' card and ask them to tell their partner the sound it makes. Display on an easel or pocket chart.

Write it
■ Say the phoneme /s/ again and ask the children to write the corresponding letter on their individual whiteboards. Emphasise the correct letter formation by saying: 'Start at the top and go down and round the snake.' Model the formation as you say it with your finger in the air. Encourage the children to practise letter formation in the air, or on their partner's back, first and then to write on their whiteboards. For additional practice at a later time, provide line guides for children to practise correct letter formation.

/s/

Snakes on slippery sand

LESSON 2 /a/

1 ALPHABET FUN (2-3 mins)

■ Begin by reciting in a lively way the 'Alphabet rhyme' on photocopiable page 25.

■ Encourage the children to do the actions for each letter and ensure that they understand that these are the names of the letters.

2 REVIEW (5-6 mins)

Hear it

■ Using the phoneme card /s/ (see photocopiable page 42), describe the picture emphasising the initial sound, 'snake'. Then say the alliterative phrase 'Snakes on slippery sand' and ask the children to repeat it with the action.

Say it

■ Using several words containing the phoneme /s/, say these slowly in 'robot talk': /s/u/n/, /s/a/n/d/, /s/i/t/. Ask the children to blend the phonemes into words and tell their partners.

■ Now ask the children to talk in 'robot talk'. Say a word, for example, 'sad', and ask them to segment it using 'robot talk' first to a partner and then all together.

Read it

■ Hold up a letter card for 's', and ask the children to tell you the sound (phoneme) it makes.

Write it

■ Say the phoneme /s/ and ask the children to write the corresponding letter on their individual whiteboards. Invite them to show you what they have written for a quick assessment.

3 NEW LETTER SOUND /a/ (6-8 mins)

Hear it

■ Show the card for the phoneme /a/ and describe the picture. Ask the children to say the sounds they can hear. Explain that we call this phoneme a vowel. Explain that this is a special letter and we have short and long vowel phonemes. We need a vowel in every word.

■ Read the alliterative phrase 'Ants and apples' emphasising the initial sound – 'ants' and 'apples'.

■ Teach the corresponding action as you say the phrase (fingers crawl up to mouth and then pretend to munch an apple).

> **Now or later**
> ■ Play the 'Yes/no game' (see page 46) for the letter 'a' for reinforcement by saying words that either do or do not begin with 'a'.

Say it

■ Ask the children to repeat the phoneme /a/ /a/ /a/. Reinforce correct pronunciation and explain we open our mouths wide and make a loud sound, as if something is nipping us /a/a/a/. Model stretching the sound. Practise saying it several times.

■ Say several words containing the phoneme /a/ in initial and medial position using 'robot talk': /a/t/, /a/n/t/, /r/a/t/. Ask the children to blend the phonemes into words and tell their partner. Although you have not taught all these sounds, it is good practice at beginning blending.

Read it

■ Display the 'a' letter card next to the 's' card and ask the children to read the two letters separately saying their sounds (rather than names). Display on an easel or pocket chart.

Write it

■ Now say the phoneme /a/ again and ask the children to write the letter. Demonstrate first by using your finger in the air, then on the board or easel. Ask the children to draw the letter in the air, and emphasise the correct letter formation and starting point. Invite them to practise and then to write on their whiteboards and show you.

■ Now try and begin the process of segmenting sounds. Say a word containing the phoneme /a/ (for example, 'at'). First ask the children to tell their partner how many phonemes in the word by counting on their fingers and then to hold up the correct number of fingers. Explain that you will be learning the sound /t/ next time.

LESSON 3 /t/

1 ALPHABET FUN *(2-3 mins)*
■ Begin by reciting in a lively way the 'Alphabet rhyme' (on photocopiable page 25).
■ Encourage the children to do the actions for each letter.

2 REVIEW *(5-6 mins)*
Hear it
■ Using the phoneme cards /a/ and /s/, say what is on the pictures emphasising the initial sounds. Then say the alliterative phrases and ask the children to repeat them with the actions.

Say it
■ Using several words containing /a/ and /s/, say these slowly in 'robot talk' for example /s/a/d/, /s/a/t/. Ask the children to blend the phonemes into words and tell their partners.
■ Now ask the children to talk in 'robot talk'. Say a word, for example, 'sag', and ask them to segment it using 'robot talk' first to a partner and then all together.

Read it
■ Hold up letter cards for 'a' and 's', ask the children to tell you the sounds (phonemes) they make.

Write it
■ Say the phonemes /a/ and /s/ and ask the children to write the corresponding letters. Invite them to show you what they have written for a quick assessment.

3 NEW LETTER SOUND /t/ *(6-8 mins)*
Hear it
■ Show the card of the phoneme /t/ and describe the picture emphasising the initial sound. Ask the children to say the sound they can hear.
■ Read the alliterative phrase 'Ten tall towers' emphasising the initial sounds – 'ten' 'tall' and 'towers'.
■ Teach the corresponding action as you say the phrase (stand on tiptoe and hold ten fingers up straight).

Say it
■ Ask the children to repeat the phoneme: /t/ /t/ /t/. Reinforce the correct pronunciation of the phoneme explain that when we say /t/ our mouths are open and our tongues are behind our teeth. It starts at the top of our mouth and goes down; the children should feel the air come out of their mouth as they do it. Make it a very short sound and whisper it, /t/t/t/. Practise saying it several times.
■ Say several words containing the phoneme /t/ in initial and final position using 'robot talk': /t/e/n/, /a/t/, /s/a/t/. Ask the children to blend the phonemes into words and tell their partner. Although you have not taught all these phonemes, it is good practice at beginning blending.

> **Now or later**
> ■ Play 'Polly puppet' on page 47, where the puppet gets the initial phoneme wrong for the words beginning with 't', for example, 'top', 'tin', 'tap'. You may like to use objects to reinforce this. This game can be played at any time during the day to reinforce hearing and saying the phoneme correctly.

Read it
■ Display the 't' letter card next to 'a' and 's' and ask the children to read the letter sounds (rather than the letter names) separately.

Write it
■ Now say the phoneme /t/ again and ask the children to write the letter. Demonstrate first by using your finger in the air, then on the board or easel. Ask the children to draw the letter in the air, and emphasise the correct letter formation and starting point. Ask them to practise and then to write on their whiteboards and show you.
■ Say a word containing the phoneme /t/ (for example, 'top'). First ask the children to tell their partner how many phonemes in the word by counting and then to hold up the correct number of fingers. Ask the children to write the word if they are able (as they have not learned all the letters yet). Explain that they will learn the sound /p/ next time.

LESSON 4 /p/

1 ALPHABET FUN (2-3 mins)
■ Begin by reciting in a lively way the 'Alphabet rhyme' on photocopiable page 25.
■ Encourage the children to do the actions for each letter.

2 REVIEW (5-6 mins)
Hear it
■ Using the phoneme cards /t/, /a/ and /s/, describe the pictures emphasising the initial sounds. Then say the alliterative phrases and ask the children to repeat them with the actions.

Say it
■ Using several words containing the phonemes taught so far, say these slowly in 'robot talk', for example: /s/a/t/, /a/t/. Ask the children to blend the phonemes into words and tell their partners.
■ Now ask the children to speak in 'robot talk'. Say a word, for example, 'sat', and ask them to segment it using 'robot talk' first to a partner and then all together.

Read it
■ Hold up letter cards for 't', 'a' and 's', and ask the children to tell you the sounds (phonemes) that they make.

Write it
■ Say the phonemes /t/, /a/ and /s/ to the children and ask them to write the corresponding letters on their individual whiteboards. Invite them to show you what they have written for a quick assessment.

3 NEW LETTER SOUND /p/ (6-8 mins)
Hear it
■ Show the card of the phoneme /p/ and describe the picture, emphasising the initial sounds. Ask the children to say the sound they hear.
■ Read the alliterative phrase 'Pet in the park', emphasising the initial sounds – 'pet' and 'park'.
■ Teach the corresponding action as you say the phrase (pretend to stroke a pet).

Say it
■ Ask the children to repeat the phoneme /p/ /p/ /p/. Reinforce correct pronunciation and explain that when you say /p/ your lips touch together quickly. It is a quiet sound like a whisper. Imagine that you are blowing a candle out on a cake and make it a very short sound, /p/p/p/. Practise saying it several times.
■ Say several words containing the phoneme /p/ in initial and final position using 'robot talk', for example: /p/a/t/, /t/a/p/, /a/s/p/. Ask the children to blend the phonemes into words and tell their partner.

Read it
■ Display the 'p' letter card next to the 't', 'a' and 's' cards and ask the children to read the letters separately saying their sounds (rather than their names).

> **Now or later**
> ■ Play 'Magnetic letters' on page 47, where the children explore making words with the phonemes taught. This can be for children to explore during independent work.

Write it
■ Say the phoneme /p/ again and ask the children to write the letter. Demonstrate first by using your finger in the air, then on the board or easel. Ask the children to draw the letter in the air and emphasise the correct letter formation and starting point. Invite them to practise and then to write on their whiteboards and show you.
■ Say a word containing the phoneme /p/ (for example, 'pat') and the other phonemes taught so far. Ask the children to tell their partner how many phonemes in the word by counting and then to hold up the correct number of fingers. Ask the children to write the word if they are able.

STAGE TWO: LESSON PLANS

LESSON 5: REVISION

1 ALPHABET FUN *(2-3 mins)*

■ Begin by reciting in a lively way the 'Alphabet rhyme' (see photocopiable page 25).

■ Encourage children to do the actions for each letter.

2 REVIEW SOUNDS *(10 mins)*

Hear it

■ Using the phoneme cards, say the name of the pictures emphasising the initial sound. Invite the children to say the word after you. Ask the children what sound they can hear. Repeat for all letters covered during the week in a brisk, pacy way.

■ Play the 'Yes/no game', 'Polly puppet' or 'Magnetic letters' on pages 46 and 47 for reinforcement.

Say it

■ Using several words containing the phonemes taught in initial, medial and final position, say these slowly in 'robot talk'.

■ Now ask the children to speak in 'robot talk' by saying a word, for example: 'pat', and ask them to segment it using 'robot talk'.

Read it

■ Using letter cards (or alternatively use the phoneme cards for pages 42–45), quickly show the children the ones learned from the week and ask them to tell you the sound each one makes.

■ Select three words for each phoneme taught that week and ask the children to read them by blending.

Write it

■ Provide the children with individual whiteboards and pens. Explain that you are going to say the phoneme and the children will write the letter. Quickly revise all letters taught that week in this way.

■ Say a word containing a recently taught phoneme. First ask the children to tell you how many phonemes there are in the word by counting on their fingers and showing you, and then ask them to write the word. Practise for all phonemes taught that week. Ask the children to write some words using the phonemes.

■ Ensure you check the children's ability to hear, read and write all phonemes taught and provide reinforcement for any who need it.

How to adapt revision lessons

When you reach the end of each week it is important to recap the phonemes taught so far, to make sure that the children are ready to move on to the next level.

For each revision lesson, follow the format on this page and adapt as necessary, depending on the phonemes learned. Ensure that you note children's progress and reinforce where necessary. One useful assessment of ability to read and blend phonemes is to read nonsense words. Examples of these are provided when the Revision lessons are mentioned.

LESSON 6 /i/

1 ALPHABET FUN *(2-3 mins)*

■ Begin by reciting in a lively way the 'Alphabet rhyme' (on photocopiable page 25).

■ Encourage children to do the actions for each letter and ensure that they understand that these are the names of the letters.

2 REVIEW *(5-6 mins)*

Hear it

■ Using the phoneme cards /p/, /t/, /a/ and /s/ on photocopiable pages 42–45, describe the pictures emphasising the initial sound. Then say the alliterative phrases and ask the children to repeat them with the actions.

Say it

■ Using several words containing the phonemes taught so far, say these slowly in 'robot talk', for example: /p/a/t/, /t/a/p/ and /s/a/t/. Ask the children to blend the phonemes into words and tell their partners.

■ Now ask the children to speak in 'robot talk'. Say a word, for example, 'pat', and ask them to segment it using 'robot talk' first to a partner and then all together.

Read it

■ Hold up the letter cards 'p', 't', 'a' and 's', and ask the children to say the sounds (phonemes) they make.

Write it

■ Say the phonemes /p/, /t/, /a/ and /s/ and ask the children to write the corresponding letters on their individual whiteboards. Ask the children to show you what they have written for a quick assessment.

3 NEW LETTER SOUND /i/ *(6-8 mins)*

Hear it

■ Show the card of the phoneme /i/ and describe the picture, emphasising the initial sounds. Ask the children to say the sounds they can hear.

■ Read the alliterative phrase 'Imps and itchy insects' emphasising the initial sound in 'imps', 'itchy' and 'insects'.

■ Teach the corresponding action as you say the phrase (jump up and down and pretend to scratch).

Say it

■ Ask the children to repeat the phoneme /i/ /i/ /i/. Reinforce correct pronunciation and explain that when you say /i/ your mouth is open a tiny bit and the corners of your mouth pull back. You can stretch the sound /i/i/i/i/. Practise saying it several times.

■ Say several words containing the phoneme /i/ in initial and medial position using 'robot talk', for example: /i/t/, /i/m/p/, /t/i/p/. Ask the children to blend the phonemes into words and tell their partner.

> **Now or later**
> ■ Play 'Polly puppet' on page 47 with the puppet incorrectly identifying objects beginning with the phoneme /i/.

Read it

■ Display the 'i' letter card next to the 'p', 't', 'a' and 's' cards and ask the children to read the letters separately saying their sounds.

Write it

■ Now say the phoneme /i/ again and ask the children to write the letter. Demonstrate first by using your finger in the air, then on the board or easel. Ask the children to draw the letter in the air and emphasise the correct letter formation and starting point. Invite the children to practise and then to write on their whiteboards and show you.

■ Say a word containing the phoneme /i/ (for example: 'tin'). First ask the children to tell their partner how many phonemes in the word by counting and then to hold up the correct number of fingers. Ask the children to write the word if they are able. Explain that you will be learning the sound /n/ next time.

STAGE TWO: LESSON PLANS

LESSON 7 /n/

1 ALPHABET FUN *(2-3 mins)*

■ Begin by reciting in a lively way the 'Alphabet rhyme' (on photocopiable page 25).

■ Encourage the children to do the actions for each letter.

2 REVIEW *(5-6 mins)*
Hear it

■ Using the phoneme cards /i/, /p/, /t/, /a/ and /s/ (see photocopiable pages 42–45), describe the pictures emphasising the initial sounds. Then say the alliterative phrases and ask the children to repeat them with the actions.

Say it

■ Using several words containing /i/, /p/, /t/, /a/ and /s/, say these slowly in 'robot talk', for example: /p/i/t/, /t/a/p/, /s/a/t/. Ask the children to blend the phonemes into words and tell their partners.

■ Now ask the children to speak in 'robot talk'. Say a word, for example, 'tip', and ask them to segment it using 'robot talk' first to a partner and then all together.

Read it

■ Hold up letter cards for 'i', 'p', 't', 'a' and 's', and ask the children to tell you the sounds (phonemes) they make.

Write it

■ Say the phonemes /i/, /p/, /t/, /a/ and /s/ and ask the children to write the corresponding letters on their individual whiteboards. Invite them to show you what they have written for a quick assessment.

3 NEW LETTER SOUND /n/ *(6-8 mins)*
Hear it

■ Show the card of the phoneme /n/ to the class and describe the picture emphasising the initial sounds. Ask the children to say the sounds they can hear.

■ Read the alliterative phrase 'Nests and nets catch nuts' emphasising the initial sound in 'nests', 'nets' and 'nuts'.

■ Teach the corresponding action as you say the phrase (pretend to throw a nut and catch in a net).

Say it

■ Ask the children to repeat the phoneme /n/ /n/ /n/. Reinforce the correct pronunciation and explain that when you say /n/, the tip of your tongue goes behind your top teeth and your tongue does not move. You can stretch the sound /n/n/n/n/. Practise saying it several times.

■ Say several words containing the phoneme /n/ in the initial and final position using 'robot talk', for example: /n/e/t/, /n/a/p/, /t/a/n/. Ask the children to blend the phonemes into words and tell their partner.

Read it

■ Display the 'n' letter card next to 'i', 'p', 't', 'a' and 's' and ask the children to read out the letter sounds separately.

> **Now or later**
> ■ Play 'Magnetic letters' (see page 47) with the phonemes taught so far. This can be explored during independent activities.

Write it

■ Say the phoneme /n/ again and ask the children to write the letter. Demonstrate first by using your finger in the air, then on the board or easel. Ask the children to draw the letter in the air and emphasise the correct letter formation and starting point. Invite the children to practise and then to write on their whiteboards and show you.

■ Say a word containing the phoneme /n/ (for example, net). First ask the children to tell their partner how many phonemes are in the word by counting and then hold up the correct number of fingers. Ask the children to write the word if they are able. Explain that you will be learning the sound /e/ next time.

LESSON 8 /e/

1 ALPHABET FUN (2-3 mins)

■ Begin by reciting in a lively way the 'Alphabet rhyme' (on photocopiable page 25).

■ Encourage the children to do the actions for each letter.

2 REVIEW (5-6 mins)
Hear it

■ Using the phoneme cards /n/, /i/, /p/, /t/, /a/ and /s/ (see photocopiable pages 42–45), describe the pictures emphasising the initial sounds. Then say the alliterative phrases and ask the children to repeat them with the actions.

Say it

■ Using several words containing the phonemes taught so far, say these slowly in 'robot talk', for example: /n/i/p/, /p/a/t/, /p/i/n/ and /s/a/t/. Ask the children to blend the phonemes into words and tell their partners.

■ Now ask the children to speak in 'robot talk'. Say a word, for example, 'nit', and ask them to segment it using 'robot talk' first to a partner and then all together.

Read it

■ Hold up letter cards for 'n', 'i', 'p', 't', 'a' and 's', and ask the children to tell you the sounds (phonemes) they make.

Write it

■ Say the phonemes taught so far and ask the children to write the corresponding letters on their individual whiteboards. Invite them to show you what they have written for a quick assessment.

3 NEW LETTER SOUND /e/ (6-8 mins)
Hear it

■ Show the card for the phoneme /e/ and describe the picture, emphasising the initial sounds. Ask the children to say the sounds they can hear.

■ Read the alliterative phrase 'Elephants eat eleven eggs', emphasising the initial sound – 'elephants', 'eat' and 'eggs'.

■ Teach the corresponding action as you say the phrase (pretend to be an elephant with one arm dangling like a trunk).

Say it

■ Ask the children to repeat the phoneme /e/ /e/ /e/. Reinforce correct pronunciation of the phoneme and explain that when we say /e/ our mouths are open a little and our teeth are apart. It looks like we are smiling. The children should feel the tip of their tongue go behind their top teeth and their tongue does not move. You can stretch the sound /e/e/e/e/. Practise saying it several times.

■ Say several words containing the phoneme /e/ in initial and medial position using 'robot talk', for example: /e/gg/, /e/n/d/, /p/e/t/, /n/e/t/. Ask the children to blend the phonemes into words and tell their partner.

Read it

■ Display the 'e' letter card next to 'n', 'i', 'p', 't', 'a' and 's' and ask the children to read out the letter sounds separately.

> **Now or later**
> ■ Play 'Magnetic letters' (see page 47) with phonemes taught so far. This can be done during independent activities.

Write it

■ Now say the phoneme /e/ again and ask the children to write the letter. Demonstrate first by using your finger in the air, then on the board or easel. Ask the children to draw the letter in the air and emphasise the correct letter formation and starting point. Invite them to practise and then to write on their whiteboards and show you.

■ Say a word containing the phoneme /e/ (for example, end). First ask the children to tell their partner how many phonemes are in the word by counting and then to hold up the correct number of fingers. Ask the children to write the word if they are able. Explain that you will be learning the sound 'd' next time.

STAGE TWO: LESSON PLANS

LESSON 9 /d/

1 ALPHABET FUN *(2-3 mins)*

■ Begin by reciting in a lively way the 'Alphabet rhyme' (on photocopiable page 25).

■ Encourage children to do the actions for each letter.

2 REVIEW *(5-6 mins)*

Hear it

■ Using the phoneme cards /e/, /n/, /i/, /p/, /t/, /a/ and /s/, describe the pictures emphasising the initial sound. Then say the alliterative phrases and ask the children to repeat them with the actions.

Say it

■ Using several words containing the phonemes taught so far, say these slowly in 'robot talk', for example: /t/e/n/, /p/i/n/ and /n/e/t/. Ask the children to blend the phonemes into words and tell their partners.

■ Now ask the children to speak in 'robot talk'. Say a word, for example, 'nit', and ask them to segment it using 'robot talk' first to a partner and then all together.

Read it

■ Hold up the letter cards 'e', 'n', 'i', 'p', 't', 'a' and 's', and ask the children to tell you the sounds (phonemes) they make.

Write it

■ Say the phonemes taught so far and ask the children to write the corresponding letters on their individual whiteboards. Invite them to show you what they have written for a quick assessment.

3 NEW LETTER SOUND /d/ *(6-8 mins)*

Hear it

■ Show the card for the phoneme /d/ to the class and describe the picture emphasising initial sounds. Ask the children to say the sounds they can hear.

■ Read the alliterative phrase 'Dogs and ducks dig dens' emphasising the initial sound – 'dogs', 'ducks', 'dig' and 'dens'.

■ Teach the corresponding action as you say the phrase (pretend to dig with two hands like a dog with paws).

Say it

■ Ask the children to repeat the phoneme /d/ /d/ /d/. Reinforce the correct pronunciation and explain that when we say /d/ we put the tip of our tongue behind our top teeth and our tongue moves down. It is similar to a /t/ but only a little air comes out of our mouth. Practise saying it several times.

■ Say several words containing the phoneme /d/ in the initial position using 'robot talk', for example: /d/i/p/, /d/e/n/, /d/r/i/ll/. Ask the children to blend the phonemes into words and tell their partner.

> **Now or later**
> ■ Play a game of 'Read with your partner' (see page 47), practising reading words containing the phonemes taught so far. This can be done at any time during the day to reinforce blending phonemes for reading.

Read it

■ Display the 'd' letter card next to 'e', 'n', 'i', 'p', 't', 'a' and 's', and ask the children to read out the letter sounds separately.

Write it

■ Now say the phoneme /d/ again and ask the children to write the letter. Demonstrate first by using your finger in the air, then on the board or easel. Ask the children to draw the letter in the air, emphasising correct letter formation and starting point. Invite them to practise and then to write on their whiteboards and show you.

■ Say a word containing the phoneme /d/ (for example, dip). First ask the children to tell their partner how many phonemes there are in the word by counting and then to hold up the correct number of fingers. Ask the children to write the word if they are able.

> **LESSON 10**
> **REVISE PHONEMES TAUGHT**
> ■ Follow the format from the previous revision lesson (see Lesson 5 on page 58) to revise all phonemes taught in the week.

LESSON 11 /m/

1 ALPHABET FUN *(2-3 mins)*

■ Begin by reciting in a lively way the 'Alphabet rhyme' on (photocopiable page 25).
■ Encourage the children to do the actions for each letter.

2 REVIEW *(5-6 mins)*

Hear it

■ Using the phoneme cards taught so far, describe the pictures emphasising the initial sounds. Then say the alliterative phrases and ask the children to repeat them with the actions.

Say it

■ Using several words containing the phonemes taught so far in initial, medial and final position, say these slowly in 'robot talk', for example: /n/i/p/, /s/e/t/, /d/a/d/. Ask the children to blend the phonemes into words and tell their partners.
■ Now ask the children to speak in 'robot talk'. Say a word, for example, 'pant', and ask them to segment it using 'robot talk' first to their partner and then all together.

Read it

■ Hold up letter cards for 'd', 'e', 'n', 'i', 'p', 't', 'a' and 's', and ask the children to tell you the sounds (phonemes) they make.
■ Write three words containing phonemes taught so far (for example: 'dent', 'post' and 'nest') on the easel or whiteboard, and ask the children to read the words out loud. Encourage them to blend the phonemes.

> **Now or later**
> ■ Play 'Magnetic letters' (see page 47) where children make words with a partner, using given letters. Alternatively, this can be done at a later time during independent activities.

Write it

■ Say the phonemes taught so far and ask the children to write the corresponding letters on their individual whiteboards. Invite them to show you what they have written for a quick assessment.

3 NEW LETTER SOUND /m/ *(6-8 mins)*

Hear it

■ Show the card of the phoneme /m/ and describe the picture emphasising the initial sounds. Ask the children say the sounds they can hear.
■ Read out the alliterative phrase 'Monkeys march up mountains' emphasising the initial sound – 'monkeys' and 'mountains'.
■ Teach the corresponding action as you say the phrase (do a funny march).

Say it

■ Ask the children to repeat the phoneme /m/ /m/ /m/. Reinforce correct pronunciation and explain when you say /m/ your lips are together and it sounds like humming. You can stretch the sound /m/m/m/. Practise saying it several times.
■ Say several words containing the phoneme /m/ using 'robot talk', for example: /m/e/, /m/a/n/. Try to include consonant blends, for example, /m/a/s/t/, and ask the children to blend the phonemes into words and tell their partner.

Read it

■ Display the 'm' card next to the phonemes taught so far and ask the children to read out the letter sounds separately.

Write it

■ Now say the phoneme /m/ again and ask the children to write the letter. Demonstrate first by using your finger in the air, then on the board or easel. Ask the children to draw the letter in the air and emphasise the correct letter formation and starting point. Invite them to practise and then to write on their whiteboards and show you.
■ You may wish to explore, particularly with more able children, the fact that /m/ can also be written 'mm' as in 'hammer' when we have two-syllable words.
■ Say a word containing the phoneme /m/ and any other phonemes that have been taught so far. Ask the children to first count the number of phonemes that are in the word and then to hold up the correct number of fingers. Ask the children to write the word if they are able.

STAGE TWO: LESSON PLANS

LESSONS 12 /g/

① ALPHABET FUN *(2-3 mins)*
■ Begin by reciting in a lively way the 'Alphabet rhyme' (on photocopiable page 25).
■ Encourage the children to do the actions for each letter.

② REVIEW *(5-6 mins)*
Hear it
■ Using the phoneme cards taught so far, describe the pictures emphasising the initial sounds. Then say the alliterative phrases and ask the children to repeat them with the actions.

Say it
■ Using several words containing the phonemes taught so far in initial, medial and final position, say these slowly in 'robot talk', for example: /m/a/t/, /a/m/p/, /P/a/m/, /m/i/s/t/. Ask the children to blend the phonemes into words and tell their partners.
■ Now ask the children to speak in 'robot talk'. Say a word, for example, 'mast', and ask them to segment it using 'robot talk' first to their partner and then all together.

Read it
■ Hold up the letter cards 'm', 'd', 'e', 'n', 'i', 'p', 't', 'a' and 's', and ask the children to tell you the sounds (phonemes) they make.
■ Write three words containing the phonemes taught so far (for example: 'post', 'imp' and 'mend') on the easel or board and ask the children to read the words out loud. Encourage them to blend the phonemes.

Write it
■ Say the phonemes taught so far and ask the children to write the corresponding letters on their individual whiteboards. Invite them to show you what they have written for a quick assessment.

③ NEW LETTER SOUND /g/ *(6-8 mins)*
Hear it
■ Show the card of the phoneme /g/ and describe the picture emphasising the initial sounds. Ask the children say the sounds they can hear.
■ Read out the alliterative phrase 'Girls giggle with goats' emphasising the initial sound – 'girls', 'giggle' and 'goats'.
■ Teach the corresponding action as you say the phrase (giggle and point to a girl).

Say it
■ Ask the children to repeat the phoneme /g/ /g/ /g/. Reinforce correct pronunciation and explain that when you say /g/ you can feel the sound right at the back of your mouth. If you put your fingers on your throat you can feel the sound /g/g/g/. Practise saying it several times.
■ Say several words containing the phoneme /g/ using 'robot talk', for example: /g/a/p/, /g/a/s/, /n/a/g/. Include consonant blends, for example, /s/n/a/g/, and ask the children to blend the phonemes into words and tell their partner.

Read it
■ Display the 'g' card next to phonemes taught so far and ask the children to read out the letter sounds separately.

> **Now or later**
> ■ Play 'Read with your partner' on page 47, practising reading words containing the phonemes taught. This can be done at any time during the day to reinforce blending phonemes for reading.

Write it
■ Now say the phoneme /g/ again and ask the children to write the letter. Demonstrate first by using your finger in the air, then on the board or easel. Ask the children to draw the letter in the air and emphasise the correct letter formation and starting point. Invite them to practise and then to write on their whiteboards and show you.
■ You may wish to explore with more able children that /g/ can also be written 'gg' as in 'egg'.
■ Say a word containing the phoneme /g/ and any other phonemes that have been taught so far. Ask the children to first count the phonemes in the word and then to hold up the correct number of fingers. Ask the children to write the word if they are able.

LESSONS 13 /o/

1 ALPHABET FUN *(2-3 mins)*

■ Begin by reciting in a lively way the 'Alphabet rhyme' (on photocopiable page 25).

■ Encourage the children to do the actions for each letter.

2 REVIEW *(5-6 mins)*

Hear it

■ Using the phoneme cards taught so far, describe the pictures emphasising the initial sounds. Then say the alliterative phrases and ask the children to repeat them with the actions.

Say it

■ Using several words containing the phonemes taught so far in initial, medial and final position, say these slowly in 'robot talk', for example: /g/a/s/, /n/a/g/, /m/i/s/t/. Ask the children to blend the phonemes into words and tell their partners.

■ Now ask the children to speak in 'robot talk'. Say a word, for example, 'get', and ask them to segment it using 'robot talk' first to their partner and then all together.

Read it

■ Hold up the letter cards 'g', 'm', 'd', 'e', 'n', 'i', 'p', 't', 'a' and 's', and ask the children to tell you the sounds (phonemes) they make.

■ Write three words containing phonemes taught so far (for example: 'egg', 'mend', 'pest') on the easel or board and ask the children to read the words out loud. Encourage them to blend the phonemes.

Write it

■ Say the phonemes taught so far and ask the children to write the corresponding letters on their individual whiteboards. Invite them to show you what they have written for a quick assessment.

3 NEW LETTER SOUND /o/ *(6-8 minutes)*

Hear it

■ Show the card of the phoneme /o/ and describe the picture emphasising the initial sounds. Ask the children to say the sounds they can hear.

■ Read out the alliterative phrase 'Octopuses on oranges' emphasising the initial sound – 'octopus' and 'oranges'.

■ Teach the corresponding action as you say the phrase (wave arms around and try and balance on one leg).

Say it

■ Ask the children to repeat the phoneme /o/ /o/ /o/. Reinforce correct pronunciation of the sound and explain when you say /o/ your mouth is open and your chin drops down a little. You can stretch the sound /o/o/o/. Practise saying it several times.

■ Say several words containing the phoneme /o/ using 'robot talk', for example: /o/n/, /p/o/t/, /d/o/g/. Include consonant blends, for example, /s/t/o/p/, and ask the children to blend the phonemes into words and tell their partner.

Read it

■ Display the 'o' card next to phonemes taught so far and ask the children to read out the letter sounds separately.

> ### Now or later
> ■ For reinforcement, play a game from pages 46–49, for example, 'Magnetic letters' where children make words with given letters with a partner. Alternatively, this can be done at a later time during independent activities.

Write it

■ Now say the phoneme /o/ again and ask the children to write the letter. Demonstrate first by using your finger in the air, then on the board or easel. Ask the children to draw the letter in the air and emphasise the correct letter formation and starting point. Invite the children to practise and then to write on their whiteboards and show you.

■ Say a word containing the phoneme /o/ and the other phonemes taught so far. Ask the children to first count the phonemes in the word and then to hold up the correct number of fingers. Invite the children to write the word if they are able.

STAGE TWO: LESSON PLANS

LESSONS 14 /c/ /k/

1 ALPHABET FUN (2-3 mins)

■ Begin by reciting in a lively way the 'Alphabet rhyme' (on photocopiable page 25).

■ Encourage the children to do the actions for each letter.

2 REVIEW (5-6 mins)

Hear it

■ Using the phoneme cards taught so far, describe the pictures emphasising the initial sounds. Then say the alliterative phrases and ask the children to repeat them with the actions.

Say it

■ Using several words containing the phonemes taught so far, say these slowly in 'robot talk', for example: /n/a/g/, /s/t/o/p/ and /m/e/n/d/. Ask the children to blend the phonemes into words.

■ Now ask the children to speak in 'robot talk'. Say a word, for example, 'pest', and ask them to segment it using 'robot talk' first to their partner and then all together.

Read it

■ Hold up the letter cards 'o', 'g', 'm', 'd', 'e', 'n', 'i', 'p', 't', 'a' and 's', and ask the children to tell you the sounds (phonemes) they make.

Write it

■ Say the phonemes taught so far and ask the children to write the corresponding letters on their individual whiteboards. Invite them to show you what they have written for a quick assessment.

3 NEW LETTER SOUND /c/ /k/ (6-8 mins)

Hear it

■ Show the picture card of the phoneme /c/ /k/ and describe the picture emphasising the initial sounds. Ask the children say the sounds they can hear.

■ Read the alliterative phrase 'Camels kick cakes' emphasising the initial sounds – 'camel', 'kick' and 'cakes'.

■ Teach the action as you say the phrase (bend and hunch your back and then kick one leg).

Say it

■ Ask the children to repeat the phoneme. Reinforce correct pronunciation and explain that when you say /k/ you can feel the sound in the back of your mouth. It sounds a bit like /g/, but when you say /k/ you can feel air coming out from your mouth. Say it like a whisper /k/k/k/. Practise it several times.

■ Say several words containing the phoneme /c/ /k/ using 'robot talk', for example: /k/i/t/, /c/a/t/, /k/i/p/, /c/a/p/. Include consonant blends, for example, /c/l/o/p/, and ask the children to blend the phonemes into words and tell their partner.

Read it

■ Display the 'c / k' card next to phonemes taught so far and ask the children to read out the letter sounds separately.

■ Talk about the letters 'c' and 'k'. Explain that both make the same sound and that sometimes we use 'c' as in 'cat' and sometimes 'k' as in 'kite'. Explain that in words which have the phonemes /a/, /o/ and /u/ we use 'c' first, such as 'cat', 'cot' and 'cup'. But in words where we hear the phonemes /i/ and /e/, we use 'k' first as in 'king' and 'Ken'. We also sometimes use both letters together to make the grapheme 'ck' at the end of one-beat (syllable) words.

Write it

■ Now say the phoneme /c/ /k/ again and ask the children to write these letters individually. Demonstrate first by using your finger in the air, then on the board or easel. Ask the children to draw the letter in the air and emphasise the correct letter formation and starting point. Invite the children to practise and then to write on their whiteboards.

■ Say a word containing the phoneme /c/ /k/ and the other phonemes taught so far. Ask the children to count the phonemes in the word and then to hold up the correct number of fingers.

LESSON 15
REVISE PHONEMES TAUGHT

■ Follow the format from Revision Lesson 5 on page 58 to revise all phonemes taught in the week.

■ Encourage the children to read nonsense words. The following could be used:

tis   pas   tad   nid   dep   min   gom

STAGE TWO: LESSON PLANS

LESSON 16 /u/

1 ALPHABET FUN *(2-3 mins)*

■ Begin by reciting in a lively way the 'Alphabet rhyme' (on photocopiable page 25).

■ Encourage the children to do the actions for each letter.

2 REVIEW *(5-6 mins)*

Hear it

■ Using the phoneme cards taught so far, describe the pictures emphasising the initial sounds. Then say the alliterative phrases and ask the children to repeat them with the actions.

Say it

■ Using several words containing the phonemes taught so far say these slowly in 'robot talk', for example: /c/a/t/, /k/i/t/ and /a/s/k/. Ask the children to blend the phonemes into words and tell their partners.

■ Now ask the children to speak in 'robot talk'. Say a word, for example, 'kick', and ask them to segment it using 'robot talk' first to their partner and then all together.

Read it

■ Hold up the letter cards 'c / k', 'o', 'g', 'm', 'd', 'e', 'n', 'i', 'p', 't', 'a' and 's', and ask the children to tell you the sounds (phonemes) they make.

■ Write three words containing the phonemes taught so far, for example, 'dog', 'stop', 'tuck' on the easel or board and ask the children to read the words out loud. Encourage them to blend the phonemes.

Write it

■ Say the phonemes taught so far and ask the children to write the corresponding letters on their individual whiteboards. Invite them to show you what they have written for a quick assessment.

3 NEW LETTER SOUND /u/ *(6-8 mins)*

Hear it

■ Show the card of the phoneme /u/ and describe the picture emphasising the initial sounds. Ask the children say the sounds they can hear.

■ Read the alliterative phrase 'Umbrellas and uncles jump' emphasising the initial sounds – 'umbrellas' and 'uncles'.

■ Teach the corresponding action as you say the phrase (pretend to hold an umbrella and jump).

Say it

■ Ask the children to repeat the phoneme /u/ /u/ /u/. Reinforce correct pronunciation of the sound and explain that when you say /u/ your mouth is open just a little. You need to push some air out as you do it /u/u/u/. Practise saying it several times.

■ Say several words containing the phoneme /u/ using 'robot talk', for example: /u/p/, /s/u/n/, /u/p/s/e/t/. Include consonant blends, for example, /s/n/u/g/, and ask the children to blend the phonemes into words and tell their partner.

Read it

■ Display the 'u' card next to phonemes taught so far and ask the children to read out the letter sounds separately.

> **Now or later**
> ■ Play a game of 'Read with your partner' on page 47, where children practise reading words containing the phonemes taught so far. This can be done at any time during the day to reinforce blending phonemes for reading.

Write it

■ Now say the phoneme /u/ again and ask the children to write the letter. Demonstrate first by using your finger in the air, then on the board or easel. Ask the children to draw the letter in the air and emphasise the correct letter formation and starting point. Invite the children to practise and then to write on their whiteboards and show you.

■ Say a word containing the phoneme /u/ and the other phonemes taught so far. Ask the children to first count the phonemes in the word and then to hold up the correct number of fingers. Invite the children to write the word if they are able.

STAGE TWO: LESSON PLANS

LESSON 17 /r/

1 ALPHABET FUN *(2-3 mins)*

■ Begin by reciting in a lively way the 'Alphabet rhyme' (on photocopiable page 25).

■ Encourage the children to do the actions for each letter.

2 REVIEW *(5-6 mins)*

Hear it

■ Using the phoneme cards taught so far, describe the pictures emphasising the initial sounds. Then say the alliterative phrases and ask the children to repeat them with the actions.

Say it

■ Using several words containing the phonemes taught so far, say these slowly in 'robot talk', for example: /s/u/n/, /k/i/ck/, /t/e/s/t/. Ask the children to blend the phonemes into words and tell their partners.

■ Now ask the children to speak in 'robot talk'. Say a word, for example, 'upset', and ask them to segment it using 'robot talk' first to their partner and then all together.

Read it

■ Hold up the letter cards 'u', 'c / k', 'o', 'g', 'm', 'd', 'e', 'n', 'i', 'p', 't', 'a' and 's', and ask the children to tell you the sounds (phonemes) they make.

■ Write three words containing the phonemes taught so far (for example: 'duck', 'pant' and 'dog') on the easel or board and ask the children to read the words out loud. Encourage them to blend the phonemes.

Write it

■ Say the phonemes taught so far and ask the children to write the corresponding letters on their individual whiteboards. Invite them to show you what they have written for a quick assessment.

3 NEW LETTER SOUND /r/ *(6-8 mins)*

Hear it

■ Show the card of the phoneme /r/ and describe the picture emphasising the initial sounds. Ask the children to say the sounds they can hear.

■ Read the alliterative phrase 'Rabbits run and rest' emphasising the initial sounds – 'rabbits', 'run' and 'rest'.

■ Teach the corresponding action as you say the phrase (pretend to be a rabbit that hops and then stops suddenly).

Say it

■ Ask the children to repeat the phoneme /r/ /r/ /r/. Reinforce correct pronunciation of the sound and explain when you make the /r/ sound your tongue lifts up in the back of your mouth. It sounds like a car going fast. You can stretch the sound /r/r/r/. Practise saying it several times.

■ Say several words containing the phoneme /r/ using 'robot talk', for example: /r/a/n/, /r/e/d/ and /r/i/p/. Include consonant blends, such as: 'pr', 'tr', 'dr', 'gr', 'spr' and 'str' (for example: /p/r/a/m/, /t/r/e/k/, /d/r/i/p/, /g/r/a/b/, /s/p/r/i/g/, /s/t/r/a/p/). Ask the children to blend the phonemes into words and tell their partner.

Read it

■ Display the 'r' letter card next to phonemes taught so far and ask the children to read out the letter sounds separately.

> ### Now or later
> ■ Play 'Magnetic letters', (page 47) with a partner by making words with given letters. Alternatively, this can be done at a later time during independent activities.

Write it

■ Now say the phoneme /r/ again and ask the children to write the letter. Demonstrate first by using your finger in the air, then on the board or easel. Ask the children to draw the letter in the air and emphasise the correct letter formation and starting point. Invite the children to practise and then to write on their whiteboards and show you.

■ Say a word containing the phoneme /r/ and the other phonemes taught so far. Ask the children to first count the phonemes in the word and then to hold up the correct number of fingers. Invite the children to write the word if they are able.

■ More able children might like to know that /r/ can be written 'rr' in words of more than one syllable.

LESSON 18 /b/

1 ALPHABET FUN *(2-3 mins)*
■ Begin by reciting in a lively way the 'Alphabet rhyme' (on photocopiable page 25).
■ Encourage the children to do the actions for each letter.

2 REVIEW *(5-6 mins)*
Hear it
■ Using the phoneme cards taught so far, describe the pictures emphasising the initial sounds. Then say the alliterative phrases and ask the children to repeat them with the actions.

Say it
■ Using several words containing the phonemes taught so far, say these slowly in 'robot talk', for example: /r/e/s/t/, /r/u/n/, /t/r/i/ck/. Ask the children to blend the phonemes into words and tell their partners.
■ Now ask the children to talk in 'robot talk'. Say a word, for example, 'grin', and ask them to segment it using 'robot talk' first to their partner and then all together.

Read it
■ Hold up letter cards for 'r', 'u', 'c / k', 'o', 'g', 'm', 'd', 'e', 'n', 'i', 'p', 't', 'a' and 's', and ask the children to tell you the sounds (phonemes) they make.
■ Write three words containing phonemes taught so far (for example, 'trim', 'must' and 'kick') on the easel or board and ask the children to read the words out loud. Encourage them to blend the phonemes.

Write it
■ Say the phonemes taught so far and ask the children to write the corresponding letters on their individual whiteboards. Invite them to show you what they have written for a quick assessment.

3 NEW LETTER SOUND /b/ *(6-8 mins)*
Hear it
■ Show the card of the phoneme /b/ and describe the picture emphasising the initial sounds. Ask the children to say the sounds they can hear.

■ Read the alliterative phrase 'Boys and bells on the bus' emphasising the initial sounds – 'boys', 'bells' and 'bus'.
■ Teach the corresponding action as you say the phrase (pretend to sit on a bus and jump up and ring the bell).

Say it
■ Ask the children to repeat the phoneme /b/ /b/ /b/. Reinforce correct pronunciation and explain that when you make this sound your lips go together and pop open. It is like /p/ but no air comes out /b/b/b/. Practise saying it several times.
■ Say several words containing the phoneme using 'robot talk', for example: /b/a/t/, /b/a/ll/, b/u/s/. Include consonant blends, for example, /b/e/l/t/, and ask the children to blend the phonemes into words and tell their partner.

Read it
■ Display the 'b' card next to phonemes taught so far and ask the children to read out the letter sounds separately.

> **Now or later**
> ■ Play a game of 'Read with your partner' on page 47, where children practise reading words containing the phonemes taught. This can be done at any time during the day to reinforce blending.

Write it
■ Now say the phoneme /b/ again and ask the children to write the letter. Demonstrate first by using your finger in the air, then on the board or easel. Ask the children to draw the letter in the air and emphasise the correct letter formation and starting point. Invite the children to practise and then to write on their whiteboards and show you.
■ Say a word containing the phoneme /b/ and the other phonemes taught so far. Ask the children to first count the phonemes in the word and then to hold up the correct number of fingers. Invite the children to write the word if they are able.
■ Explore the different graphemes that represent the phoneme /b/ with more able children. Explain that in words of more than one syllable we use 'bb' as in 'rabbit'.

LESSON 19 /f/

1 ALPHABET FUN *(2-3 mins)*
■ Begin by reciting in a lively way the 'Alphabet rhyme' (on photocopiable page 25).
■ Encourage the children to do the actions for each letter.

2 REVIEW *(5-6 mins)*
Hear it
■ Using the phoneme cards taught so far, describe the pictures emphasising the initial sounds. Then say the alliterative phrases and ask the children to repeat them with the actions.

Say it
■ Using several words containing the phonemes taught so far say these slowly in 'robot talk', for example: /b/u/g/, /b/i/g/, /r/e/s/t/. Ask the children to blend the phonemes into words.
■ Now ask the children to speak in 'robot talk'. Say a word, for example, 'grab', and ask them to segment it using 'robot talk' first to their partner and then all together.

Read it
■ Hold up the letter cards and ask the children to tell you the sounds (phonemes) they make.
■ Write three words containing phonemes taught so far (for example: 'drop', 'rap' and 'neck') on the easel or board and ask the children to read the words out loud. Encourage them to blend the phonemes.

Write it
■ Say the phonemes taught so far and ask the children to write the corresponding letters on their individual whiteboards. Invite them to show you what they have written for a quick assessment.

3 NEW LETTER SOUND /f/ *(6-8 mins)*
Hear it
■ Show the card of the phoneme /f/ and describe the picture emphasising the initial sounds. Ask the children to say the sounds they can hear.
■ Read the alliterative phrase 'Five floppy fish flap' emphasising the initial sounds.

■ Teach the corresponding action as you say the phrase (flap arms like a fish).

Say it
■ Ask the children to repeat the phoneme /f/ /f/ /f/. Reinforce correct pronunciation of the sound and explain when you say /f/ your teeth touch your bottom lip. You make the /f/ sound by pushing air between your teeth. You can stretch the sound /f/f/f/. Practise saying it several times.
■ Say several words containing the phoneme /f/ in the initial position using 'robot talk', for example: /f/u/n/, /fa/t/ and /f/i/t/. Include consonant blends, for example, /f/r/o/ck/, and ask the children to blend the phonemes into words and tell their partner.

Read it
■ Display the 'f' card next to phonemes taught so far and ask the children to read out the letter sounds separately.

Write it
■ Now say the phoneme /f/ again and ask the children to write the letter. Demonstrate first by using your finger in the air, then on the board or easel. Ask the children to draw the letter in the air and emphasise the correct letter formation and starting point. Invite the children to practise and then to write on their whiteboards and show you.
■ Say a word containing the phoneme /f/ and other phonemes taught so far. Ask the children to first count the phonemes in the word and then to hold up the correct number of fingers. Invite them to write the word if they are able.
■ Explore the different graphemes that represent phoneme /f/ such as 'ph'. Write some other words on the easel that use the grapheme 'ph'. You may also like to explore with more able children that, as in 'rabbit', with two syllable words we write /f/ with 'ff', for example, 'coffee'.

LESSON 20
REVISE PHONEMES TAUGHT
■ Follow the format from Revision Lesson 5 on page 58 to revise all phonemes taught in the week.
■ Encourage the children to read nonsense words. The following could be used:
fub   bip   rof   duf   bup   fon

LESSON 21 /l/

1 ALPHABET FUN *(2-3 mins)*

■ Begin by reciting in a lively way the 'Alphabet rhyme' (on photocopiable page 25).

■ Encourage the children to do the actions for each letter.

2 REVIEW *(5-6 mins)*

Hear it

■ Using the phoneme cards taught so far, describe the pictures emphasising the initial sounds. Then say the alliterative phrases and ask the children to repeat them with the actions.

Say it

■ Using several words containing the phonemes taught so far, say these slowly in 'robot talk', for example: /f/u/r/, /b/r/i/ck/ and /f/r/o/g/. Ask the children to blend the phonemes into words and tell their partners.

■ Now ask the children to speak in 'robot talk.' Say a word, for example 'grin', and ask them to segment it using 'robot talk' first to their partner and then all together.

Read it

■ Hold up the letter cards 'f', 'b', 'r', 'u', 'c / k', 'o', 'g', 'm', 'd', 'e', 'n', 'i', 'p', 't', 'a' and 's', and ask the children to tell you the sounds (phonemes) they make.

■ Write three words containing the phonemes taught so far (for example, 'brag', 'pram' and 'gran') on the easel or board and ask the children to read the words out loud. Encourage them to blend the phonemes.

Write it

■ Say the phonemes taught so far and ask the children to write the corresponding letters on their individual whiteboards. Invite them to show you what they have written for a quick assessment.

3 NEW LETTER SOUND /l/ *(6-8 mins)*

Hear it

■ Show the card of the phoneme /l/ and describe the picture emphasising the initial sounds. Ask the

children to say out loud to the rest of the group the sounds that they can hear.

■ Read the alliterative phrase 'Lick the lemon lolly' emphasising the initial sounds – 'lick', 'lemon' and 'lolly'.

■ Teach the corresponding action as you say the phrase (pretend to lick a lolly).

Say it

■ Ask the children to repeat the phoneme /l/ /l/ /l/. Reinforce correct pronunciation of the sound and explain when you say /l/ your tongue moves to the top of your mouth. It stays there as you make the sound in the back of your mouth. You can stretch the sound /l/l/l/. Practise saying it several times.

■ Say several words containing the phoneme /l/ using 'robot talk', for example: /l/i/ck/, /l/o/ck/, /l/e/f/t/, /f/l/a/t/. Ask the children to blend the phonemes into words and tell their partner.

Read it

■ Display the 'l' card next to phonemes taught so far and ask the children to read out the letter sounds separately.

> **Now or later**
>
> ■ For reinforcement, play 'Magnetic letters' on page 47, where children make words with given letters with a partner. Alternatively, this can be done at a later time during independent activities.

Write it

■ Now say the phoneme /l/ again and ask the children to write the letter. Demonstrate first by using your finger in the air, then on the board or easel. Ask the children to draw the letter in the air and emphasise the correct letter formation and starting point. Ask children to practise writing on their whiteboards and show you.

■ Say a word containing the phoneme /l/ and other phonemes taught so far. Ask the children to first count the phonemes in the word and then to hold up the correct number of fingers. Invite the children to write the word if they are able.

■ Explore the different graphemes that represent the phoneme /l/ where 'll' is used, as in 'spell' and 'bell' at the end of words.

STAGE TWO: LESSON PLANS

LESSON 22 /h/

1 ALPHABET FUN (2-3 mins)
■ Begin by reciting in a lively way the 'Alphabet rhyme' (on photocopiable page 25).
■ Encourage the children to do the actions for each letter.

2 REVIEW (5-6 mins)
Hear it
■ Using the phoneme cards taught so far, describe the pictures emphasising the initial sounds. Then say the alliterative phrases and ask the children to repeat them with the actions.

Say it
■ Using several words containing the phonemes taught so far, say these slowly in 'robot talk', for example: /l/i/ck/, /b/e/s/t/ and /f/l/a/g/. Ask the children to blend the phonemes into words and tell their partners.
■ Now ask the children to speak in 'robot talk'. Say a word, for example, 'left', and ask them to segment it using 'robot talk' first to their partner and then all together.

Read it
■ Hold up the letter cards 'l', 'f', 'b', 'r', 'u', 'c / k', 'o', 'g', 'm', 'd', 'e', 'n', 'i', 'p', 't', 'a' and 's', and ask the children to tell you the sounds (phonemes) they make.
■ Write three words containing phonemes taught so far (for example: 'rest', 'leg' and 'flap') on the easel or board and ask the children to read the words out loud. Encourage them to blend the phonemes.

Write it
■ Say the phonemes taught so far and ask the children to write the corresponding letters on their individual whiteboards. Invite them to show you what they have written for a quick assessment.

3 NEW LETTER SOUND /h/ (6-8 mins)
Hear it
■ Show the card of the phoneme /h/ and describe the picture emphasising the initial sounds. Ask the children to say the sounds they can hear.

■ Read the alliterative phrase 'Hopping happy hens' emphasising the initial sounds – 'hopping', 'happy' and 'hens'.
■ Teach the corresponding action as you say the phrase (pretend to hop and squawk like a hen).

Say it
■ Ask the children to repeat the phoneme /h/ /h/ /h/. Reinforce correct pronunciation of the sound and explain when you make the sound /h/ your mouth is open a little. You push air out of your mouth to say /h/. You can stretch the sound /h/h/h/. Practise saying it several times.
■ Say several words containing the phoneme /h/ using 'robot talk', for example: /h/a/n/d/, /h/a/t/ and /h/e/l/p/. Ask the children to blend the phonemes into words and tell their partner.

Read it
■ Display the 'h' card next to phonemes taught so far and ask the children to read out the letter sounds separately.

> ### Now or later
> ■ Play a game of 'Silly sentences' on page 48, practising reading words containing the phonemes taught so far. This can be done at any time during the day to reinforce blending.

Write it
■ Now say the phoneme /h/ again and ask the children to write the letter. Demonstrate first by using your finger in the air, then on the board or easel. Ask the children to draw the letter in the air and emphasise the correct letter formation and starting point. Invite children to practise writing on their whiteboards and show you.
■ Say a word containing the phoneme /h/ and other phonemes taught so far. Ask the children to first count the phonemes in the word and then to hold up the correct number of fingers. Invite the children to write the word if they are able.

LESSON 23 /sh/

1 ALPHABET FUN (2-3 mins)

■ Begin by reciting in a lively way the 'Alphabet rhyme' (on photocopiable page 25).
■ Encourage the children to do the actions for each letter.

2 REVIEW (5-6 mins)

Hear it

■ Using the phoneme cards taught so far, describe the pictures emphasising the initial sounds. Then say the alliterative phrases and ask the children to repeat them with the actions.

Say it

■ Using several words containing the phonemes taught so far, say these slowly in 'robot talk', for example: /h/a/n/d/, /b/e/ll/, /l/i/ck/. Ask the children to blend the phonemes into words and tell their partners.
■ Now ask the children to speak in 'robot talk'. Say a word, for example, 'left', and ask them to segment it using 'robot talk' first to their partner and then all together.

Read it

■ Hold up the letter cards 'h', 'l', 'f', 'b', 'r', 'u', 'c / k', 'o', 'g', 'm', 'd', 'e', 'n', 'i', 'p', 't', 'a' and 's', and ask the children to tell you the sounds (phonemes) they make.
■ Write three words containing phonemes taught so far (for example, 'help', 'flat', 'hug') on the easel or board and ask the children to read the words out loud. Encourage them to blend the phonemes.

Write it

■ Say the phonemes taught so far and ask the children to write the corresponding letters on their individual whiteboards. Invite them to show you what they have written for a quick assessment.

3 NEW LETTER SOUND /sh/ (6-8 mins)

Hear it

■ Show the card of the phoneme /sh/ and describe the picture emphasising the initial sounds. Ask the children to say the sounds they can hear.

■ Read the alliterative phrase 'Sharks and shells on the shore' emphasising the initial sounds – 'sharks', 'shells' and 'shore'.
■ Teach the corresponding action as you say the phrase (open your mouth and show your teeth and with arms outstretched and hands together, move arms).

Say it

■ Ask the children to repeat the phoneme /sh/ /sh/ /sh/. Reinforce correct pronunciation of the sound and explain that when you make the sound /sh/ your teeth are together and you push air out of your mouth. It is the sound you make when you want someone to be quiet. You can stretch the sound /sh/sh/sh/. Practise saying it several times.
■ Say several words containing the phoneme /sh/ using 'robot talk', for example: /sh/i/p/, /sh/e/ll/, /d/i/sh/ and ask the children to blend the phonemes into words and tell their partner.

Read it

■ Display the 'sh' card next to phonemes taught so far and ask the children to read out the letter sounds separately.
■ Explain that phonemes which are commonly written with two letters (such as /sh/ as in /sh/e/) are called digraphs.

Write it

■ Now say the phoneme /sh/ again and ask the children to write the letters. Demonstrate first by using your finger in the air, then on the board or easel. Ask the children to draw the letter in the air and emphasise the correct letter formation and starting point. Invite the children to then write on their whiteboards and show you.
■ Say a word containing the phoneme /sh/ and other phonemes taught so far. Ask the children to first count the phonemes in the word and then to hold up the correct number of fingers. Invite the children to write the word if they are able.
■ Ensure that the children are able to count the phonemes when they contain digraphs. Encourage them to write the word out on their individual whiteboards.
■ Point out to more able children that sometimes we do not use the letters 'sh' to write the /sh/ phoneme, we use 'ch' as in 'chef'.

LESSON 24 /z/

1 ALPHABET FUN *(2-3 mins)*
■ Begin by reciting in a lively way the 'Alphabet rhyme' (on photocopiable page 25).
■ Encourage the children to do the actions for each letter.

2 REVIEW *(5-6 mins)*
Hear it
■ Using the phoneme cards taught so far, describe the pictures emphasising the initial sounds. Then say the alliterative phrases and ask the children to repeat them with the actions.

Say it
■ Using several words containing the phonemes taught so far, say these slowly in 'robot talk', for example: /d/i/sh/, /sh/e/ll/ and /h/e/l/p/. Ask the children to blend the phonemes into words and tell their partners.
■ Now ask the children to speak in 'robot talk'. Say a word, for example, 'crash', and ask them to segment it using 'robot talk' first to their partner and then all together.

Read it
■ Hold up the letter cards 'sh', 'h', 'l', 'f', 'b', 'r', 'u', 'c / k', 'o', 'g', 'm', 'd', 'e', 'n', 'i', 'p', 't', 'a' and 's', and ask the children to tell you the sounds (phonemes) they make.
■ Write three words containing phonemes taught so far (for example: 'ship', 'belt' and 'rest') on the easel or board and ask the children to read the words out loud. Encourage them to blend the phonemes.

Write it
■ Say the phonemes taught so far and ask the children to write the corresponding letters on their individual whiteboards. Invite them to show you what they have written for a quick assessment.

3 NEW LETTER SOUND /z/ *(6-8 mins)*
Hear it
■ Show the card of the phoneme /z/ and describe the picture emphasising the initial sounds. Ask the children to say the sounds they can hear.

■ Read the alliterative phrase 'Zebras buzz in zoos' emphasising the initial sounds – 'zebras' and 'zoos', and the final sound 'buzz'.
■ Teach the corresponding action as you say the phrase (pretend to gallop round and make buzzing noise).

Say it
■ Ask the children to repeat the phoneme /z/ /z/ /z/. Reinforce correct pronunciation and explain that when you make the sound /z/ your teeth are together and your tongue is near the front of your mouth and behind your teeth. You push air through your teeth and it makes a buzzing noise. You can stretch the sound /z/z/z/. Practise saying it several times.
■ Say several words containing the phoneme /z/ using 'robot talk', for example: /z/i/p/, /z/a/p/, /z/oo/m/. Ask the children to blend the phonemes into words and tell their partner.

Read it
■ Display the 'z' card next to phonemes taught so far and ask the children to read out the letter sounds separately.

Write it
■ Now say the phoneme /z/ again and ask the children to write the letter. Demonstrate first by using your finger in the air, then on the board or easel. Ask the children to draw the letter in the air and emphasise the correct letter formation and starting point. Invite the children to practise and then to write on their whiteboards and show you.
■ Say a word containing the phoneme /z/ and other phonemes taught so far. Ask the children to first count the phonemes in the word and then to hold up the correct number of fingers. Invite the children to write the word if they are able.
■ You might like to explore with more able children that sometimes we do not use the letter 'z' to write this phoneme, we use 'zz' in two-syllable words as in 'fizzy' or 's' as in 'is'.

LESSON 25
REVISE PHONEMES TAUGHT
■ Follow the format from Revision Lesson 5 on page 58 to revise all phonemes taught in the week.

LESSON 26 /w/

① ALPHABET FUN *(2-3 mins)*

■ Begin by reciting in a lively way the 'Alphabet rhyme' (on photocopiable page 25).

■ Encourage the children to do the actions for each letter.

② REVIEW *(5-6 mins)*
Hear it

■ Using the phoneme cards taught so far, describe the pictures emphasising the initial sounds. Then say the alliterative phrases and ask the children to repeat them with the actions.

Say it

■ Using several words containing the phonemes taught so far, say these slowly in 'robot talk', for example: /z/a/p/, /sh/e/ll/ and /f/l/a/p/. Ask the children to blend the phonemes into words and tell their partners.

■ Now ask the children to speak in 'robot talk'. Say a word, for example, 'zest', and ask them to segment it using 'robot talk' first to their partner and then all together.

Read it

■ Hold up the letter cards 'z', 'sh', 'h', 'l', 'f', 'b', 'r', 'u', 'c / k', 'o', 'g', 'm', 'd', 'e', 'n', 'i', 'p', 't', 'a' and 's', and ask the children to tell you the sounds (phonemes) they make.

■ Write three words containing phonemes taught so far (for example, 'zip', 'fish' and 'splash') on the easel or board and ask the children to read the words out loud. Encourage them to blend the phonemes.

Write it

■ Say the phonemes taught so far and ask the children to write the corresponding letters on their individual whiteboards. Invite them to show you what they have written for a quick assessment.

③ NEW LETTER SOUND /w/ *(6-8 mins)*
Hear it

■ Show the card of the phoneme /w/ and describe the picture emphasising the initial sounds. Ask the

children to say the sounds they can hear.

■ Read the alliterative phrase 'Water wheels went whoosh' emphasising the initial sounds in 'water', 'wheels', 'went' and 'whoosh'.

■ Teach the corresponding action as you say the phrase (circle arms round and say 'whoosh').

Say it

■ Ask the children to repeat the phoneme /w/ /w/ /w/. Reinforce correct pronunciation and explain that when you say the sound /w/ your lips are close together in a little circle, then they open up /w/w/w/. Practise saying it several times.

■ Say several words containing the phoneme /w/ using 'robot talk', (for example: /w/e/b/, /w/i/sh/ and /w/e/s/t/) and ask the children to blend the phonemes into words and tell their partner.

Read it

■ Display the 'w' card next to phonemes taught so far and ask the children to read out the letter sounds separately.

> **Now or later**
> ■ Play a game of 'Read with your partner' on page 47, practising reading words containing phonemes taught so far. This can be done at any time during the day to reinforce blending.

Write it

■ Now say the phoneme /w/ again and ask the children to write the letter. Demonstrate first by using your finger in the air, then on the board or easel. Ask the children to draw the letter in the air and emphasise the correct letter formation and starting point. Invite the children to practise and then to write on their whiteboards and show you.

■ Say a word containing the phoneme /w/ and other phonemes taught so far. Ask the children to first count the phonemes in the word and then to hold up the correct number of fingers. Invite the children to write the word if they are able.

■ You might like to explore with more able children that sometimes we do not use the letter 'w' to write this phoneme, we use 'u' as in 'queen', or 'wh' as in 'wheel'.

STAGE TWO: LESSON PLANS

LESSON 27 /ch/

1 ALPHABET FUN *(2-3 mins)*

■ Begin by reciting in a lively way the 'Alphabet rhyme' (on photocopiable page 25).

■ Encourage the children to do the actions for each letter.

2 REVIEW *(5-6 mins)*

Hear it

■ Using the phoneme cards taught so far, describe the pictures emphasising the initial sounds. Then say the alliterative phrases and ask the children to repeat them with the actions.

Say it

■ Using several words containing the phonemes taught so far, say these slowly in 'robot talk', for example: /w/i/sh/, /b/u/zz/ and /l/i/ck/. Ask the children to blend the phonemes into words and tell their partners.

■ Now ask the children to speak in 'robot talk'. Say a word, for example, 'crash', and ask them to segment it using 'robot talk' first to their partner and then all together.

Read it

■ Hold up the letter cards and ask the children to tell you the sounds (phonemes) they make.

■ Write three words containing the phonemes taught so far (for example: 'wag', 'zip' and 'shop') on the easel or board and ask the children to read the words out loud. Encourage them to blend the phonemes.

Write it

■ Say the phonemes taught so far and ask the children to write the corresponding letters on their individual whiteboards. Invite them to show you what they have written for a quick assessment.

3 NEW LETTER SOUND /ch/ *(6-8 mins)*

Hear it

■ Show the card of the phoneme /ch/ and describe the picture emphasising the initial sounds. Ask the children to say the sounds they can hear.

■ Read the alliterative phrase 'Chop chips and cheese' emphasising the initial sounds in 'chop', 'chips' and 'cheese'.

■ Teach the corresponding action as you say the phrase (pretend to chop with a knife).

Say it

■ Ask the children to repeat the phoneme /ch/ /ch/ /ch/. Reinforce correct pronunciation and explain when you make this sound your lips stick out a little. Your teeth are together at first and then they open up. It sounds like a steam train /ch/ch/ch/. Practise saying it several times.

■ Say several words containing the phoneme /ch/ using 'robot talk' (for example: /ch/o/p/, /ch/i/ck/, /s/u/ch/) and ask the children to blend the phonemes into words and tell their partners.

Read it

■ Display the 'ch' card next to phonemes taught so far and ask the children to read out the letter sounds separately.

■ Explain that phonemes which are commonly written with two letters (such as /ch/ as in /ch/o/p/) are called digraphs.

Write it

■ Now say the phoneme /ch/ again and ask the children to write the letter. Demonstrate first by using your finger in the air, then on the board or easel. Ask the children to draw the letter in the air and emphasise the correct letter formation and starting point. Invite the children to practise and then to write on their whiteboards and show you.

■ Say a word containing the phoneme /ch/ and other phonemes taught so far. Ask the children to first count the phonemes in the word and then to hold up the correct number of fingers. Ensure that the children are able to count the phonemes when they contain digraphs. Invite the children to write the word if they are able.

■ You might like to explore with more able children that sometimes we do not use the letters 'ch' to write the /ch/ phoneme, we use 'tch' as in 'watch' which uses three letters. We call this a trigraph.

> **Now or later**
> ■ For reinforcement, play a game of 'Which grapheme?' on page 48. You may need to spend a further day reinforcing this digraph.

LESSON 28 /j/

1 ALPHABET FUN *(2-3 mins)*

■ Begin by reciting in a lively way the 'Alphabet rhyme' on photocopiable page 25.

■ Encourage the children to do the actions for each letter.

2 REVIEW *(5-6 mins)*

Hear it

■ Using the phoneme cards taught so far, describe the pictures emphasising the initial sounds. Then say the alliterative phrases and ask the children to repeat them with the actions.

Say it

■ Using several words containing the phonemes taught so far, say these slowly in 'robot talk', for example: /ch/o/p/, /w/i/sh/ and /z/e/s/t/. Ask the children to blend the phonemes into words and tell their partners.

■ Now ask the children to speak in 'robot talk'. Say a word, for example, 'chest', and ask them to segment it using 'robot talk' first to their partner and then all together.

Read it

■ Hold up the letter cards 'ch', 'w', 'z', 'sh', 'h', 'l', 'f', 'b', 'r', 'u', 'c / k', 'o', 'g', 'm', 'd', 'e', 'n', 'i', 'p', 't', 'a' and 's', and ask the children to tell you the sounds (phonemes) they make.

■ Write three words containing the phonemes taught so far (for example: 'chip', 'west' and 'splash') on the easel or board and ask the children to read the words out loud. Encourage them to blend the phonemes.

Write it

■ Say the phonemes taught so far and ask the children to write the corresponding letters on their individual whiteboards. Invite them to show you what they have written for a quick assessment.

3 NEW LETTER SOUND /j/ *(6-8 mins)*

Hear it

■ Show the card of the phoneme /j/ and describe the picture emphasising the initial sounds. Ask the children to say the sounds they can hear.

■ Read the alliterative phrase 'Jelly jiggles in the jug' emphasising the initial sounds in 'jelly', 'jiggles' and 'jug'.

■ Teach the corresponding action as you say the phrase (pretend to hold a jug which wobbles).

Say it

■ Ask the children to repeat the phoneme /j/ /j/ /j/. Reinforce correct pronunciation and explain that when you say the sound /j/ your lips stick out a little. Your tongue is near the top of your mouth and it moves when you open your mouth /j/j/j/. Practise saying it several times.

■ Say several words containing the phoneme /j/ using 'robot talk' (for example: /j/u/g/, /j/u/m/p/, /j/u/s/t/) and ask the children to blend the phonemes into words and tell their partner.

Read it

■ Display the 'j' letter card next to phonemes taught so far and ask the children to read out the letter sounds separately.

Write it

■ Now say the phoneme /j/ again and ask the children to write the letter. Demonstrate first by using your finger in the air, then on the board or easel. Ask the children to draw the letter in the air and emphasise the correct letter formation and starting point. Invite the children to practise and then to write on their whiteboards and show you.

■ Say a word containing the phoneme /j/ and other phonemes taught so far. Ask the children to first count the phonemes in the word and then to hold up the correct number of fingers. Invite the children to write the word if they are able.

■ Explore with more able children that sometimes we do not use the letter 'j' to write this phoneme, we use 'g' as in 'giant', or 'dge' as in 'bridge' (a trigraph).

> **Now or later**
> ■ For reinforcement, play a game of 'Find the sound in the rhyme' on page 49.

STAGE TWO: LESSON PLANS

LESSON 29 /v/

1 ALPHABET FUN (2-3 mins)
■ Begin by reciting in a lively way the 'Alphabet rhyme' (on photocopiable page 25).
■ Encourage the children to do the actions for each letter.

2 REVIEW (5-6 mins)
Hear it
■ Using the phoneme cards taught so far, describe the pictures emphasising the initial sounds. Then say the alliterative phrases and ask the children to repeat them with the actions.

Say it
■ Using several words containing the phonemes taught so far, say these slowly in 'robot talk', for example: /j/u/g/, /ch/e/s/t/ and /w/a/tch/. Ask the children to blend the phonemes into words and tell their partners.
■ Now ask the children to talk in 'robot talk'. Say a word, for example, 'Jack', and ask them to segment it using 'robot talk' first to their partner and then all together.

Read it
■ Hold up the letter cards taught so far and ask the children to tell you the sounds (phonemes) they make.
■ Write three words containing phonemes taught so far (for example: 'jam', 'chick' and 'wish') on the easel or board and ask the children to read the words out loud. Encourage them to blend the phonemes.

Write it
■ Say the phonemes taught so far and ask the children to write the corresponding letters on their individual whiteboards. Invite them to show you what they have written for a quick assessment.

3 NEW LETTER SOUND /v/ (6-8 mins)
Hear it
■ Show the card of the phoneme /v/ and describe the picture emphasising the initial sounds. Ask the children to say the sounds they can hear.

■ Read the alliterative phrase 'Vinegar on the van and vest' emphasising the initial sounds in 'vinegar', 'van' and 'vest'.
■ Teach the corresponding action as you say the phrase (try and wipe off spilt vinegar).

Say it
■ Ask the children to repeat the phoneme /v/ /v/ /v/. Reinforce correct pronunciation and explain when you say /v/ your teeth touch your bottom lip. You make the /v/ sound by pushing air between your teeth. You can stretch the sound /v/v/v/. Practise saying it several times.
■ Say several words containing the phoneme /v/ using 'robot talk' (for example: /v/a/n/, /v/e/s/t/ and /v/e/t/) and ask the children to blend the phonemes into words and tell their partner.

Read it
■ Display the 'v' card next to phonemes taught so far and ask the children to read out the letter sounds separately.

Write it
■ Now say the phoneme /v/ again and ask the children to write the letter. Demonstrate first by using your finger in the air, then on the board or easel. Ask the children to draw the letter in the air and emphasise the correct letter formation and starting point. Invite the children to practise and then to write on their whiteboards and show you.
■ Say a word containing the phoneme /v/ and other phonemes taught so far. Ask the children to first count the phonemes in the word and then to hold up the correct number of fingers. Invite the children to write the word if they are able.
■ Explore with more able children that sometimes we use the letters 've' to write this phoneme, as in 'love' or 'sleeve'.

LESSON 30
REVISE PHONEMES TAUGHT
■ Follow the format from Revision Lesson 5 on page 58 to revise all phonemes taught in the week.
■ Encourage the children to read nonsense words. The following could be used:
jush   huv   wosh   vuz   chof

LESSON 31 /y/

1 ALPHABET FUN *(2-3 mins)*
■ Begin by reciting in a lively way the 'Alphabet rhyme' (on photocopiable page 25).
■ Encourage the children to do the actions for each letter.

2 REVIEW *(5-6 mins)*
Hear it
■ Using the phoneme cards taught so far, describe the pictures emphasising the initial sounds. Then say the alliterative phrases and ask the children to repeat them with the actions.

Say it
■ Using several words containing the phonemes taught so far, say these slowly in 'robot talk', for example: /v/e/s/t/, /j/u/s/t/ and /w/a/tch/. Ask the children to blend the phonemes into words and tell their partners.
■ Now ask the children to speak in 'robot talk'. Say a word, for example, 'vent', and ask them to segment it using 'robot talk' first to their partner and then all together.

Read it
■ Hold up the letter cards 'v', 'j', 'ch', 'w', 'z', 'sh', 'h', 'l', 'f', 'b', 'r', 'u', 'c / k', 'o', 'g', 'm', 'd', 'e', 'n', 'i', 'p', 't', 'a' and 's', and ask the children to tell you the sounds (phonemes) they make.
■ Write three words containing phonemes taught so far (for example: 'verb', 'flash' and 'chick') on the easel or board and ask the children to read the words out loud. Encourage them to blend the phonemes.

Write it
■ Say the phonemes taught so far and ask the children to write the corresponding letters on their individual whiteboards. Invite them to show you what they have written for a quick assessment.

3 NEW LETTER SOUND /y/ *(6-8 mins)*
Hear it
■ Show the card of the phoneme /y/ and describe the picture emphasising the initial sounds. Ask the

children to say the sounds they can hear.
■ Read the alliterative phrase 'Yell for yummy yoghurt' emphasising the initial sounds in 'yell', 'yummy' and 'yoghurt'.
■ Teach the corresponding action as you say the phrase (shout 'yum, yum' and rub your tummy).

Say it
■ Ask the children to repeat the phoneme /y/ /y/ /y/. Reinforce correct pronunciation and explain when you make the /y/ sound your mouth is open a little and your tongue is near the top of your mouth. Your tongue touches the sides of your teeth. Your mouth is open a little more at the end of the sound /y/y/y/. Practise saying it several times.
■ Say several words containing the phoneme /y/ using 'robot talk' (for example: /y/e/s/, /y/e/ll/ and /y/e/l/p/) and ask the children to blend the phonemes into words and tell their partners.

Read it
■ Display the 'y' card next to phonemes taught so far and ask the children to read out the letter sounds separately.

> **Now or later**
> ■ Play a game of 'Read with your partner' on page 47, practising reading words containing phonemes taught. This can be done at any time during the day to reinforce blending.

Write it
■ Now say the phoneme /y/ again and ask the children to write the letter. Demonstrate first by using your finger in the air, then on the board or easel. Ask the children to draw the letter in the air and emphasise the correct letter formation and starting point. Invite the children to practise and then to write on their whiteboards and show you.
■ Say a word containing the phoneme /y/ and other phonemes taught so far. Ask the children to first count the phonemes in the word and then to hold up the correct number of fingers. Invite the children to write the word if they are able.

LESSON 32 /th/

1 ALPHABET FUN *(2-3 mins)*

■ Begin by reciting in a lively way the 'Alphabet rhyme' (on photocopiable page 25).

■ Encourage the children to do the actions for each letter.

2 REVIEW *(5-6 mins)*

Hear it

■ Using the phoneme cards taught so far, describe the pictures emphasising the initial sounds. Then say the alliterative phrases and ask the children to repeat them with the actions.

Say it

■ Using several words containing the phonemes taught so far, say these slowly in 'robot talk', for example: /y/e/ll/, /v/e/s/t/ and /ch/o/p/. Ask the children to blend the phonemes into words and tell their partners.

■ Now ask the children to speak in 'robot talk'. Say a word, for example, 'bridge', and ask them to segment it using 'robot talk' first to their partner and then all together.

Read it

■ Hold up the letter cards taught so far and ask the children to tell you the sounds (phonemes) they make.

■ Write three words containing the phonemes taught so far (for example: 'yum', 'van' and 'judge') on the easel or board and ask the children to read the words out loud. Encourage them to blend the phonemes.

Write it

■ Say the phonemes taught so far and ask the children to write the corresponding letters on their individual whiteboards. Invite them to show you what they have written for a quick assessment.

3 NEW LETTER SOUND /th/ *(6-8 mins)*

Hear it

■ Show the card of the phoneme /th/ and describe the picture emphasising the initial sounds. Ask the

children to say the sounds they can hear.

■ Read the alliterative phrase 'Thimble on a thumb' emphasising the initial sound of 'thimble' and 'thumb'.

■ Teach the corresponding action as you say the phrase (point to a pretend thimble on your thumb).

Say it

■ Ask the children to repeat the phoneme /th/ /th/ /th/. Reinforce correct pronunciation and explain that when you make the sound /th/ as in 'thin', you put your tongue between your teeth and stick it out. You push air between your tongue and teeth. You can stretch the sound /th/th/th/. Practise saying it several times, check that children are not saying 'f'.

■ Say several words containing the phoneme /th/ using 'robot talk' (for example: /th/i/n/, /th/i/ck/ and /m/o/th/) and ask the children to blend the phonemes into words and tell their partner.

Read it

■ Display the 'th' card next to phonemes taught so far and ask the children to read out the letter sounds separately.

■ Explain that phonemes which are commonly written with two letters (such as /th/ as in /th/i/n/) are called digraphs.

> **Now or later**
> ■ For reinforcement, select a game from pages 46–49, for example, 'Magnetic letters', for children to play with a partner making words with given letters.

Write it

■ Now say the phoneme /th/ again and ask the children to write the letters. Demonstrate first by using your finger in the air, then on the board or easel. Ask the children to draw the letters in the air and emphasise the correct letter formation and starting point. Invite the children to practise and then to write on their whiteboards and show you.

■ Say a word containing the phoneme /th/ and other phonemes taught so far. Ask the children to first count the phonemes in the word and then to hold up the correct number of fingers. Ensure that children are able to count the phonemes when they contain digraphs. Invite the children to write the word if they are able.

LESSON 33 /th/

1 ALPHABET FUN *(2-3 mins)*
■ Begin by reciting in a lively way the 'Alphabet rhyme' (on photocopiable page 25).
■ Encourage the children to do the actions for each letter.

2 REVIEW *(5-6 mins)*
Hear it
■ Using the phoneme cards taught so far, describe the pictures emphasising the initial sounds. Then say the alliterative phrases and ask the children to repeat them with the actions.

Say it
■ Using several words containing the phonemes taught so far, say these slowly in 'robot talk', for example: /th/i/ck/, /v/e/s/t/ and /w/a/tch/. Ask the children to blend the phonemes into words and tell their partners.
■ Now ask the children to speak in 'robot talk'. Say a word, for example, 'church', and ask them to segment it using 'robot talk' first to their partner and then all together.

Read it
■ Hold up the letter cards taught so far and ask the children to tell you the sounds (phonemes) they make.
■ Write three words containing phonemes taught so far (for example: 'thin', 'yes' and 'rich') on the easel or board and ask the children to read the words out loud. Encourage them to blend the phonemes.

Write it
■ Say the phonemes taught so far and ask the children to write the corresponding letters on their individual whiteboards. Invite them to show you what they have written for a quick assessment.

3 NEW LETTER SOUND /th/ *(6-8 mins)*
Hear it
■ Show the card of the phoneme /th/ and describe the picture emphasising the initial sounds. Ask the children to say the sounds they can hear.

■ Read the alliterative phrase 'Feather with this' emphasising the initial sound in 'this'.
■ Teach the corresponding action as you say the phrase (pretend to tickle with a soft feather).

Say it
■ Ask the children to repeat the phoneme /th/ /th/ /th/. Reinforce correct pronunciation and explain when you make this sound as in 'this' your tongue touches the top of your mouth and it vibrates. You can feel the sound in your throat. You can stretch the sound /th/th/th/. Practise saying it several times, ensuring that the children differentiate it from the unvoiced /th/ taught previously.
■ Say several words containing the phoneme /th/ using 'robot talk' (for example: /th/e/n/, /th/a/t/ and /w/i/th/) and ask the children to blend the phonemes into words and tell their partner.

Read it
■ Display the 'th' card next to phonemes taught so far and ask the children to read out the letter sounds separately.
■ Explain that phonemes which are commonly written with two letters (such as /th/ as in /th/i/s/) are called digraphs.

Now or later
■ For reinforcement, select a game from pages 46–49, for example, 'Magnetic letters', for children to play with a partner making words with given letters. You may need to spend a further day reinforcing this digraph.

Write it
■ Now say the phoneme /th/ again and ask the children to write the letters. Demonstrate first by using your finger in the air, then on the board or easel. Ask the children to draw the letters in the air and emphasise the correct letter formation and starting point. Invite the children to practise and then to write on their whiteboards and show you.
■ Say a word containing the phoneme /th/ and other phonemes taught so far. Ask the children to first count the phonemes in the word and then to hold up the correct number of fingers. Ensure that children are able to count the phonemes when they contain digraphs. Invite the children to write the word if they are able.

STAGE TWO: LESSON PLANS

LESSON 34 /ng/

① ALPHABET FUN *(2-3 mins)*

■ Begin by reciting in a lively way the 'Alphabet rhyme' (on photocopiable page 25).

■ Encourage the children to do the actions for each letter.

② REVIEW *(5-6 mins)*

Hear it

■ Using the phoneme cards taught so far, describe the pictures emphasising the initial sounds. Then say the alliterative phrases and ask the children to repeat them with the actions.

Say it

■ Using several words containing the phonemes taught, say these slowly in 'robot talk', for example: /w/i/th/, /y/e/s/ and /k/i/ck/. Ask the children to blend the phonemes into words and tell their partners.

■ Now ask the children to talk in 'robot talk'. Say a word, for example, 'rush', and ask them to segment it using 'robot talk' first to their partner and then all together.

Read it

■ Hold up the letter cards 'th', 'th', 'y', 'v', 'j', 'ch', 'w', 'z', 'sh', 'h', 'l', 'f', 'b', 'r', 'u', 'c / k', 'o', 'g', 'm', 'd', 'e', 'n', 'i', 'p', 't', 'a' and 's', and ask the children to tell you the sounds (phonemes) they make.

■ Write three words containing phonemes taught so far (for example: 'this', 'thin' and 'chef') on the easel or board and ask the children to read the words out loud. Encourage them to blend the phonemes.

Write it

■ Say the phonemes taught so far and ask the children to write the corresponding letters on their individual whiteboards. Invite them to show you what they have written for a quick assessment.

③ NEW LETTER SOUND /ng/ *(6-8 mins)*

Hear it

■ Show the card of the phoneme /ng/ and describe the picture emphasising the initial sounds. Ask the children to say the sounds they can hear.

■ Read the alliterative phrase 'King with a ring' emphasising the final sounds in 'king' and 'ring'.

■ Teach the corresponding action as you say the phrase (pretend to put a crown on your head and a ring on your finger).

Say it

■ Ask the children to repeat the phoneme /ng/ /ng/ /ng/. Reinforce correct pronunciation and explain that when you make this sound it is like a humming sound at the back of your throat but you make it with your mouth open. You can stretch the sound /ng/ng/ng/. Practise saying it several times.

■ Say several words containing the phoneme /ng/ using 'robot talk' (for example: /s/i/ng/, /s/t/r/i/ng/ and /b/u/ng/) and ask the children to blend the phonemes into words and tell their partner.

Read it

■ Display the 'ng' card next to phonemes taught so far and ask the children to read out the letter sounds separately.

■ Explain that phonemes which are commonly written with two letters (such as /ng/ as in /r/i/ng/) are called digraphs.

Write it

■ Now say the phoneme /ng/ again and ask the children to write the letters. Demonstrate first by using your finger in the air, then on the board or easel. Ask the children to draw the letters in the air and emphasise the correct letter formation and starting point. Invite the children to practise and then to write on their whiteboards and show you.

■ Say a word containing the phoneme /ng/ and other phonemes taught so far. Ask the children to first count the phonemes in the word and then to hold up the correct number of fingers. Ensure that children are able to count the phonemes when they contain digraphs. Invite the children to write the word if they are able.

■ Point out that sometimes we just use the letter 'n' to write this phoneme, as in 'sink'.

Now or later

■ For reinforcement, play a game of 'Spell it!' on page 49. You may need to spend an extra day on this digraph.

LESSON 35 /zh/

1 ALPHABET FUN *(2-3 mins)*

■ Begin by reciting in a lively way the 'Alphabet rhyme' on photocopiable page 25.
■ Encourage the children to do the actions for each letter.

2 REVIEW *(5-6 mins)*

Hear it

■ Using the phoneme cards taught so far, describe the pictures emphasising the initial sounds. Then say the alliterative phrases and ask the children to repeat them with the actions.

Say it

■ Using several words containing the phonemes taught so far, say these slowly in 'robot talk', for example: /r/i/ng/, /th/i/s/ and /s/n/a/p/. Ask the children to blend the phonemes into words and tell their partners.
■ Now ask the children to talk in 'robot talk'. Say a word, for example, 'spring', and ask them to segment it using 'robot talk' first to their partner and then all together.

Read it

■ Hold up the letter cards 'ng', 'th', 'th', 'y', 'v', 'j', 'ch', 'w', 'z', 'sh', 'h', 'l', 'f', 'b', 'r', 'u', 'c / k', 'o', 'g', 'm', 'd', 'e', 'n', 'i', 'p', 't', 'a' and 's', and ask the children to tell you the sounds (phonemes) they make.
■ Write three words containing the phonemes taught so far (for example: 'then', 'rust' and 'cloth') on the easel or board and ask the children to read the words out loud. Encourage them to blend the phonemes.

Write it

■ Say the phonemes taught so far and ask the children to write the corresponding letters on their individual whiteboards. Invite them to show you what they have written for a quick assessment.

3 NEW LETTER SOUND /zh/ *(6-8 mins)*

Hear it

■ Show the card of the phoneme /zh/ and describe the picture emphasising the initial sounds. Ask the children to say the sounds they can hear.
■ Read the alliterative phrase 'Pleasure to find treasure'.
■ Teach the corresponding action as you say the phrase (pretend to open a box and find treasure and say, 'Wow!').

Say it

■ Ask the children to repeat the phoneme /zh/ /zh/ /zh/. Reinforce correct pronunciation and explain that when you make this sound your lips are open in a little circle and you blow air through your mouth. Your mouth opens wider at the end of the sound /zh/zh/zh/. Practise saying it several times.
■ Say several words containing the phoneme /zh/ using 'robot talk' (for example: /m/ea/s/ure/, /t/r/ea/s/ure/, /t/e/l/e/v/i/s/io/n/) and ask the children to blend the phonemes into words.

Read it

■ Display the 'zh' card next to phonemes taught so far and ask the children to read out the letter sounds separately.

Write it

■ Now say the phoneme /zh/ again and ask the children to write the letters. Demonstrate first by using your finger in the air, then on the board or easel. Ask the children to draw the letters in the air and emphasise the correct letter formation and starting point. Invite the children to practise and then to write on their whiteboards and show you.

Note: This phoneme is not commonly taught at an early age. You may wish to delay teaching therefore until later in Stage 3.

WEEK 8 ASSESSMENT

■ Revise the phonemes taught in the week, following the format from Revision Lesson 5 on page 58. Then, ensure that you carry out the assessment on page 99 before proceeding to Stage 3. Provide more revision and reinforcement lessons for children who are not secure with the phonemes in Stage 2.

Never camp
with ants

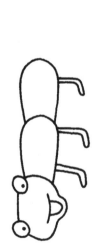

Words which the children will require support to read:
never, camp, with, the

Tip, tap, tip, tap.

2

Tap, tap, tap.

1

Ned and Nat sat in the tent.

4

It's a din!

3

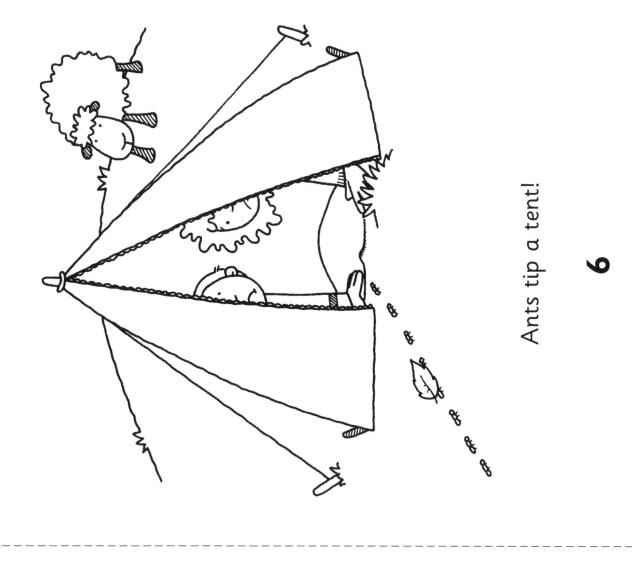

Ants tip a tent!

6

An ant in the tent.

5

PHONICS: A COMPLETE SYNTHETIC PROGRAMME FOR AGES 4+

SCHOLASTIC
www.scholastic.co.uk

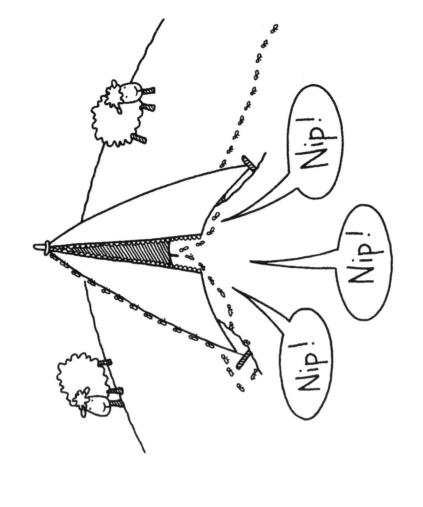

8

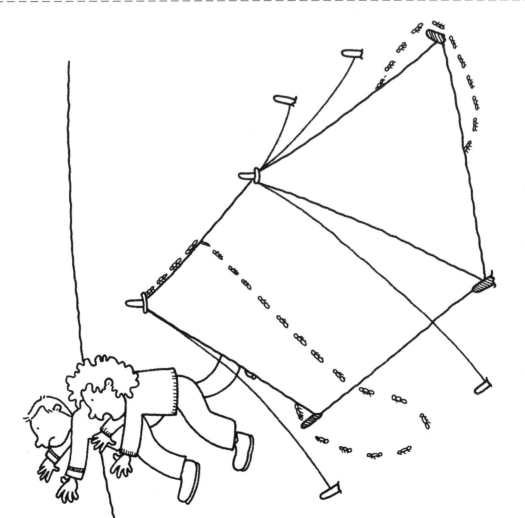

Sad Ned and Nat!

7

Rocks in the fog

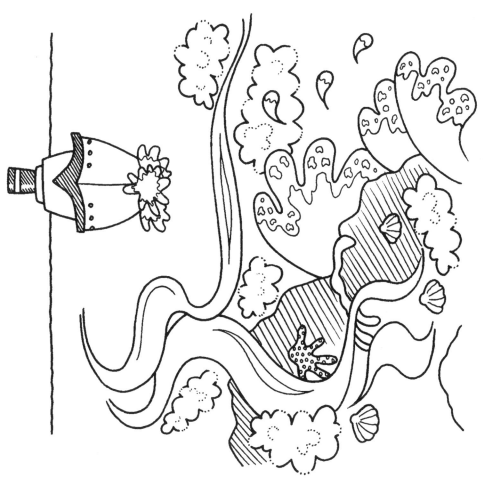

Words which the children will require support to read:
the, we, good

2

Rub-a-dub duck.
Rub-a-dub-duck.
Rub-a-dub duck for luck.

1

"Stop! Stop."
"Big rocks!."

4

"No! Fog!"
"Rocks! – Stop!"

3

"We must mend the straps."

6

STAGE TWO: PHOTOCOPIABLE MINIBOOKS ■ ■ ■

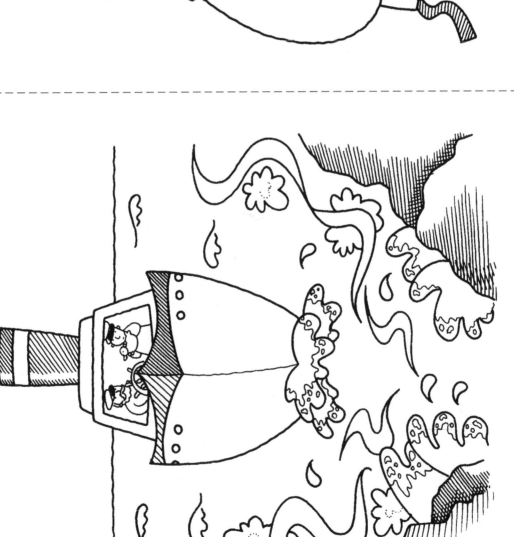

"Can we get in the gap?"

5

"It's good I gave the duck a rub for luck!"

8

"No fog!"

7

The king, the sheep and the hen

Words which the children will require support to read: when, there, sheep, sleep, treasure, watch, he, she, of

Then, a hen went up to the rock in a van.
With a jump, she left the van.
The sheep jumped at the hen. He fell flat on
his back.

2

The king of the land gets a big, flat rock for
the top of his treasure.
It had no lock so he left a sheep on top to
watch.
The sheep went to sleep.

1

PHONICS: A COMPLETE SYNTHETIC PROGRAMME FOR AGES 4+

■SCHOLASTIC
www.scholastic.co.uk

Help

Help

4

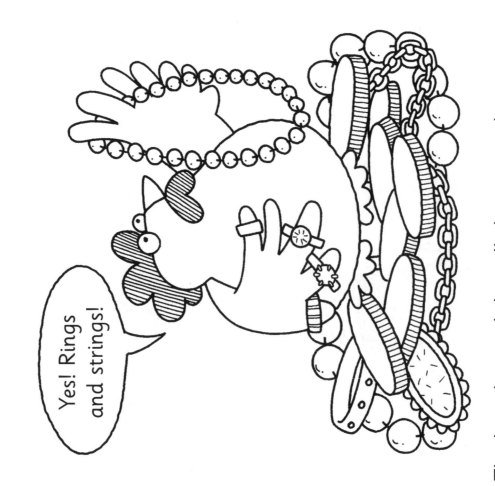

Yes! Rings and strings!

The hen dug and dug till she got to the treasure.

3

and the sheep is a rug...

6

When the king got back there was no treasure left.

5

SCHOLASTIC
www.scholastic.co.uk

8

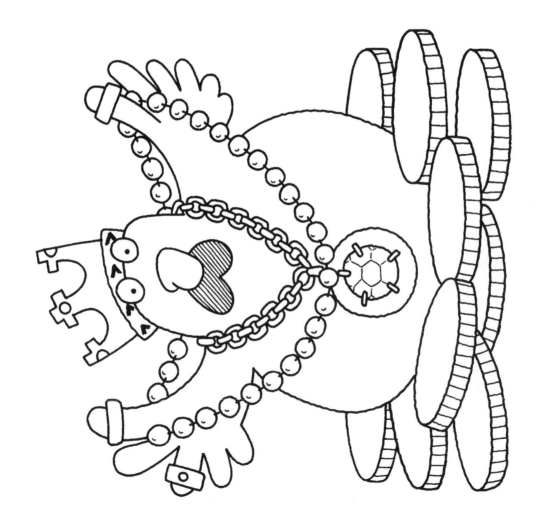

... and the hen is king!

7

STAGE TWO:
ASSESSMENT

These assessments are part of overall observations of the children's progress. Use these assessments at the end of Stage 2 to ensure that all of the children are ready to progress on to Stage 3.

/s/a/t/	/p/a/t/	/t/a/p/	/n/e/s/t/
/f/i/sh/	/ch/i/n/	/r/a/bb/i/t/	
/b/r/i/ng/	/th/e/n/	/d/e/s/k/	

ASSESSMENT 5

A PHONEME-GRAPHEME CORRESPONDENCE
What to do
■ Show the children the letters below and ask them what sound they make (you may prefer to use individual letter cards).
■ Mark any words they struggle with in the table A on page 100. Record their overall achievement in the 'Correct answers' table on page 100 for a record of their overall assessment.

Phoneme			
a	m	f	j
t	g	l	v
p	o	h	y
l	c k	sh	th (thin)
n	u	z	th (then)
e	r	w	ng
d	b	ch	z

B BLENDING
What to do
■ Tell the children that you are going to talk in 'robot talk' and read the words below. They need to tell you what the word is each time.
■ Mark down how many they blend correctly or those which they struggle with in table B on page 100. Record their overall achievement in the 'Correct answers' table at the bottom of page 100 for a record of their overall assessment. (Ensure they don't see the assessment sheet.)

C READING WORDS (BLENDING)
What to do
■ Ask the child to read the following nonsense words (you may prefer to put these on a separate card).
■ Record how well they do in the 'Correct answers' table at the bottom of page 100 for a record of their overall assessment.

tas	tep	nid	pim
dest	leck	snib	gell
sprog	bratch	chub	zish

D SEGMENTING WORDS (SPELLING)
What to do
■ Explain that you will say a word and the children should say it in 'robot talk' and then try to write it.
■ Record how well they do in the 'Correct answers' table at the bottom of page 100 for a record of their overall assessment.

1. mad	2. rug	3. imp	4. drill	5. clap
6. sing	7. lick	8. crash	9. chop	10. chef

Child's name:	Date:

ASSESSMENT 5

A PHONEME-GRAPHEME CORRESPONDENCE

Phoneme	Comment	Phoneme	Comment	Phoneme	Comment	Phoneme	Comment
a		m		f		j	
t		g		l		v	
p		o		h		y	
i		c k		sh		th (thin)	
n		u		z		th (then)	
e		r		w		ng	
d		b		ch		z	

B BLENDING

Phonemes	Word	Blended correctly?	Phonemes	Word	Blended correctly?
/s/a/t/	sat	(practice test)	/ch/i/n/	chin	
/p/a/t/	pat		/r/a/bb/i/t/	rabbit	
/t/a/p/	tap		/b/r/i/ng/	bring	
/n/e/s/t/	nest		/th/e/n/	then	
/f/i/sh/	fish		/d/e/s/k/	desk	

Correct answers	
A Phoneme/grapheme correspondence	
B Blending phonemes	
C Reading words (blending)	
D Segmenting words (spelling)	
Total	

Overall comments:

Areas for development:
NB Children need to show proficiency in each of these areas before progressing further.

STAGE THREE
LONG VOWEL SOUNDS

STAGE THREE:
SUBJECT KNOWLEDGE

It is the long vowel sounds of the English language that present the most difficulties to children and adults alike. Stage 3 of the programme teaches the remaining 15 vowel sounds with their many different graphemes or spelling choices. The use of the rap (see page 107) to support children learning these phonemes and graphemes, accompanied with an action, can help even very young children to become familiar with these phonemes.

MAPPING THE PHONEMES TO GRAPHEMES

The 'Phoneme–grapheme chart' on photocopiable page 105 shows the 15 long vowel phonemes and the most common spelling choices for each (there are other possible spelling choices, but it is important to ensure that the most frequent are clearly taught).

Check your familiarity with long vowel sounds by filling in the blank phoneme chart 'Matching graphemes to phonemes' photocopiable page 106. Sort the list of words provided into the correct places. To further consolidate your knowledge, try the following quiz (answers on page 192).

Phoneme quiz
1. Name a word containing the long vowel phoneme /a/ spelled 'ai'.
2. Which trigraph can be used to make the long vowel phoneme /i/?
3. Name two graphemes for the long vowel phoneme /ow/.
4. Name a word containing a split digraph, making the long vowel phoneme /o/.
5. Which digraphs can be used to represent the long vowel phoneme /er/?
6. Which graphemes can be used to represent the long vowel phoneme /e/?
7. Name five graphemes for the phoneme /er/ in words containing an unstressed syllable.
8. Name three words containing the long vowel phomeme /i/ each spelled differently.
9. Name four words each containing different split digraphs.
10. Which letter is commonly used to make the long vowel sound /e/ at the end of words?

COUNTING PHONEMES ACCURATELY

As well as being able to accurately map phonemes to graphemes, it is important to ensure that knowledge of spelling of words does not interfere with accurate counting of phonemes. Take, for example the word 'bright': it is easy to confuse here the blend at the beginning (br) with one sound, but wherever two sounds can be distinctly heard, these are separate phonemes. So the word 'bright' contains four phonemes: /b/r/igh/t/.

Now check your knowledge by segmenting the following words:

Word	Divide into phonemes	Number of phonemes
brain		
tree		
crime		
float		
wait		
groan		
stew		
shark		
stern		
horse		
shout		
bear		
square		
green		
teacher		

(See Appendix on page 192 for the answers.)

THE SCHWA PHONEME

The schwa phoneme, most commonly written as 'er', as in 'sister', is one of the trickiest phonemes for children to understand. This is because it is contained in words of more than one syllable; it is the unstressed vowel in such words and it can be written in many ways. The common alternatives are: 'ar' (in collar), 'e' (as in garden), 'u' (as in fungus) and

'or' (as in doctor). As the phoneme is contained in the unstressed part of the word, it is often difficult to hear and differentiate correctly.

The schwa phoneme is included here to ensure that all 44 phonemes are included, and because of its frequency in our language. However, you may feel that your children are not ready to learn multi-syllabic words and you might choose to leave the specific teaching of this phoneme until later. It is deliberately left to the end of the programme for this reason.

BLENDING AND SEGMENTING SOUNDS

Blending and segmenting remain vital elements of this stage of the programme and a key way of ensuring that children apply the skills they are being taught. You might find it helpful to find other opportunities during the day to reinforce this. For example, when lining up children to go into assembly, ask a child to blend a word you say in phonemes (such as /p/l/ay/ – the child says 'play').

USE OF ROBOT TALK

As with Stage 2 of this programme, 'robot talk' remains an important tool to support children blending and segmenting sounds. Continue to use it at this stage with the robot only talking in phonemes and the children then blending the sounds to make words. This requires constant practice with every new sound taught. In addition children will need to continue to hear words and then say them in 'robot talk'. This will aid their application of phonics to writing and spelling words.

RAP

Learning long vowel sounds is the most complex area of phonics and to aid this process, we have provided a 'Long vowel sounds rap' on photocopiable page 107 which the children will enjoy learning. Constant practice at saying this rap will support them in remembering the phonemes and their most common spelling choices/graphemes.

To teach the long vowel rap

1. Say the phoneme twice, for example: 'ay' 'ay'
2. Say the mnemonic, for example: 'Play with hay'
3. Say the letter names, for example: 'AY'.

When teaching split digraph

1. Say the phoneme twice, for example: 'a–e' 'a–e'
2. Say the mnemonic, for example: 'Take a cake'
3. Say the letter names, for example 'A–E' (say 'A' skip a letter 'E')

The rap for the first two long vowel phonemes is as follows:

> 'ay' 'ay' Play with hay AY
> 'ai' 'ai' What did you say? AI

The rap will build up as children learn more phonemes.

ACTIONS

To support the recall of the long vowel phonemes further, illustrations of the actions are provided on the 'Phoneme-grapheme cards' on pages 108–116, similar to Stage 2, as well as being provided on the 'Long vowel sounds rap' on photocopiable page 107. These actions should be taught as each phoneme is introduced so that the children say the rap and do the accompanying action, for example:

| 'ee' 'ee' | F**ee**l the tr**ee** | EE | pretend to hug a tree |
| 'ea' 'ea' | H**ea**t the m**ea**t | EA | pretend to stir with a spoon |

TEACHING ORDER GRID

As for Stage 2 of the programme, it is vital that children are given constant practice of the phonemes they have learned; therefore, here again, each lesson will begin with a quick revision of previous sounds. This should be short, fast and fun, to maintain the children's interest. The use of the rap and actions will support this.

In addition, the programme again is structured to allow you time to teach reinforcement and practice lessons every week (or five days). For some weeks, time has been allowed for two days of revision to ensure the children have fully grasped the phonemes taught. The grid on pages 9 and 10 shows the order of teaching for the long vowel phonemes and where the reinforcement lessons fall.

It is recommended that you maintain a quick pace, however it is important you also ensure that the children are able to recall and use the phonemes as you go along and, of course, some children will be

STAGE THREE: SUBJECT KNOWLEDGE

able to learn at a faster pace than others. Accurate assessment of children's progress is therefore vital in order to ensure that the programme suits the children's needs.

COMMON SPELLING CHOICES/ GRAPHEMES

Another difficulty with phonics in the English language is the many different ways of representing the same phoneme, that is: the different spelling choices or graphemes for the same sound. This teaching programme introduces the most common spelling choice (grapheme) first for each of the long vowel phonemes. You may prefer to initially teach this grapheme only, depending on the maturity of the children and later teach all the spelling choices. Note that sometimes the phoneme which is represented between slashes, for example /ee/ and the grapheme, represented in inverted commas, 'ee' may be the same.

To make this clear, as the different graphemes for each phoneme are introduced, enlarge a photocopy and cut out the 'Phoneme-grapheme cards' on pages 108–116, and display a large laminated version of each card on a chart under their respective phoneme (follow the layout of the Phoneme-grapheme chart on page 105). This will help the children to see the different spelling choices for each sound.

This does not include all the possible spelling choices for each phoneme, only the most common

and therefore, if appropriate, you may wish to add further graphemes as they arise. You may also wish to begin to introduce spelling rules to help make sense of the many choices, such as 'ay' is found at the end of words and 'ai' in the middle. You will need to continue to build on this throughout Key Stage 1 and in Key Stage 2 as children work through a spelling programme. This phonics programme forms the foundations of that process.

MINIBOOKS

As with Stage 2 of this programme, it is helpful if parents can support their children's learning at home. The grid below shows how the words used in the minibooks, on photocopiable pages 167–186, link to the phonemes taught. These minibooks can then be given to the children to take home. See page 38 for more information on how to use and make the minibooks. Once again, there are a few words (mainly high frequency words) which are recommended to be taught as sight vocabulary (see also page 120) that children will need support with.

Corresponding lessons	Book	New words	Words children will need support with
36–55 New phonemes: /ae/, /ee/, /ie/, /oe/	4	baby, day, feel, see, she, lie, cried, light, bright, right, my, dry, tiger, idea, boat, coat, snow, row, know, cold, old, go, floated	one, too, said, won't, look
56–70 New phonemes: /u/, /ue/, /a-e/, /i-e/, /o-e, /u-e/	5	book, cook, took, should, could, would, true, make, cake, time, nice, bone, cube, put, long, shape, eat, like, take	Woof, said
71–91 New phonemes: /ow/, /oi/, /ur/, /au/, /ar/	6	out, house, boy, girl, shirt, bird, first, heard, early, search, worm, Paul, door, floor, Lorna, warn, fall, called, dark, join, shout, saw, lawn	was, watched, said
92–106 New phonemes: /air/, /ear/, /ure/, /er/	7	fair, chair, bear, wear, tear, fare, fear, ear, dear, here, mere, cheer, sure, cure, sister, doctor	Mary, said, fix, magic

ASSESSMENT

There are four assessments to be undertaken at weeks 12, 16, 19 and 22, (see pages 187–191). This is to ensure that the children are able to fully understand, recall and apply the phonemes before proceeding. You will also need to continually assess children's progress. Where children have not fully grasped taught phonemes, further lessons will be needed, and the use of the phonic games will help reinforcement.

STAGE THREE: SUBJECT KNOWLEDGE

PHONEME-GRAPHEME CHART

Vowel 1 /ae/	Vowel 2 /ee/	Vowel 3 /ie/	Vowel 4 /oe/	Vowel 5 /u/	Vowel 6 /ue/	Vowel 7 /ow/	Vowel 8 /oi/	Vowel 9 /ur/	Vowel 10 /au/	Vowel 11 /ar/	Vowel 12 /air/	Vowel 13 /ear/	Vowel 14 /ure/	Vowel 15 /er/
ay (day)	ee (see)	ie (tie)	oa (boat)	oo (book)	oo (moon)	ow (cow)	oi (coin)	ur (burn)	au (haul)	ar (car)	air (hair)	ear (fear)	ure (sure)	er (sister)
ai (tail)	ea (beach)	igh (light)	ow (snow)	ou (would)	ue (clue)	ou (shout)	oy (boy)	ir (girl)	or (horn)		ear (bear)	ere (here)	our (tour)	e (wooden)
a (baby)	e (me)	y (my)	o (cold)	u (put)	ew (grew)			er (term)	oor (door)		are (share)	eer (deer)		u (circus)
a-e (make)	y (pony)	i (tiger)	o-e (bone)		u-e (tune)			ear (heard)	ar (warn)					ar (collar)
		i-e (time)						or (work)	aw (claw)					or (doctor)
									a (call)					

NB Each column includes different graphemes (spelling choices) for the same phoneme.

STAGE THREE: PHOTOCOPIABLES

LONG VOWEL SOUNDS ●■

MATCHING GRAPHEMES TO PHONEMES

/ae/	/ee/	/ie/	/oe/	/u/	/ue/	/ow/	/oi/

/ur/	/au/	/ar/	/air/	/ear/	/ure/	/er/

■ Place each of the following words which contain a long vowel phoneme or schwa phoneme in the corresponding phoneme column (see page 102 for details):

able east right know ago fuel rook ark hurl maul vow doubt wear pure fungus take fee pie
foal roof should shirt born toil chair cover garden tray dollar dry phone few earth draw shout
pear jeer tour mummy

Answers: /ae/ – able, take, tray; /ee/ – east, fee, mummy; /ie/ – right, pie, dry; /oe/ – foal, know, ago, phone; /ue/ – roof, fuel, few; /u/ – should, rook, put; /ar/ – ark, garden; /ur/ – hurl, earth, shirt; /au/ – maul, born, draw; /ow/ – vow, doubt, shout; /oi/ – toil; /air/ – pear, wear, chair; /ear/ – jeer; /ure/ – tour, pure; /er/ – dollar, cover, fungus.

PHONICS: A COMPLETE SYNTHETIC PROGRAMME FOR AGES 4+

LONG VOWEL SOUNDS RAP

Week	Phoneme (say twice)	Phrase	Letter names	Action
9	'ay' 'ay'	**Play** with h**ay**	AY	Pretend to lift a pile of hay
	'ai' 'ai'	What did you s**ay**?	AI	Hand cupped around ear
	'a' 'a'	**A**corn in an **a**cre	A	Pretend to hold a tiny acorn
10	'ee' 'ee'	F**ee**l the tr**ee**	EE	Pretend to hug a tree
	'ea' 'ea'	H**ea**t the m**ea**t	EA	Pretend to stir with a spoon
	'e' 'e'	H**e** and m**e**	E	Point to someone
	'y' 'y'	Bon**y** pon**y**	Y	Pretend to ride a pony
11	'ie' 'ie'	T**ie** the t**ie**	IE	Pretend to tie a tie
	'igh' 'igh'	L**igh**t helps s**igh**t	IGH	Make a circle with thumb and forefinger and hold around eyes
	'y' 'y'	M**y** what a fl**y**	Y	Buzz like a fly
	'i' 'i'	K**i**nd t**i**ger	I	Pretend to wave to a tiger
12	'oa' 'oa'	Fl**oa**t the b**oa**t	OA	Arms outstretched and pretend to float
	'ow' 'ow'	R**ow** it sl**ow**	OW	Move arms in a rowing motion
	'o' 'o'	C**o**ld n**o**se!	O	Finger on nose
13	'oo' 'oo'	T**oo**k the b**oo**k	OO	Pretend to take a book
	'ou' 'ou'	C**ou**ld you? W**ou**ld you?	OU	Hold hands together as if pleading
	'u' 'u'	P**u**t it, p**u**t it	U	Point to a table
14	'oo' 'oo'	R**oo**m on the m**oo**n	OO	Point up to the moon
	'ue' 'ue'	S**ue**'s cl**ue**	UE	Finger to mouth and frown
	'ew' 'ew'	He gr**ew** and gr**ew**!	EW	Pretend to grow taller and taller
15	'a–e' 'a–e'	T**a**ke a c**a**ke	A–E*	Pretend to eat a cake
	'i–e' 'i–e'	M**i**ke's b**i**ke	I–E*	Pretend to ride a bike
	'o–e' 'o–e'	St**o**ne on a b**o**ne	O–E*	Hop several times, pointing to leg
	'u–e' 'u–e'	C**u**te t**u**ne	U–E*	Pretend to play a tune on a recorder
16	'ow' 'ow'	Not n**ow** br**ow**n c**ow**	OW	Hold up finger as if telling off a cow
	'ou' 'ou'	Sh**ou**t **ou**t l**ou**d	OU	Hands to face and pretend to shout
	'oi' 'oi'	J**oi**n the c**oi**n	OI	Pretend to hold a coin between fingers
	'oy' 'oy'	R**oy**'s a b**oy**	OY	Point to a boy
17	'ur' 'ur'	T**ur**n the f**ur**	UR	Pretend to stroke some fur
	'ir' 'ir'	Tw**ir**l the g**ir**l	IR	Twirl round
	'er' 'er'	P**er**m for the t**er**m	ER	Pat hair and stand up smartly
	'ear' 'ear'	S**ear**ch the **ear**th	EAR	Pretend to search and peer in the distance
	'or' 'or'	W**or**k, w**or**k, w**or**k	OR	Pretend to write fast
18	'au' 'au'	S**au**ce, lots of s**au**ce	AU	Pretend to pat the bottom of the sauce bottle
	'or' 'or'	The h**or**n is w**or**n	OR	Pretend to look at an animal's horn
	'oor' 'oor'	D**oor** on the m**oor**	OOR	Pretend to open a door
	'ar' 'ar'	W**ar**n the w**ar**d	AR	Hands to mouth as if shouting to warn people
19	'aw' 'aw'	Dr**aw** the cl**aw**	AW	Hold up fingers and bend like a claw
	'a' 'a'	C**a**ll the b**a**ll	A	Pretend to hold up a ball
	'ar' 'ar'	P**ar**k the c**ar**	AR	Pretend to drive the car with hands on wheel
20	'air' 'air'	F**air** h**air**	AIR	Pretend to brush hair
	'ear' 'ear'	B**ear** in a p**ear**	EAR	Point and look amazed
	'are' 'are'	F**are** sh**are**	ARE	Pretend to give some money
21	'ear' 'ear'	H**ear** with your **ear**	EAR	Pull on ear lobe
	'ere' 'ere'	H**ere**, h**ere**	ERE	Beckon with finger
	'eer' 'eer'	Ch**eer** the d**eer**	EER	Clap several times
22	'ure' 'ure'	S**ure**, s**ure**	URE	Nod head several times
	'our' 'our'	T**our** and det**our**	OUR	Walk in a circle
	'er' 'er'	Teach**er**, doctor, sist**er** too	ER	Point to different people

* For split digraphs say: 'A skip a letter E'; 'I skip a letter E'; 'O skip a letter E'; 'U skip a letter E'.
NB This rap is in order of teaching therefore split digraphs have been placed together.

STAGE THREE: PHOTOCOPIABLES

Phoneme-grapheme cards

ay

'ay' 'ay'
Play with hay   AY

ai

'ai' 'ai'
What did you say?   AI

a

'a' 'a'
Acorn in an acre   A

ee

'ee' 'ee'
Feel the tree   EE

ea

'ea' 'ea'
Heat the meat   EA

e

'e' 'e'
He and me   E

PHONICS: A COMPLETE SYNTHETIC PROGRAMME FOR AGES 4+

Phoneme-grapheme cards

y	ie
'y' 'y' Bony pony Y	'ie' 'ie' Tie the tie IE
igh	y
'igh' 'igh' Light helps sight IGH	'y' 'y' My what a fly Y
i	oa
'i' 'i' Kind tiger I	'oa' 'oa' Float the boat OA

STAGE THREE: PHOTOCOPIABLES

Phoneme-grapheme cards

OW

'ow' 'ow'
Row it slow   OW

O

'o' 'o'
Cold nose   O

OO

'oo' 'oo'
Took the book   OO

ou

'ou' 'ou'
Could you? Would you?   OU

u

'u' 'u'
Put it, put it   U

OO

'oo' 'oo'
Room on the moon   OO

Phoneme-grapheme cards

ue

'ue' 'ue'
Sue's clue   UE

ew

'ew' 'ew'
He grew and grew!   EW

a–e

'a–e' 'a–e'
Take a cake A–E

i–e

'i–e' 'i–e'
Mike's bike   I–E

o–e

'o–e' 'o–e'
Stone on a bone   O–E

u–e

'u–e' 'u–e'
Cute tune   U–E

Phoneme-grapheme cards

ow

'ow' 'ow'
Not now brown cow   OW

ou

'ou' 'ou'
Shout out loud   OU

oi

'oi' 'oi'
Join the coin   OI

oy

'oy' 'oy'
Roy's a boy   OY

ur

'ur' 'ur'
Turn the fur   UR

ir

'ir' 'ir'
Twirl the girl   IR

STAGE THREE: PHOTOCOPIABLES

SCHOLASTIC
www.scholastic.co.uk

PHONICS: A COMPLETE SYNTHETIC PROGRAMME FOR AGES 4+

Phoneme-grapheme cards

er

GROVE SCHOOL — NEW TERM

'er' 'er'
Perm for the term   ER

ear

'ear' 'ear'
Search the earth   EAR

or

'or' 'or'
Work, work, work   OR

au

'au' 'au'
Sauce, lots of sauce   AU

or

'or' 'or'
The horn is worn   OR

oor

'oor' 'oor'
Door on the moor   OOR

STAGE THREE: PHOTOCOPIABLES

Phoneme-grapheme cards

ar

'ar' 'ar'
Warn the ward   AR

aw

'aw' 'aw'
Draw the claw   AW

a

'a' 'a'
Call the ball   A

ar

'ar' 'ar'
Park the car   AR

air

'air' 'air'
Fair hair   AIR

ear

'ear' 'ear'
Bear in a pear   EAR

Phoneme-grapheme cards

are

'are' 'are'
Fare share   ARE

ear

'ear' 'ear'
Hear with your ear   EAR

ere

'ere' 'ere'
Here, here   ERE

eer

'eer' 'eer'
Cheer the deer   EER

STAGE THREE: PHOTOCOPIABLES

Phoneme-grapheme cards

ure

'ure' 'ure'

Sure, sure   URE

oor

'our' 'our'

Tour and detour   OUR

er

'er' 'er'

Teacher, doctor, sister too   ER

PHONICS: A COMPLETE SYNTHETIC PROGRAMME FOR AGES 4+

STAGE THREE:
LESSON PLANS

LESSON 36 'ay'

1 NEW PHONEME /ae/ GRAPHEME 'ay'
(10 mins)
Hear it
■ Explain to the children that they are going to learn a fun rap. You may like to give an example by saying a rap or listening to a pop rap.
■ Introduce the children to the new phoneme /ae/ with the grapheme 'ay' by saying several words that contain it, for example: 'may', 'say' and 'play'.

Say it
■ Say the phoneme /ae/, grapheme 'ay', emphasising correct articulation, and then show the children the corresponding phoneme picture card and mnemonic phrase 'Play with hay' (see the 'Phoneme-grapheme cards' on photocopiable pages 108–116). Ask the children to repeat it several times with you.
■ Say the letter names of the new grapheme: 'AY' and introduce the action (pretend to lift a pile of hay).
■ Now say the full rap for this grapheme (see instructions in Subject knowledge on page 103 and the 'Long vowel rap' on photocopiable page 107) and ask the children to do the action: 'ay' 'ay' Play with hay AY.
■ Say several words containing the phoneme /ae/ with the grapheme 'ay', slowly in 'robot talk' (for example: /d/ay/, /m/ay/ and /t/r/ay/) and ask the children to blend the phonemes into words and tell their partners.
■ Now ask the children to speak in 'robot talk'. Say a word, for example, 'play', and ask them to segment it using 'robot talk' to their partner.

Read it
■ Write words that contain the phoneme /ae/ with the grapheme 'ay' on the easel or board (for example: 'pay', 'say' and 'day') and ask the children to read out the phonemes by blending them together and to tell their partner.
■ Display the picture card of the grapheme 'ay' on the wall chart to build up a Phoneme-grapheme chart for

the long vowel phonemes (see Subject knowledge page 104 for more details). Ask the children to tell you the grapheme for the phoneme /ae/ and repeat the mnemonic phrase 'ay'.

Write it
■ Say a word containing the new phoneme /ae/, grapheme 'ay'. Ask the children to repeat it and then segment it into phonemes using 'robot talk', for example: play – /p/l/ay/. Ask the children to first count the number of phonemes that are in the word by counting on their fingers and then to hold up the correct number of fingers.
■ Now say the word again and ask the children to write it on their whiteboards and underline the grapheme that represents the phoneme /ae/.
■ Ask the children to tell you the grapheme for the phoneme /ae/. Encourage them to refer to the Phoneme-grapheme chart on to support spelling.

ay

'ay' 'ay'
Play with hay   AY

LESSON 37 'ai'

① REVIEW *(5 mins)*
Hear it
■ Review the phoneme /ae/, grapheme 'ay' by saying the first line of the 'Long vowel rap' in a lively fun way with the children: 'ay' 'ay' Play with hay AY.

■ Help the children to practise hearing the sounds by saying a range of words, some of which contain the phoneme /ae/, grapheme 'ay', and some that do not, for example: 'day', 'sold', 'bone', 'way', 'cake', 'play'. Ask them to put their hands up every time they hear the phoneme /ae/.

Say it
■ Say several words containing the phoneme /ae/ with the grapheme 'ay' slowly in 'robot talk', for example: /p/l/ay/, /w/ay/, /s/ay/. Ask the children to blend the phonemes into words and tell their partners.

■ Now ask the children to speak in 'robot talk'. Say a word, for example, 'may', and ask them to segment it using 'robot talk' first to their partner and then all together.

Read it
■ Write the following words on the board or easel and show the children: 'play', 'say', 'hay'.

■ Ask the children to read the words out loud to their partner. Encourage them to blend the phonemes.

Write it
■ Say a word containing the phoneme /ae/ with grapheme 'ay', for example, 'ray'. Ask the children to repeat it and then segment it into phonemes using 'robot talk'. Ask the children to count the phonemes in the word and to hold up the correct number of fingers. Then write the answer on their whiteboard.

② NEW GRAPHEME 'ai' *(10 mins)*
Hear it
■ Explain to the children that they are going to learn some more of the rap.

■ Introduce the new grapheme 'ai' by saying several words that contain it: 'sail', 'mail', 'tail'. Explain that this is the same phoneme as 'ay' but they are learning a different way to spell it.

Say it
■ Say the phoneme /ae/, grapheme 'ai', emphasising correct articulation, and then show the children the corresponding phoneme-grapheme picture card and mnemonic phrase, 'What did you say?' Ask the children to repeat it several times with you.

■ Say the letter names of the new grapheme: 'AI' and introduce the action (hand cupped around ear).

■ Now say the full rap for this grapheme and ask the children to do the action: 'ai' 'ai' What did you say? AI.

■ Using several words containing the phoneme /ae/, grapheme 'ai', say these slowly in 'robot talk' (for example: /s/n/ai/l/, /m/ai/l/ and /t/r/ai/l/) and ask the children to blend the phonemes into words and tell their partners.

■ Now ask the children to speak in 'robot talk'. Say a word, for example, 'wail', and ask them to segment it using 'robot talk' to their partner.

Read it
■ Write words that contain the phoneme /ae/ with the grapheme 'ai' on the easel or board (for example: 'rail', 'pail', 'sail') and ask the children to read out the phonemes and blend them together with their partner. Ensure that the children can identify the grapheme 'ai'.

■ Display the picture card of the grapheme 'ai' on the wall underneath the grapheme 'ay' to build up the Phoneme-grapheme chart for the long vowel phonemes. Ask the children to tell you the graphemes for the phoneme /ae/ and repeat the mnemonic phrase for 'ai'.

Write it
■ Say a word containing the phoneme /ae/ with grapheme 'ai'. Ask the children to repeat it and then segment it into phonemes using 'robot talk', for example: pail - /p/ai/l/. Ask the children to first count the phonemes in the word and then to hold up the correct number of fingers.

■ Now say the word again and ask the children to write it on their whiteboards and underline the grapheme that represents the phoneme /ae/.

■ Ask the children to tell you the graphemes for the phoneme /ae/. Encourage them to refer to the Phoneme-grapheme chart on the wall to support spelling.

LESSON 38 'a'

1 REVIEW (5 mins)
Hear it
■ Review the long vowel phonemes taught so far by saying the vowel rap in a lively fun way with the children.

■ Help the children to practise hearing the sounds by saying a range of words, some of which contain the phoneme /ae/, graphemes 'ay' or 'ai' and some that do not, for example: 'day', 'sail', 'tree', 'fork', 'rail', 'girl', 'hay'. Ask them to put their hands up every time they hear the phoneme /ae/.

Say it
■ Say several words containing the long vowel phonemes slowly in 'robot talk', for example: /r/ai/l/, /s/ay/ and /f/ai/l/. Ask the children to blend the phonemes into words and tell their partners.

■ Now ask the children to speak in 'robot talk'. Say a word, for example, 'sail', and ask them to segment it using 'robot talk' first to their partner and then all together.

Read it
■ Write the following words on the board or easel and show the children: 'mail', 'wail', 'play'.

■ Ask the children to read the words out loud to their partner. Encourage them to blend the phonemes.

Write it
■ Say a word containing the phoneme /ae/ with the grapheme 'ai', for example: 'fail'. Ask the children to repeat it and then segment it into phonemes using 'robot talk'. Ask the children to count the phonemes in the word and to hold up the correct number of fingers. Then write the answer on their whiteboard.

2 NEW GRAPHEME 'a' (10 mins)
Hear it
■ Explain to the children that they are going to learn some more of the rap.

■ Introduce the new grapheme 'a' by saying several words that contain it for example, 'baby', 'able' and 'acorn'. Explain that this is the same sound (phoneme) as the graphemes 'ay' and 'ai' but a different spelling.

Say it
■ Say the phoneme /ae/, grapheme 'a' emphasising correct articulation, and then show the children the corresponding phoneme picture card and mnemonic phrase, 'Acorn in an acre'. Ask the children to repeat it several times with you.

■ Say the letter name of the new grapheme: 'A' and introduce the action (pretend to hold a tiny acorn).

■ Now say the full rap for this grapheme and ask the children to do the action: 'a' 'a' Acorn in an acre A.

■ Using several words containing the phoneme /ae/ grapheme 'a', say these slowly in 'robot talk' (for example: /b/a/b/y/ and /a/b/le/) and ask the children to blend the phonemes into words and tell their partners.

■ Now ask the children to talk in 'robot talk'. Say a word, for example, 'baby', and ask them to segment it using 'robot talk' to their partner.

Read it
■ Write words that contain the phoneme /ae/, grapheme 'a', on the easel or board (for example: 'apron', 'able' and 'acre') and ask the children to read out the phonemes by blending them together with their partner. Ensure that the children can identify the grapheme 'a'.

■ Display the picture card of the grapheme 'a' underneath the graphemes 'ay' and 'ai' to build up the Phoneme-grapheme chart for the long vowel phonemes. Ask the children to tell you the graphemes for the phoneme /ae/ and repeat the mnemonic phrase for 'a'.

Write it
■ Say a word containing the phoneme /ae/, grapheme 'a'. Ask the children to repeat it and then segment it into phonemes using 'robot talk', for example: able – /a/b/le/. Ask the children to first count the phonemes in the word and then to hold up the correct number of fingers.

■ Now say the word again and ask the children to write it on their whiteboards and underline the grapheme that represents the phoneme /ae/.

■ Ask the children to tell you the graphemes for the phoneme /ae/. Encourage them to refer to the Phoneme-grapheme chart on the wall to support spelling.

STAGE THREE: LESSON PLANS

LESSONS 39/40
REVISION

1 REVIEW *(5 mins)*

Hear it

■ Review the phonemes taught so far by saying the 'Long vowel rap' in a lively fun way with the children.

■ Help the children to practise hearing the phonemes by saying a range of words, some of which contain the phonemes and corresponding graphemes taught during the week and some that do not. Ask them to put their hands up every time they hear the appropriate phoneme.

Say it

■ Say several words containing the graphemes taught so far slowly in 'robot talk'. Ask the children to blend the phonemes into words and tell their partners.

■ Now ask the children to speak in 'robot talk'. Say several words to the children and ask them to segment them using 'robot talk' first to their partner and then all together.

Read it

■ Write words that contain the long vowel phonemes taught so far on the board or easel and show the children.

■ Ask the children to read the words out loud to their partner. Encourage them to blend the phonemes together.

Write it

■ Say several words containing the phonemes taught so far. Invite the children to repeat them and then to segment them into phonemes using 'robot talk'. Ask the children to first count the phonemes in the word and then to hold up the correct number of fingers. Ask them to write the answer on their individual whiteboards.

■ Dictate a short sentence for the children to write which includes the phonemes taught and some irregular sight words (see table below). Sight words are words which are irregular in their spellings and therefore need to be learned as a whole word. This is also a good opportunity to reinforce use of capital letters to start sentences and full stops to end.

Sight Words				
said	are	come	the	was
because	once	people	some	your
their	there	two	want	what
where	who			

NB Some of the above can be read phonetically but, as they are unusual spellings, it would be helpful to learn these as whole words.

How to adapt revision lessons

When you reach the end of each week it is important to recap the phonemes and graphemes taught so far, to make sure that the children are ready to move on to the next level.

For each revision lesson, follow the format above and adapt as necessary, depending on the phonemes and corresponding graphemes learned. Ensure that you note children's progress and reinforce where necessary.

LESSON 41 'ee'

1 REVIEW *(5 mins)*
Hear it
■ Review the long vowel sounds taught so far by saying the vowel rap in a lively fun way with the children.

■ Help the children to practise hearing the sounds by saying a range of words, some of which contain the phoneme /ae/ graphemes 'ay', 'ai' or 'a' and some that do not, for example: 'able', 'cow', 'day', 'sail', 'tree', 'fork', 'rail', 'girl'. Ask them to put their hands up every time they hear the phoneme /ae/.

Say it
■ Say several words containing the long vowel phonemes slowly in 'robot talk', for example: /b/a/b/y/, /r/ai/l/, /t/r/ay/. Ask the children to blend the phonemes into words and tell their partners.

■ Now ask the children to speak in 'robot talk'. Say a word, for example, 'may', and ask them to segment it using 'robot talk' first to their partner and then all together.

Read it
■ Write the following words on the board or easel and show the children: 'apron', 'mail', 'say'.

■ Ask the children to read the words out loud to their partner. Encourage them to blend the phonemes.

Write it
■ Say a word containing the phoneme /ae/ with the grapheme 'a', for example: 'able'. Ask the children to repeat it and then segment it into phonemes using 'robot talk'. Ask the children to first count the phonemes in the word and then to hold up the correct number of fingers. Ask them to write the answer on their individual whiteboards.

2 NEW PHONEME /ee/ GRAPHEME 'ee'
(10 mins)
Hear it
■ Explain to the children that they are going to learn some more of the rap.

■ Introduce the new phoneme /ee/ represented by the grapheme 'ee' by saying several words that contain it for example 'tree', 'agree', 'see'.

Say it
■ Say the phoneme /ee/, grapheme 'ee', emphasising correct articulation, and then show the children the corresponding phoneme picture card and mnemonic phrase, 'Feel the tree'. Ask the children to repeat it several times with you.

■ Say the letter names of the new grapheme: 'EE' and introduce the action (pretend to hug a tree).

■ Now say the full rap for this grapheme and ask the children to do the action: 'ee' 'ee' Feel the tree EE.

■ Using several words containing the phoneme /ee/ with grapheme 'ee', say these slowly in 'robot talk' (for example: /s/ee/, /f/ee/l/ and /t/r/ee/) and ask the children to blend the phonemes into words and tell their partners.

■ Now ask the children to talk in 'robot talk'. Say a word, for example, 'feel', and ask them to segment it using 'robot talk' to their partner.

Read it
■ Write words that contain the phoneme /ee/, grapheme 'ee', on the easel or board for example, 'sleep', 'tree' and 'see' and ask the children to read out the phonemes by blending them together and to tell their partner. Ensure that the children can identify the grapheme 'ee'.

■ Display the picture card of the grapheme 'ee' next to the phonemes taught so far, beginning a new column (see the Phoneme-grapheme chart on photocopiable page 105 for layout) to build up the phoneme chart for the long vowel phonemes. Ask the children to tell you the grapheme for the phoneme /ee/ and say the mnemonic phrase for 'ee'.

Write it
■ Say a word containing the phoneme /ee/, grapheme 'ee'. Ask the children to repeat it and then segment it into phonemes using 'robot talk', for example: tree – /t/r/ee/. Ask the children to first count the phonemes in the word and then to hold up the correct number of fingers.

■ Now say the word again and ask them to write it on their whiteboards and underline the grapheme that represents the phoneme /ee/.

■ Ask the children to tell you the grapheme for the phoneme /ee/. Encourage them to refer to the Phoneme-grapheme chart on the wall to support spelling.

LESSON 42 'ea'

1 REVIEW (5 mins)

Hear it

■ Review the long vowel phonemes taught so far by saying the vowel rap in a lively fun way with the children.

■ Help the children to practise hearing the sounds by reading a range of words, some of which contain the phoneme /ee/, grapheme 'ee' and some that do not for example: 'see', 'day', 'feel', 'sail', 'tree', 'far' 'deep'. Ask them to put their hands up every time they hear the phoneme /ee/.

Say it

■ Say several words containing the long vowel phonemes slowly in 'robot talk', for example: /d/ee/p/, /t/r/ee/, /f/r/ee/. Ask the children to blend the phonemes into words and tell their partners.

■ Now ask the children to speak in 'robot talk'. Say a word, for example, 'sleep', and ask them to segment it using 'robot talk' first to their partner and then all together.

Read it

■ Write the following words on the board or easel and show the children: 'sleep', 'deep', 'keep'.

■ Ask the children to read the words out loud to their partner. Encourage them to blend the phonemes together.

Write it

■ Say a word containing the phoneme /ee/ with the grapheme 'ee', for example: 'sheep'. Ask the children to repeat it and then segment it into phonemes using 'robot talk'. Ask the children to first count the phonemes in the word and then to hold up the correct number of fingers. Ask them to write the answer on their individual whiteboards.

2 NEW GRAPHEME 'ea' (10 mins)

Hear it

■ Explain to the children that they are going to learn some more of the rap.

■ Introduce the new grapheme 'ea' by saying several words that contain it for example 'beach', 'teach', 'reach'.

Say it

■ Say the phoneme /ee/, grapheme 'ea', emphasising correct articulation, and then show the children the corresponding phoneme picture card and mnemonic phrase 'Heat the meat'. Ask the children to repeat it several times with you.

■ Say the letter names of the new grapheme: 'EA' and introduce the action (pretend to stir with a spoon).

■ Now say the full rap for this grapheme and ask the children to do the action: 'ea' 'ea' Heat the meat EA.

■ Using several words containing the phoneme /ee/, grapheme 'ea', say these slowly in 'robot talk' for example: /r/ea/ch/, /b/ea/ch/ and /m/ea/t/) and ask the children to blend the phonemes into words and tell their partners.

■ Now ask the children to speak in 'robot talk'. Say a word, for example, 'meal' and ask them to segment it using 'robot talk' to their partner.

Read it

■ Write words that contain the phoneme /ee/, grapheme 'ea', on the easel or board (for example: 'cheap', 'east' and 'beam') and ask the children to read out the phonemes by blending them together with their partner. Ensure that the children can identify the grapheme 'ea'.

■ Display the picture card of the grapheme 'ea' on the wall underneath the grapheme 'ee' to build up the phoneme chart for the long vowel phonemes. Ask the children to tell you the graphemes for the phoneme /ee/ and say the mnemonic phrase for 'ea'.

Write it

■ Say a word containing the phoneme /ee/, grapheme 'ea'. Ask the children to repeat it and then segment into phonemes using 'robot talk', for example: 'beach' – /b/ea/ch/. Ask the children to first count the phonemes in the word and then to hold up the correct number of fingers.

■ Now say the word again and ask them to write it on their whiteboards and underline the grapheme that represents the phoneme /ee/.

■ Ask the children to tell you the graphemes for the phoneme /ee/. Encourage them to refer to the Phoneme-grapheme chart on the wall to support spelling.

LESSON 43 'e'

1 REVIEW *(5 mins)*
Hear it
■ Review the long vowel phonemes taught so far by saying the vowel rap in a lively fun way with the children.

■ Help the children to practise hearing the sounds by reading a range of words, some of which contain the phoneme /ee/, graphemes 'ee' or 'ea' and some that do not, for example: 'bead', 'day', 'fork', 'cheap', 'tree'. Ask them to put their hands up every time they hear the phoneme /ee/.

Say it
■ Say several words containing the long vowel phonemes slowly in 'robot talk', for example: /b/ea/ch/, /d/ee/p/, /r/ea/ch/. Ask the children to blend the phonemes into words and tell their partners.

■ Now ask the children to speak in 'robot talk'. Say a word, for example, 'teach', and ask them to segment it using 'robot talk' first to their partner and then all together.

Read it
■ Write the following words on the board or easel and show the children: 'reach', 'bead', 'east'.

■ Ask the children to read the words out loud to their partner. Encourage them to blend the phonemes.

Write it
■ Say a word containing the phoneme /ee/ with the grapheme 'ea', for example: 'teach'. Ask the children to repeat it and then segment it into phonemes using 'robot talk'. Ask the children to count the phonemes in the word and to hold up the correct number of fingers. Then write the answer on their whiteboard.

2 NEW GRAPHEME 'e' *(10 mins)*
Hear it
■ Explain to the children that they are going to learn some more of the rap.

■ Introduce the new grapheme 'e' by saying several words that contain it for example 'we', 'me', 'she'.

Say it
■ Say the phoneme /ee/, grapheme 'e', emphasising

correct articulation, and then show the children the corresponding phoneme picture card and mnemonic phrase, 'He and me'. Ask the children to repeat it several times with you.

■ Say the letter name of the new grapheme: 'E' and introduce the action (point to someone).

■ Now say the full rap for this grapheme and ask the children to do the action: 'e' 'e' He and me E.

■ Using several words containing the phoneme /ee/, grapheme 'e', say these slowly in 'robot talk' for example: /h/e/, /m/e/ and /b/e/ and ask the children to blend the phonemes into words and tell their partners.

■ Now ask the children to speak in 'robot talk' to their partner. Say a word, for example, 'she', and ask them to segment it using 'robot talk'.

Read it
■ Write words that contain the phoneme /ee/, grapheme 'e', on the easel or board (for example: 'be', 'he' and 'she') and ask the children to read the phonemes by blending them together with their partner. Ensure that the children can identify the grapheme 'e'.

■ Display the picture card of the grapheme 'e' underneath the graphemes 'ee' and 'ea' to build up the Phoneme–grapheme chart for the long vowel phonemes. Ask the children to tell you the graphemes for the phoneme /ee/ and repeat the mnemonic phrase for 'e'.

Write it
■ Say a word containing the phoneme /ee/, grapheme 'e'. Ask the children to repeat it and then segment it into phonemes using 'robot talk', for example: 'he' – /h/e/. Ask the children to first count the phonemes in the word and then to hold up the correct number of fingers.

■ Now say the word again and ask them to write it on their whiteboards and underline the grapheme that represents the phoneme /ee/.

■ Ask the children to tell you the graphemes for the phoneme /ee/. Encourage them to refer to the Phoneme–grapheme chart on the wall to support spelling.

STAGE THREE: LESSON PLANS

LESSON 44 'y'

1 REVIEW (5 mins)
Hear it
■ Review the long vowel phonemes taught so far by saying the vowel rap in a lively fun way with the children.

■ Help the children to practise hearing the sounds by reading a range of words, some of which contain the phoneme /ee/, graphemes 'ee', 'ea' and 'e', and some that do not, for example: 'we', 'tray', 'me', 'rail', 'he', 'teach'. Ask them to put their hands up every time they hear the phoneme /ee/.

Say it
■ Say several words containing the long vowel phonemes slowly in 'robot talk', for example: /m/e/, /h/e/, /b/e/. Ask the children to blend the phonemes into words and tell their partners.

■ Now ask the children to speak in 'robot talk'. Say a word, for example, 'she', and ask them to segment it using 'robot talk' first to their partner and then all together.

Read it
■ Write the following words on the board or easel and show the children: 'he', 'be', 'we'.

■ Ask the children to read the words out loud to their partner. Encourage them to blend the phonemes.

Write it
■ Say a word containing the phoneme /ee/ with the grapheme 'e', for example: 'she'. Ask the children to repeat it and then segment it into phonemes using 'robot talk'. Ask the children to count the phonemes in the word and hold up the correct number of fingers, then to write the answer on their whiteboards.

2 NEW GRAPHEME 'y' (10 mins)
Hear it
■ Explain to the children that they are going to learn more of the rap.

■ Introduce the grapheme 'y' by saying several words that contain it for example, 'pony', 'stony', 'misty'.

Say it
■ Say the phoneme /ee/, grapheme 'y', emphasising correct articulation, and then show the children the corresponding phoneme picture card and mnemonic phrase, 'Bony pony'. Repeat it several times.

■ Say the letter name of the new grapheme: 'Y' and introduce the action (pretend to ride a pony).

■ Now say the full rap for this grapheme and ask the children to do the action: 'y' 'y' Bony pony Y.

■ Say several words containing the phoneme /ee/, grapheme 'y', slowly in 'robot talk' for example: /b/o/n/y/ and /p/o/n/y/ and ask the children to blend the phonemes into words and tell their partners.

■ Now ask the children to talk in 'robot talk' to their partner. Say a word, for example, 'mummy', and ask them to segment it using 'robot talk' to their partner.

Read it
■ Write words that contain the phoneme /ee/, grapheme 'y', on the easel or board (for example: 'misty', 'tasty' and 'frosty') and ask the children to read out the phonemes by blending them together with their partner. Ensure that the children can identify the grapheme 'y'.

■ Display the picture card of the grapheme 'y' on the wall underneath the graphemes 'e', 'ea' and 'ee' to build up the phoneme chart for the long vowel phonemes. Ask the children to tell you the graphemes for the phoneme and repeat the mnemonic phrase for 'y'.

Write it
■ Say a word containing the phoneme /ee/, grapheme 'y'. Ask the children to repeat it and then segment it into phonemes using 'robot talk' for example: 'frosty'. Ask the children to count the phonemes and to hold up the correct number of fingers.

■ Now say the word again and ask them to write it on their whiteboards and underline the grapheme that represents the phoneme /ee/.

■ Ask the children to tell you the graphemes for the phoneme /ee/. Encourage them to refer to the Phoneme–grapheme chart to support spelling.

LESSON 45
REVISE PHONEMES TAUGHT
■ Follow the format from Revision Lessons 39/40 on page 120 to revise all phonemes and corresponding graphemes taught in the week.

LESSON 46 'ie'

1 REVIEW (5 mins)

Hear it

■ Review the long vowel phonemes taught so far by saying the vowel rap in a lively fun way with the children.

■ Help the children to practise hearing the sounds by choosing one of the long vowel sounds taught so far. Say a range of words, some which contain the phoneme and some which do not. Ask the children to put up their hand when they hear the appropriate phoneme.

Say it

■ Say several words containing the long vowel phonemes taught so far slowly in 'robot talk', for example: /m/i/s/t/y/, /m/e/, /t/ea/ch/, /sh/ee/p/. Ask the children to blend the phonemes into words and tell their partners.

■ Now ask the children to speak in 'robot talk'. Say a word, for example, 'pony', and ask them to segment it using 'robot talk' first to their partner and then all together.

Read it

■ Write the following words on the board or easel and show the children: 'speed', 'real', 'we', 'misty'.

■ Ask the children to read the words out loud to their partner. Encourage them to blend the phonemes together.

Write it

■ Say a word containing the phoneme /ee/ with the grapheme 'y', for example, 'bony'. Ask the children to repeat it and then segment it into phonemes using 'robot talk'. Ask the children to first count the phonemes in the word and then to hold up the correct number of fingers. Ask them to write the answer on their individual whiteboards.

2 NEW PHONEME /ie/ GRAPHEME 'ie'
(10 mins)

Hear it

■ Explain to the children that they are going to learn more of the rap.

■ Introduce the new phoneme /ie/ represented by grapheme 'ie' by saying several words that contain it for example 'lie', 'pie', 'tie'.

Say it

■ Say the phoneme /ie/, grapheme 'ie', emphasising correct articulation, and then show the children the corresponding phoneme picture card and mnemonic phrase 'Tie the tie'. Ask the children to repeat it several times with you.

■ Say the letter names of the new grapheme: 'IE' and introduce the action (pretend to tie a tie).

■ Now say the full rap for this grapheme and ask the children to do the action: 'ie' 'ie' Tie the tie IE.

■ Using several words containing the phoneme /ie/, grapheme 'ie', say these slowly in 'robot talk' (for example: /t/ie/, /c/r/ie/d/ and /p/ie/) and ask the children to blend the phonemes into words and tell their partners.

■ Now ask the children to speak in 'robot talk' to their partner. Say a word, for example, 'lie', and ask them to segment it using 'robot talk' to their partner.

Read it

■ Write words that contain the phoneme /ie/, grapheme 'ie', on the easel or board (for example: 'pie', 'cried' and 'die') and ask the children to read out the phonemes by blending them together with their partner. Ensure that the children can identify the grapheme 'ie'.

■ Display the picture card of the grapheme 'ie' on the wall beginning a new column to build up the Phoneme-grapheme chart for the long vowel phonemes. Ask the children to tell you the grapheme for the phoneme /ie/ and repeat the mnemonic phrase for 'ie'.

Write it

■ Say a word containing the phoneme /ie/, grapheme 'ie'. Ask the children to repeat it and then segment it into phonemes using 'robot talk', for example: 'pie'. Ask the children to first count the phonemes in the word and then to hold up the correct number of fingers.

■ Now say the word again and ask them to write it on their whiteboards and underline the grapheme that represents the phoneme /ie/.

■ Ask the children to tell you the grapheme for the phoneme /ie/. Encourage them to refer to the Phoneme-grapheme chart on the wall to support spelling.

LESSON 47 'igh'

1 REVIEW *(5 mins)*

Hear it
■ Review the long vowel phonemes taught so far by saying the vowel rap in a lively fun way with the children.

■ Help the children to practise hearing the sounds by reading a range of words, some of which contain the long vowel phoneme /ie/, grapheme 'ie' and some that do not, for example: 'tie', 'tray', 'lie', 'rail', 'pie'. Ask them to put their hands up every time they hear the phoneme /ie/.

Say it
■ Say several words containing the long vowel phonemes slowly in 'robot talk', for example: /p/ie/, /t/ie/, /d/ie/. Ask the children to blend the phonemes into words and tell their partners.

■ Now ask the children to speak in 'robot talk'. Say a word, for example, 'cried', and ask them to segment it using 'robot talk' first to their partner and then all together.

Read it
■ Write the following words on the board or easel and show the children: 'cried', 'tied', 'pie', 'lie'.

■ Ask the children to read the words out loud to their partner. Encourage them to blend the phonemes together.

Write it
■ Say a word containing the phoneme /ie/ with the grapheme 'ie', for example: 'pie'. Ask the children to repeat it and then segment it into phonemes using 'robot talk'. Ask the children to first count the phonemes in the word and then to hold up the correct number of fingers. Ask them to write the answer on their individual whiteboards.

2 NEW GRAPHEME 'igh' *(10 mins)*

Hear it
■ Explain to the children that they are going to learn more of the rap.

■ Introduce the grapheme 'igh' by saying several words that contain it for example, 'sigh', 'light', 'tight', 'right'.

Say it
■ Say the phoneme /ie/, grapheme 'igh', emphasising correct articulation, and then show the children the corresponding phoneme picture card and mnemonic phrase 'Light helps sight'. Ask the children to repeat it several times with you.

■ Say the letter names of the new grapheme: 'IGH' and introduce the action (make a circle with thumb and forefinger and hold around eyes).

■ Now say the full rap for this grapheme and ask the children to do the action: 'igh' 'igh' Light helps sight IGH.

■ Using several words containing the phoneme /ie/, grapheme 'igh', say these slowly in 'robot talk' for example: /l/igh/t/, /t/igh/t/ and /s/igh/t/ and ask the children to blend the phonemes into words and tell their partners.

■ Now ask the children to talk in 'robot talk'. Say a word, for example, 'right', and ask them to segment it using 'robot talk' to their partner.

Read it
■ Write words that contain the phoneme /ie/, grapheme 'igh', on the easel or board for example: 'bright', 'fight' and 'light' and ask the children to read out the phonemes by blending them together with their partner. Ensure that the children can identify the grapheme 'igh' and talk about three letters making the sound – a trigraph.

■ Display the picture card of the grapheme 'igh' on the wall underneath the grapheme 'ie' to build up the Phoneme-grapheme chart for the long vowel phonemes. Ask the children to tell you the graphemes for the phoneme /ie/ and repeat the mnemonic phrase for 'igh'.

Write it
■ Say a word containing the phoneme /ie/, grapheme 'igh'. Ask the children to repeat it and then segment into phonemes using 'robot talk', for example: 'sight' – /s/igh/t/. Ask the children to first count the phonemes in the word and then to hold up the correct number of fingers.

■ Now say the word again and ask them to write it on their whiteboards and underline the grapheme that represents the phoneme /ie/.

■ Ask the children to tell you the graphemes for the phoneme /ie/. Encourage them to refer to the Phoneme-grapheme chart on the wall to support spelling.

LESSON 48 'y'

1 REVIEW *(5 mins)*

Hear it

■ Review the long vowel phonemes taught so far by saying the vowel rap in a lively fun way with the children.

■ Help the children to practise hearing the sounds by reading a range of words, some of which contain the phoneme /ie/, graphemes 'ie' or 'igh', and some that do not, for example: 'tie', 'tray', 'might', 'rail', 'night'. Ask them to put their hands up every time they hear the phoneme /ie/.

Say it

■ Say several words containing the long vowel phonemes slowly in 'robot talk', for example: /m/igh/t/, /f/l/igh/t/ and /b/r/igh/t/. Ask the children to blend the phonemes into words and tell their partners.

■ Now ask the children to speak in 'robot talk'. Say a word, for example, 'right', and ask them to segment it using 'robot talk' first to their partner and then all together.

Read it

■ Write the following words on the board or easel and show the children: 'might', 'sight', 'right', 'tight'.

■ Ask the children to read the words out loud to their partner. Encourage them to blend the phonemes together.

Write it

■ Say a word containing the phoneme /ie/ with the grapheme 'igh', for example, 'fight'. Ask the children to repeat it and then segment it into phonemes using 'robot talk'. Ask the children to first count the phonemes in the word and then to hold up the correct number of fingers. Ask them to write the answer on their individual whiteboards.

2 NEW GRAPHEME 'y' *(10 mins)*

Hear it

■ Explain to the children that they are going to learn more of the rap.

■ Introduce the new grapheme by saying several words that contain it ('my', 'shy', 'fly', 'cry').

Say it

■ Say the phoneme /ie/, grapheme 'y', emphasising correct articulation, and then show the children the corresponding phoneme picture card and mnemonic phrase, 'My what a fly'. Ask the children to repeat it several times with you.

■ Say the letter name of the new grapheme: 'Y' and explain that this letter can make the long /e/ as in 'pony' and the long /i/ as in 'fly'. Introduce the action (pretend to buzz like a fly).

■ Now say the full rap for this grapheme and ask the children to do the action: 'y' 'y' My what a fly Y.

■ Using several words containing the phoneme /ie/, grapheme 'y', say these slowly in 'robot talk' for example: /m/y/, /f/l/y/ and /c/r/y/ and ask the children to blend the phonemes into words and tell their partners.

■ Now ask the children to speak in 'robot talk'. Say a word, for example, 'cry', and ask them to segment it using 'robot talk' to their partner.

Read it

■ Write words that contain the phoneme /ie/, grapheme 'y', on the easel or board (for example: 'shy', 'fly' and 'dry') and ask the children to read out the phonemes by blending them together with their partner. Ensure that the children can identify the grapheme 'y'.

■ Display the picture card of the grapheme 'y' on the wall under the graphemes 'igh', and 'ie' to build up the Phoneme–grapheme chart for the long vowel phonemes. Ask the children to tell you the graphemes for the phoneme /ie/ and repeat the mnemonic phrase for 'y'.

Write it

■ Say a word containing the phoneme /ie/, grapheme 'y'. Ask the children to repeat it and then segment it into phonemes using 'robot talk', for example: 'fly' – /f/l/y/. Ask the children to first count the phonemes in the word and then to hold up the correct number of fingers.

■ Now say the word again and ask them to write it on their whiteboards and underline the grapheme that represents the phoneme /ie/.

■ Ask the children to tell you the graphemes for the phoneme /ie/. Encourage them to refer to the Phoneme–grapheme chart on the wall to support spelling.

STAGE THREE: LESSON PLANS

LESSON 49 'i'

1 REVIEW (5 mins)

Hear it

■ Review the long vowel phonemes taught so far by saying the vowel rap in a lively fun way with the children.

■ Help the children to practise hearing the sounds by reading a range of words some of which contain the phoneme /ie/, graphemes 'igh', 'ie' or 'y' and some that do not, for example: 'fly', 'tree', 'bright'; 'cry', 'pie', 'stone', 'try', 'play'. Ask them to put their hands up every time they hear the phoneme /ie/.

Say it

■ Say several words containing the long vowel phonemes slowly in 'robot talk', for example: /d/r/y/, /t/r/y/ and /f/l/y/. Ask the children to blend the phonemes into words and tell their partners.

■ Now ask the children to speak in 'robot talk'. Say a word, for example, 'cry', and ask them to segment it using 'robot talk' first to their partner and then all together.

Read it

■ Write the following words on the board or easel and show the children: 'dry', 'shy', 'my'.

■ Ask the children to read the words out loud to their partner. Encourage them to blend the phonemes.

Write it

■ Say a word containing the phoneme /ie/ with the grapheme 'y', for example: 'fry'. Ask the children to repeat it and then segment it into phonemes using 'robot talk'. Ask the children to count the phonemes in the word and to hold up the correct number of fingers. Then write the answer on their whiteboard.

2 NEW GRAPHEME 'i' (10 mins)

Hear it

■ Explain to the children that they are going to learn more of the rap.

■ Introduce the new grapheme by saying several words that contain it for example, 'tiger', 'idea', 'hi'.

Say it

■ Say the phoneme /ie/, grapheme 'i' emphasising correct articulation, and then show the children the corresponding phoneme picture card and mnemonic phrase 'Kind tiger'. Repeat this several times.

■ Say the letter name of the new grapheme: 'i' and introduce the action (pretend to wave to a tiger).

■ Now say the full rap for this grapheme and ask the children to do the action: 'i' 'i' Kind tiger I.

■ Using several words containing the phoneme /ie/, grapheme 'i', say these slowly in 'robot talk' for example: /t/i/g/er/, /c/i/d/er/ and /h/i/ and ask the children to blend the phonemes into words and tell their partners.

■ Now ask the children to speak in 'robot talk'. Say a word, for example, 'idea', and ask them to segment it using 'robot talk' to their partner.

Read it

■ Write words that contain the phoneme /ie/, grapheme 'i', on the easel or board (for example: 'hi', 'tiger' and 'cider') and ask the children to read out the phonemes by blending them together with their partner. Ensure that the children can identify the grapheme 'i'.

■ Display the picture card of the grapheme 'i' on the wall underneath the grapheme 'y' 'igh' and 'ie' to build up the Phoneme–grapheme chart for the long vowel phonemes. Ask the children to tell you the graphemes for the phoneme /ie/ and repeat the mnemonic phrase for 'i'.

Write it

■ Say a word containing the phoneme /ie/, grapheme 'i'. Ask the children to repeat it and then segment it into phonemes using 'robot talk', for example: 'kind' – /k/i/n/d/. Ask the children to first count the phonemes in the word and then to hold up the correct number of fingers.

■ Now say the word again and ask them to write it on their whiteboards and underline the grapheme that represents the phoneme /ie/.

■ Ask the children to tell you the graphemes for the phoneme /ie/. Encourage them to refer to the Phoneme–grapheme chart to support spelling.

> ## LESSON 50
> ### REVISE PHONEMES TAUGHT
> ■ Follow the format from Revision Lessons 39/40 on page 120 to revise all phonemes and corresponding graphemes taught in the week.

LESSON 51 'oa'

1 REVIEW *(5 mins)*

Hear it

■ Review the long vowel phonemes taught so far by saying the vowel rap in a lively fun way with the children.

■ Help the children to practise hearing the sounds by choosing one of the long vowel sounds taught so far. Say a range of words, some which contain the phoneme and some which do not. Ask the children to put up their hand when they hear the appropriate phoneme.

Say it

■ Say several words containing the long vowel phonemes taught so far slowly in 'robot talk', for example: /p/ie/, /f/l/y/ and /s/igh/t/. Ask the children to blend the phonemes into words and tell their partners.

■ Now ask the children to speak in 'robot talk'. Say a word, for example: 'try', and ask them to segment it using 'robot talk' first to their partner and then all together.

Read it

■ Write the following words on the board or easel and show the children: 'find', 'my', 'light', 'tie'.

■ Ask the children to read the words out loud to their partner. Encourage them to blend the phonemes together.

Write it

■ Say a word containing the phoneme /ie/ with the grapheme 'i', for example, 'tiger'. Ask the children to repeat it and then segment into phonemes using 'robot talk'. Ask the children to count the phonemes in the word and to hold up the correct number of fingers. Then write the answer on their whiteboard.

2 NEW PHONEME /oe/ GRAPHEME 'oa'
(10 mins)

Hear it

■ Explain to the children that they are going to learn more of the rap.

■ Introduce the new grapheme by saying several words that contain it for example, 'boat', 'coat', 'float'.

Say it

■ Say the phoneme /oe/, grapheme 'oa', emphasising correct articulation, and then show the children the corresponding phoneme picture card and mnemonic phrase 'Float the boat'. Ask the children to repeat it several times with you.

■ Say the letter names of the new grapheme: 'OA' and introduce the action (stretch out arms and pretend to float).

■ Now say the full rap for this grapheme and ask the children to do the action: 'oa' 'oa' Float the boat OA.

■ Using several words containing the phoneme /oe/, grapheme 'oa', say these slowly in 'robot talk' for example: /f/l/oa/t/, /b/oa/t/ and /c/oa/t/ and ask the children to blend the phonemes into words and tell their partners.

■ Now ask the children to speak in 'robot talk'. Say a word, for example, 'coat', and ask them to segment it using 'robot' talk' to their partner.

Read it

■ Write words that contain the phoneme /oe/, grapheme 'oa', on the easel or board for example: 'foal', 'goat' and 'groan' and ask the children to read out the phonemes by blending them together with their partner. Ensure that the children can identify the grapheme 'oa'.

■ Display the picture card of the grapheme 'oa' on the wall beginning a new column to build up the Phoneme-grapheme chart for the long vowel phonemes. Ask the children to tell you the grapheme for the phoneme /oe/ and repeat the mnemonic phrase for 'oa'.

Write it

■ Say a word containing the phoneme /oe/, grapheme 'oa'. Ask the children to repeat it and then segment it into phonemes using 'robot talk', for example: 'float'. Ask the children to first count the phonemes in the word and then to hold up the correct number of fingers.

■ Now say the word again and ask them to write it on their whiteboards and underline the grapheme that represents the phoneme /oe/.

■ Ask the children to tell you the grapheme for the phoneme /oe/. Encourage them to refer to the Phoneme-grapheme chart on the wall to support spelling.

LESSON 52 'ow'

1 REVIEW *(5 mins)*
Hear it
■ Review the long vowel phonemes taught so far by saying the vowel rap in a lively fun way with the children.

■ Help the children to practise hearing the sounds by saying a range of words some of which contain phoneme /oe/, grapheme 'oa' and some that do not, for example: 'boat', 'kind', 'goat', 'fly', 'tree', 'float', 'tie', 'tray', 'coat'. Ask them to put their hands up every time they hear the phoneme /oe/.

Say it
■ Say several words containing the long vowel phonemes slowly in 'robot talk', for example: /r/oa/d/, /g/oa/t/ and /th/r/oa/t/. Ask the children to blend the phonemes into words and tell their partners.

■ Now ask the children to speak in 'robot talk'. Say a word, for example, 'loaf', and ask them to segment it using 'robot talk' first to their partner and then all together.

Read it
■ Write the following words on the board or easel and show the children: 'soap', 'groan', 'goal'.

■ Ask the children to read the words out loud to their partner. Encourage them to blend the phonemes together.

Write it
■ Say a word containing the phoneme /oe/ with the grapheme 'oa', for example: 'road'. Ask the children to repeat it and then segment it into phonemes using 'robot talk'. Ask the children to first count the phonemes in the word and then to hold up the correct number of fingers. Ask them to write the answer on their individual whiteboards.

2 NEW GRAPHEME 'ow' *(10 mins)*
Hear it
■ Explain to the children that they are going to learn more of the rap.

■ Introduce the new grapheme 'ow' by saying several words that contain it for example snow, flow, row, glow.

Say it
■ Say the phoneme /oe/, grapheme 'ow', emphasising correct articulation, and then show the children the corresponding phoneme picture card and mnemonic phrase 'Row it slow'. Ask the children to repeat it several times with you.

■ Say the letter names of the new grapheme: 'OW' and introduce the action (move arms in a rowing motion).

■ Now say the full rap for this grapheme and ask the children to do the action: 'ow' 'ow' Row it slow OW.

■ Using several words containing the phoneme /oe/, grapheme 'ow', say these slowly in 'robot talk' for example: /l/ow/, /s/l/ow/ and /c/r/ow/ and ask the children to blend the phonemes into words and tell their partners.

■ Now ask the children to speak in 'robot talk'. Say a word, for example, 'glow', and ask them to segment it using 'robot talk' to their partner.

Read it
■ Write words that contain the phoneme /oe/, grapheme 'ow', on the easel or board for example: 'crow', 'flow' and 'snow' and ask the children to read out the phonemes by blending them together with their partner. Ensure that the children can identify the grapheme 'ow'.

■ Display the picture card of the grapheme 'ow' on the wall underneath the grapheme 'oa' to build up the Phoneme–grapheme chart for the long vowel phonemes. Ask the children to tell you the graphemes for the phoneme /oe/ and repeat the mnemonic phrase for 'ow'.

Write it
■ Say a word containing the phoneme /oe/, grapheme 'ow'. Ask the children to repeat it and then segment into phonemes using 'robot talk', for example: 'grow' – /g/r/ow/. Ask the children to first count the phonemes in the word and then to hold up the correct number of fingers.

■ Now say the word again and ask them to write it on their whiteboards and underline the grapheme that represents the phoneme /oe/.

■ Ask the children to tell you the graphemes for the phoneme /oe/. Encourage them to refer to the Phoneme–grapheme chart on the wall to support spelling.

STAGE THREE: LESSON PLANS ●▪

LESSON 53 'o'

1 REVIEW (5 mins)

Hear it

■ Review the long vowel phonemes taught so far by saying the vowel rap in a lively fun way with the children.

■ Help the children to practise hearing the sounds by reading a range of words, some of which contain the phoneme /oe/, graphemes 'oa' and 'ow' and some that do not, for example: 'tie', 'glow', 'beach', 'boat', 'snow', 'tree'. Ask them to put their hands up every time they hear the phoneme /oe/.

Say it

■ Say several words containing the long vowel phonemes slowly in 'robot talk', for example: /r/ow/, /b/l/ow/, /f/l/ow/. Ask the children to blend the phonemes into words and tell their partners.

■ Now ask the children to speak in 'robot talk'. Say a word, for example, 'snow', and ask them to segment it using 'robot talk' first to their partner and then all together.

Read it

■ Write the following words on the board or easel and show the children: 'snow', 'bowl', 'row'.

■ Ask the children to read the words out loud to their partner. Encourage them to blend the phonemes.

Write it

■ Say a word containing the phoneme /oe/ with the grapheme 'ow', for example, 'grow'. Ask the children to segment the word into phonemes using 'robot talk'. Ask the children to count the phonemes in the word and to hold up the correct number of fingers. Then write the answer on their individual whiteboards.

2 NEW GRAPHEME 'o' (10 mins)

Hear it

■ Explain to the children that they are going to learn more of the rap.

■ Introduce the new grapheme by saying several words that contain it for example 'cold', 'sold', 'only'.

Say it

■ Say the phoneme /oe/, grapheme 'o' emphasising correct articulation, and then show the children the corresponding phoneme picture card and mnemonic phrase 'Cold nose!' Repeat this several times.

■ Say the letter name of the new grapheme: 'O' and introduce the action (place your finger on your nose).

■ Now say the full rap for this grapheme and ask the children to do the action: 'o' 'o' Cold nose! O.

■ Using several words containing the phoneme /oe/, grapheme 'o', say these slowly in 'robot talk' for example: /c/o/l/d/, /n/o/s/e/ and /s/o/l/d/ and ask the children to blend the phonemes into words and tell their partners.

■ Now ask the children to speak in 'robot talk'. Say a word, for example, 'sold', and ask them to segment it using 'robot talk' to their partner.

Read it

■ Write words that contain the phoneme /oe/, grapheme 'o', on the easel or board and ask the children to read out the phonemes by blending them together with their partner. Ensure that the children can identify the grapheme 'o'.

■ Display the picture card of the grapheme 'o' on the wall underneath the graphemes 'ow' and 'oa' to build up the Phoneme-grapheme chart for the long vowel phonemes. Ask the children to tell you the graphemes for the phoneme /oe/ and repeat the mnemonic phrase for 'o'.

Write it

■ Say a word containing the phoneme /oe/, grapheme 'o'. Ask the children to repeat it and then segment it into phonemes using 'robot talk', for example: 'only'. Ask the children to count the phonemes in the word and to hold up the correct number of fingers.

■ Now say the word again and ask them to write it on their whiteboards and underline the grapheme that represents the phoneme /oe/.

■ Ask the children to tell you the graphemes for the phoneme /oe/. Encourage them to refer to the Phoneme-grapheme chart to support spelling.

LESSON 54/55
REVISE PHONEMES TAUGHT

■ Follow the format from Revision Lessons 39/40 on page 120 to revise all phonemes and corresponding graphemes taught in the week.

■ Ensure that you carry out Assessment 1 on page 187 before continuing with Stage 3.

STAGE THREE: LESSON PLANS

LESSON 56 'oo'

1 REVIEW *(5 mins)*

Hear it

■ Review the long vowel phonemes taught so far by saying the vowel rap in a lively fun way with the children.

■ Help the children to practise hearing the sounds by choosing one of the long vowel sounds taught so far. Say a range of words, some which contain the phoneme and some which do not. Ask the children to put up their hand when they hear the appropriate phoneme.

Say it

■ Say several words containing the long vowel phonemes taught so far slowly in 'robot talk', for example: /b/oa/t/, /s/n/ow/ and /o/n/l/y/. Ask the children to blend the phonemes into words and tell their partners.

■ Now ask the children to speak in 'robot talk'. Say a word, for example, 'foal', and ask them to segment it using 'robot talk' first to their partner and then all together.

Read it

■ Write the following words on the board or easel and show the children: 'moan', 'flow', 'sold'.

■ Ask the children to read the words out loud to their partner. Encourage them to blend the phonemes together.

Write it

■ Say a word containing the phoneme /oe/ with the grapheme 'o', for example: 'ago'. Ask the children to repeat it and then segment it into phonemes using 'robot talk'. Ask the children to first count the phonemes in the word and then to hold up the correct number of fingers. Ask them to write the answer on their individual whiteboards.

2 NEW PHONEME /u/ GRAPHEME 'oo'
(10 mins)

Hear it

■ Explain to the children that they are going to learn more of the rap.

■ Introduce the new grapheme by saying several words that contain it for example 'book', 'rook', 'shook', 'cook'.

Say it

■ Say the phoneme /u/, grapheme 'oo' emphasising correct articulation, and then show the children the corresponding phoneme picture card and mnemonic phrase 'Took the book'. Ask the children to repeat it several times with you.

■ Say the letter names of the new grapheme: 'OO' and introduce the action (pretend to take a book).

■ Now say the full rap for this grapheme and ask the children to do the action: 'oo' 'oo' Took the book OO.

■ Using several words containing the phoneme /u/, grapheme 'oo', say these slowly in 'robot talk' (for example: /b/oo/k/, /t/oo/k/ and /l/oo/k/) and ask the children to blend the phonemes into words and tell their partners.

■ Now ask the children to speak in 'robot talk'. Say a word, for example, 'hook', and ask them to segment it using 'robot talk' to their partner.

Read it

■ Write words that contain the phoneme /u/, grapheme 'oo', on the easel or board (for example: 'cook', 'hood' and 'book') and ask the children to read out the phonemes by blending them together with their partner. Ensure that the children can identify the grapheme 'oo'.

■ Display the picture card of the grapheme 'oo' on the wall beginning a new column to build up the Phoneme–grapheme chart for the long vowel phonemes. Ask the children to tell you the grapheme for the phoneme /u/ and repeat the mnemonic phrase for 'oo'.

Write it

■ Say a word containing the phoneme /u/, grapheme 'oo'. Ask the children to repeat it and then segment it into phonemes using 'robot talk', for example 'took'. Ask the children to first count the phonemes in the word and then to hold up the correct number of fingers.

■ Now say the word again and ask them to write it on their whiteboards and underline the grapheme that represents the phoneme /u/.

■ Ask the children to tell you the grapheme for the phoneme /u/. Encourage them to refer to the Phoneme–grapheme chart on the wall to support spelling.

LESSON 57 'ou'

1 REVIEW *(5 mins)*

Hear it

■ Review the long vowel phonemes taught so far by saying the vowel rap in a lively fun way with the children.

■ Help the children to practise hearing the sounds by reading a range of words, some of which contain the phoneme /u/, grapheme 'oo' and some that do not, for example: 'book', 'took', 'my', 'rook', 'shook', 'light'. Ask them to put their hands up every time they hear the phoneme /u/.

Say it

■ Say several words containing the long vowel phonemes slowly in 'robot talk', for example: /b/oo/k/, /sh/oo/k/ and /h/oo/k/. Ask the children to blend the phonemes into words and tell their partners.

■ Now ask the children to talk in 'robot talk'. Say a word, for example, 'look', and ask them to segment it using 'robot talk' first to their partner and then all together.

Read it

■ Write the following words on the board or easel and show the children: 'look', 'rook', 'book', 'shook', 'hook'.

■ Ask the children to read the words out loud to their partner. Encourage them to blend the phonemes together.

Write it

■ Say a word containing the phoneme /u/ with the grapheme 'oo', for example: 'hood'. Ask the children to repeat it and then segment it into phonemes using 'robot talk'. Ask the children to first count the phonemes in the word and then to hold up the correct number of fingers. Ask them to write the answer on their individual whiteboards.

2 NEW GRAPHEME 'ou' *(10 mins)*

Hear it

■ Explain to the children that they are going to learn more of the rap.

■ Introduce the new grapheme 'ou' by saying several words that contain it for example 'could', 'should', 'would'.

Say it

■ Say the phoneme /u/, grapheme 'ou', emphasising correct articulation, and then show the children the corresponding phoneme picture card and mnemonic phrase, 'Could you? Would you?' Ask the children to repeat it several times with you.

■ Say the letter names of the new grapheme: 'OU' and introduce the action (hold hands together as if pleading).

■ Now say the full rap for this grapheme and ask the children to do the action: 'ou' 'ou' Could you? Would you? OU.

■ Using several words containing the phoneme /u/, grapheme 'ou', say these slowly in 'robot talk' for example: /c/ou/l/d/, /w/ou/l/d/ and /sh/ou/l/d/ and ask the children to blend the phonemes into words and tell their partners.

■ Now ask the children to speak in 'robot talk'. Say a word, for example, 'should', and ask them to segment it using 'robot talk' to their partner.

Read it

■ Write words that contain the phoneme /u/, grapheme 'ou', on the easel or board (for example: 'could', 'would' and 'should') and ask the children to read out the phonemes by blending them together with their partner. Ensure that the children can identify the grapheme 'ou'.

■ Display the picture card of the grapheme 'ou' on the wall underneath the grapheme 'oo', to build up the Phoneme-grapheme chart for the vowel phonemes. Ask the children to tell you the graphemes for the phoneme /u/ and say the mnemonic phrase for 'ou'.

Write it

■ Say a word containing the phoneme /u/, grapheme 'ou'. Ask the children to repeat it and then segment it into phonemes using 'robot talk', for example: 'would'. Ask the children to first count the phonemes in the word and then to hold up the correct number of fingers.

■ Now say the word again and ask them to write it on their whiteboards and underline the grapheme that represents the phoneme /u/.

■ Ask the children to tell you the graphemes for the phoneme /u/. Encourage them to refer to the Phoneme-grapheme chart to support spelling.

STAGE THREE: LESSON PLANS

LESSON 58 'u'

① REVIEW (5 mins)

Hear it

■ Review the long vowel phonemes taught so far by saying the vowel rap in a lively fun way with the children.

■ Help the children to practise hearing the sounds by reading a range of words, some of which contain the phoneme /u/. graphemes 'oo' or 'ou', and some that do not, for example: 'could', 'beach', 'acorn', 'should', 'pony', 'book'. Ask them to put their hands up every time they hear the phoneme /u/.

Say it

■ Say several words containing the phonemes slowly using 'robot talk' for example: /sh/ou/l/d/, /c/ou/ld/ and /w/ou/ld/. Ask the children to blend the phonemes into words and tell their partners.

■ Now ask the children to speak in 'robot talk'. Say a word, for example, 'should' and ask them to segment it using 'robot talk' first to their partner and then all together.

Read it

■ Write the following words on the board or easel and show the children: 'could', 'should', 'would'.

■ Ask the children to read the words out loud to their partner. Encourage them to blend the phonemes.

Write it

■ Say a word containing the phoneme /u/ with the grapheme 'ou', for example, 'should'. Ask the children to repeat it and then segment it into phonemes using 'robot talk'. Ask the children to count the phonemes and to hold up the correct number of fingers. Then write the answer on their whiteboards.

② NEW GRAPHEME 'u' (10 mins)

Hear it

■ Explain to the children that they are going to learn more of the rap.

■ Introduce the new grapheme by saying a word that contains it, for example: 'put'.

Say it

■ Say the phoneme /u/, grapheme 'u', emphasising correct articulation, and then show the children the corresponding phoneme picture card and mnemonic phrase 'Put it, put it'. Ask the children to repeat it several times with you.

■ Say the letter name of the new grapheme: 'U' and introduce the action (point to a table).

■ Now say the full rap for this grapheme and ask the children to do the action: 'u' 'u' Put it, put it U.

■ Using words containing the phoneme /u/, grapheme 'u', say these slowly in 'robot talk', for example /p/u/t/, and ask the children to blend the phonemes into words and tell their partners.

■ Now ask the children to speak in 'robot talk'. Say the word 'put' and ask them to segment it using 'robot talk' to their partner.

Read it

■ Write the word 'put' on the easel or board and ask the children to read out the phonemes by blending them together with their partner. Ensure that the children can identify the grapheme 'u'.

■ Display the picture card of the grapheme 'u' on the wall underneath the graphemes 'ou' and 'oo', to build up the Phoneme-grapheme chart for the long vowel phonemes. Ask the children to tell you the graphemes for the phoneme /u/ and repeat the mnemonic phrase for 'u'.

Write it

■ Say a word containing the phoneme /u/, grapheme 'u'. Ask the children to repeat it and then segment into phonemes using 'robot talk', for example: 'put' – /p/u/t/. Ask the children to first count the phonemes in the word and then to hold up the correct number of fingers.

■ Now say the word again and ask them to write it on their whiteboards and underline the grapheme that represents the phoneme /u/.

■ Ask the children to tell you the graphemes for the phoneme /u/. Encourage them to refer to the Phoneme-grapheme chart on the wall to support spelling.

LESSON 59/60
REVISE PHONEMES TAUGHT

■ Follow the format from Revision Lessons 39/40 on page 120 to revise all phonemes and corresponding graphemes taught in the week.

LESSON 61 'oo'

1 REVIEW (5 mins)
Hear it
■ Review the long vowel phonemes taught so far by saying the vowel rap in a lively fun way with the children.

■ Help the children to practise hearing the sounds by choosing one of the long vowel sounds taught so far. Say a range of words, some which contain the phoneme and some which do not. Ask the children to put up their hand when they hear the appropriate phoneme.

Say it
■ Say several words containing the long vowel phonemes taught so far slowly in 'robot talk', for example: /sh/ou/ld/, /b/oo/k/, /p/u/t/. Ask the children to blend the phonemes into words and tell their partners.

■ Now ask the children to speak in 'robot talk'. Say a word for example, 'cook', and ask them to segment it using 'robot talk' first to their partner and then all together.

Read it
■ Write the following words on the board or easel and show the children: 'put', 'hood', 'would'.

■ Ask the children to read the words out loud to their partner. Encourage them to blend the phonemes.

Write it
■ Say a word containing the phoneme /u/ with the grapheme 'u', for example: 'put'. Ask the children to repeat it and then segment it into phonemes using 'robot talk'. Ask the children to count the phonemes in the word and to hold up the correct number of fingers. Then write the answer on their whiteboard.

2 NEW PHONEME /ue/ GRAPHEME
'oo' (10 mins)
Hear it
■ Explain to the children that they are going to learn more of the rap.

■ Introduce the new phoneme /ue/, grapheme 'oo' by saying several words that contain it for example, 'moon', 'soon', 'roof', 'school'.

Say it
■ Say the phoneme /ue/, grapheme 'oo', emphasising correct articulation, and then show the children the corresponding phoneme picture card and mnemonic phrase 'Room on the moon'. Ask the children to repeat it several times with you.

■ Say the letter names of the new grapheme: 'OO' and introduce the actions (point up to the moon).

■ Now say the full rap for this grapheme and ask the children to do the action: 'oo' 'oo' Room on the moon OO.

■ Link this sound with the previous phoneme /u/ as in 'book', by saying 'oo'–'oo', cuckoo. This helps children to differentiate the two sounds.

■ Using several words containing the phoneme /ue/, grapheme 'oo', say these slowly in 'robot talk' (for example: /s/oo/n/, /r/oo/m/, /m/oo/n/) and ask the children to blend the phonemes into words and tell their partners.

■ Now ask the children to speak in 'robot talk'. Say a word, for example, 'soon', and ask them to segment it using 'robot talk' to their partner.

Read it
■ Write words that contain the phoneme /ue/, grapheme 'oo', on the easel or board, (for example: 'food', 'soon', 'hoop') and ask the children to read out the phonemes by blending them together with their partner. Ensure that the children can identify the grapheme 'oo'.

■ Display the picture card of the grapheme 'oo'. Begin a new column to build up the Phoneme-grapheme chart for the long vowel phonemes. Ask the children to tell you the grapheme for the phoneme /ue/ and repeat the mnemonic phrase for 'oo'.

Write it
■ Say a word containing the phoneme /ue/, grapheme 'oo'. Ask the children to repeat it and then segment it into phonemes using 'robot talk', for example: 'moon'. Ask the children to first count the phonemes in the word and then to hold up the correct number of fingers.

■ Now say the word again and ask them to write it on their whiteboards and underline the grapheme that represents the phoneme /ue/.

■ Ask the children to tell you the grapheme for the phoneme /ue/. Encourage them to refer to the Phoneme-grapheme chart on the wall to support spelling.

STAGE THREE: LESSON PLANS

LESSON 62 'ue'

1 REVIEW (5 mins)

Hear it

■ Review the long vowel phonemes taught so far by saying the vowel rap in a lively fun way with the children.

■ Help the children to practise hearing the sounds by reading a range of words, some of which contain the phoneme /ue/, grapheme 'oo' and some that do not, for example: 'moon', 'tie', 'soon', 'beach', 'kind', 'roof', 'tree'. Ask them to put their hands up every time they hear the phoneme /ue/.

Say it

■ Say several words containing the phonemes slowly in 'robot talk', for example: /s/oo/n/, /r/oo/f/, /s/ch/oo/l/. Ask the children to blend the phonemes into words and tell their partners.

■ Now ask the children to speak in 'robot talk'. Say a word, for example, 'tool', and ask them to segment it using 'robot talk' first to their partner and then all together.

Read it

■ Write the following words on the whiteboard or easel and show the children: 'pool', 'cool', 'spoon', 'shoot'.

■ Ask the children to read the words out loud to their partner. Encourage them to blend the phonemes together.

Write it

■ Say a word containing the phoneme /ue/ with the grapheme 'oo', for example, 'mood'. Ask the children to repeat it and then segment it into phonemes using 'robot talk'. Ask the children to first count the phonemes in the word and then to hold up the correct number of fingers. Ask them to write the answer on their individual whiteboards.

2 NEW GRAPHEME 'ue' (10 mins)

Hear it

■ Explain to the children that they are going to learn more of the rap

■ Introduce the new grapheme 'ue' by saying several words that contain it for example 'clue', 'true', 'glue'.

Say it

■ Say the phoneme /ue/, also represented by the grapheme 'ue', emphasising correct articulation and then show the children the corresponding phoneme picture card and mnemonic phrase, 'Sue's clue'. Ask the children to repeat it several times with you.

■ Say the letter names of the new grapheme: 'UE' and introduce the action (place finger to mouth and frown as if thinking).

■ Now say the full rap for this grapheme and ask the children to do the action: 'ue' 'ue' Sue's clue UE.

■ Using several words containing the phoneme /ue/, grapheme 'ue', say these slowly in 'robot talk' for example: /c/ue/, /t/r/ue/, /f/ue/l/ and ask the children to blend the phonemes into words and tell their partners.

■ Now ask the children to speak in 'robot talk'. Say a word, for example, 'cue', and ask them to segment it using 'robot talk' to their partner.

Read it

■ Write words that contain the phoneme /ue/, grapheme 'ue', on the easel or board (for example: 'glue', 'clue', 'fuel') and ask the children to read out the phonemes by blending them together with their partner. Ensure that the children can identify the grapheme 'ue'.

■ Display the picture card of the grapheme 'ue' on the wall underneath the grapheme 'oo' to build up the Phoneme-grapheme chart for the long vowel phonemes. Ask the children to tell you the graphemes for the phoneme /ue/ and repeat the mnemonic phrase for 'ue'.

Write it

■ Say a word containing the phoneme /ue/, grapheme 'ue'. Ask the children to repeat it and then segment it into phonemes using 'robot talk', for example: 'glue' – /g/l/ue/. Ask the children to first count the phonemes in the word and then to hold up the correct number of fingers.

■ Now say the word again and ask them to write it on their whiteboards and underline the grapheme that represents the phoneme /ue/.

■ Ask the children to tell you the graphemes for the phoneme /ue/. Encourage them to refer to the Phoneme-grapheme chart on the wall to support spelling.

LESSON 63 'ew'

1 REVIEW (5 mins)
Hear it
■ Review the long vowel phonemes taught so far by saying the vowel rap in a lively fun way with the children.
■ Help the children to practise hearing the sounds by reading a range of words, some of which contain the long vowel phoneme /ue/, graphemes 'oo' or 'ue', and some that do not. Ask them to put their hands up every time they hear the phoneme /ue/.

Say it
■ Say several words containing the long vowel phonemes slowly in 'robot talk', for example: /c/l/ue/, /t/r/ue/, /b/l/ue/. Ask the children to blend the phonemes into words and tell their partners.
■ Now ask the children to speak in 'robot talk'. Say a word, for example, 'fuel', and ask them to segment it using 'robot talk' first to their partner and then all together.

Read it
■ Write the following words on the board or easel and show the children: 'true', 'clue', 'Sue', 'glue'.
■ Ask the children to read the words out loud to their partner. Encourage them to blend the phonemes.

Write it
■ Say a word containing the phoneme /ue/ with the grapheme 'ue', for example: 'clue'. Ask the children to repeat it and then segment it into phonemes using 'robot talk'. Ask the children to count the phonemes in the word and to hold up the correct number of fingers. Then write the answer on their whiteboard.

2 NEW GRAPHEME 'ew' (10 mins)
Hear it
■ Explain to the children that they are going to learn more of the rap.
■ Introduce the new grapheme 'ew' by saying several words that contain it for example, 'grew', 'drew', 'few'.

Say it
■ Say the phoneme /ue/, grapheme 'ew', emphasising correct articulation, and then show the children the corresponding phoneme picture card and mnemonic phrase, 'He grew and grew'. Ask the children to repeat it several times with you.
■ Say the letter names of the new grapheme: 'EW' and introduce the action (pretend to grow taller and taller).
■ Now say the full rap for this grapheme and ask the children to do the action: 'ew' 'ew' He grew and grew EW.
■ Using several words containing the phoneme /ue/, grapheme 'ew', say these slowly in 'robot talk' for example: /s/t/ew/, /g/r/ew/, /f/l/ew/ and ask the children to blend the phonemes into words and tell their partners.
■ Now ask the children to speak in 'robot talk'. Say a word, for example, 'stew', and ask them to segment it using 'robot talk' to their partner.

Read it
■ Write words that contain the phoneme /ue/, grapheme 'ew', on the easel or board (for example: 'drew', 'few', 'chew', 'pew') and ask the children to read out the phonemes by blending them together with their partner. Ensure that the children can identify the grapheme 'ew'.
■ Display the picture card of the grapheme 'ew' on the wall under the graphemes 'ue' and 'oo' to build up the Phoneme–grapheme chart. Ask the children to tell you the graphemes for the phoneme /ue/ and repeat the mnemonic phrase for 'ew'.

Write it
■ Say a word containing the phoneme /ue/, grapheme 'ew'. Ask the children to repeat it and then segment it into phonemes using 'robot talk'. Ask the children to first count the phonemes in the word and then to hold up the correct number of fingers.
■ Now say the word again and ask them to write it on their whiteboards and underline the grapheme that represents the phoneme /ue/.
■ Ask the children to tell you the graphemes for the phoneme /ue/. Encourage them to refer to the Phoneme–grapheme chart to support spelling.

LESSON 64/65
REVISE PHONEMES TAUGHT
■ Follow the format from Revision Lessons 39/40 on page 120 to revise all phonemes and corresponding graphemes taught in the week

STAGE THREE: LESSON PLANS

LESSON 66 'a-e'

1 REVIEW (5 mins)

Hear it

■ Begin this session by saying that this week they are learning some special phonemes called split digraphs.

■ Review the long vowel phonemes taught so far by saying the vowel rap in a lively fun way.

■ Help the children to practise hearing the sounds by choosing one of the long vowel sounds taught so far. Say a range of words, some which contain the phoneme and some which do not. Ask the children to put up their hand when they hear the appropriate phoneme.

Say it

■ Say several words containing the long vowel phonemes taught so far slowly in 'robot talk', for example: /d/r/ew/, /c/ue/, /m/oo/n/. Ask the children to blend the phonemes into words.

■ Now ask the children to speak in 'robot talk'. Say a word, for example, 'crew', and ask them to segment it using 'robot talk' talk to their partner.

Read it

■ Write the following words on the board or easel and show the children: 'few', 'cue', 'hoop'.

■ Ask the children to read the words out loud to their partner. Encourage them to blend the phonemes.

Write it

■ Say a word containing the phoneme /ue/ with the grapheme 'ew', for example: 'drew'. Ask the children to repeat it and then segment it into phonemes using 'robot talk'. Ask the children to count the phonemes in the word and then to hold up the correct number of fingers, then to write it on their whiteboards.

2 PHONEME /ae/ GRAPHEME 'a-e'

(10 mins)

Hear it

■ Explain to the children that they are going to learn more of the rap.

■ Introduce the new grapheme by saying several words that contain it for example 'make', 'take', 'cake'. Explain that this is the phoneme /ae/ and they have already learned three ways to spell it: 'ay', 'ai' and 'a' but they are now learning another way to spell it.

Say it

■ Say the phoneme /ae/, grapheme 'a-e', emphasising correct articulation, and then show the children the corresponding phoneme picture card and mnemonic phrase, 'Take a cake'. Repeat it several times.

■ Say the letter names of the new grapheme: 'A-E' (say 'A skip a letter E') and introduce the action (pretend to eat a cake).

■ Explain that this is a special grapheme as the two letters are split by another letter, such as in the word 'cake', we call it a 'split digraph'.

■ Now say the full rap for this grapheme and ask the children to do the action: 'a-e' 'a-e' Take a cake A-E.

■ Using several words containing the phoneme /ae/, grapheme 'a-e', say these slowly in 'robot talk' for example: /m/a/k/e/, /sh/a/k/e/, /h/a/t/e/ and ask the children to blend the phonemes into words and tell their partners.

■ Now ask the children to speak in 'robot talk'. Say a word, for example, 'take' and ask them to segment using 'robot talk' to their partner.

Read it

■ Write words that contain the phoneme /ae/, grapheme 'a-e', on the easel or board for example: 'take', 'make', 'fake', and ask the children to read out the phonemes by blending them together with their partner. Ensure that the children can identify the grapheme 'a-e' and show them clearly that these are split by the letter 'k', but sometimes it is the letter 't' as in 'hate'.

■ Display the picture card of the grapheme 'a-e' on the wall under the the phoneme /ae/ (the first column) of the Phoneme-grapheme chart. Ask the children to tell you the graphemes for the phoneme /ae/ and repeat the mnemonic phrase for 'a-e'.

Write it

■ Say a word containing the phoneme /ae/ grapheme 'a-e'. Ask the children to repeat it and then segment it into phonemes using 'robot talk', for example, take.

■ Now say the word again and ask them to write it on their whiteboards and underline the grapheme that represents the phoneme /ae/.

■ Ask the children to tell you the graphemes for the phoneme /ae/. Encourage them to refer to the Phoneme-grapheme chart to support spelling.

LESSON 67 'i–e'

1 REVIEW *(5 mins)*

Hear it

■ Review the long vowel phonemes taught so far by saying the vowel rap in a lively fun way with the children.

■ Help the children to practise hearing the sounds by reading a range of words, some of which contain the phoneme /ae/, grapheme 'a–e' and some that do not for example: 'fly', 'take', 'tree', 'make', 'snow', 'hate'. Ask them to put their hands up every time they hear the phoneme /ae/.

Say it

■ Say several words containing the long vowel phonemes slowly in 'robot talk', for example: /m/a/k/e/, /h/a/t/e/. Ask the children to blend the phonemes into words and tell their partners.

■ Now ask the children to speak in 'robot talk'. Say a word, for example, 'cake', and ask them to segment it using 'robot talk' first to their partner and then all together.

Read it

■ Write the following words on the board or easel and show the children: 'wake', 'fake', 'hate'.

■ Ask the children to read the words out loud to their partner. Encourage them to blend the phonemes.

Write it

■ Say a word containing the phoneme /ae/ with the grapheme 'a–e', for example: 'make'. Ask the children to repeat it and then segment it into phonemes using 'robot talk'. Ask the children to count the phonemes in the word and to hold up the correct number of fingers. Then write the answer on their whiteboard.

2 PHONEME /ie/ GRAPHEME 'i–e'

(10 mins)

Hear it

■ Explain to the children that they are going to learn more of the rap.

■ Introduce the grapheme 'i–e' by saying several words that contain it. Explain that this is the phoneme /ie/ and they have already learned four ways to spell it: 'ie', 'igh' 'y' and 'i'.

Say it

■ Say the phoneme /ie/, grapheme 'i–e', emphasising correct articulation, and then show the children the corresponding phoneme picture card and mnemonic phrase, 'Mike's bike'. Ask the children to repeat it several times with you.

■ Say the letter names of the new grapheme: 'I–E' (say 'I skip a letter E') and introduce the action (pretend to ride a bike).

■ Now say the full rap for this grapheme and ask the children to do the action: 'i–e' 'i–e' Mike's bike I–E.

■ Using several words containing the phoneme /ie/, grapheme 'i–e', say these slowly in 'robot talk' (for example: /M/i/k/e/, /b/i/k/e/ and /l/i/k/e/) and ask the children to blend the phonemes into words and tell their partners.

■ Now ask the children to speak in 'robot talk'. Say a word, for example, 'fine', and ask them to segment it using 'robot talk' to their partners.

Read it

■ Write words that contain the phoneme /ie/, grapheme 'i–e', on the easel or board (for example: bike, trike, file) and ask the children to read out the phonemes by blending them together with their partner. Ensure that the children can identify the grapheme 'i–e' and talk about the phoneme being split by another letter and that this is a split-digraph.

■ Display the picture card of the grapheme 'i–e' on the wall under the phoneme /ie/ (the third column) to build up the Phoneme–grapheme chart for the long vowel phonemes. Ask the children to tell you the graphemes for the phoneme /ie/ and repeat the mnemonic phrase for 'i–e'.

Write it

■ Say a word containing the phoneme /ie/, grapheme 'i–e'. Ask the children to repeat it and then segment it into phonemes using 'robot talk', for example: 'hive' – /h/i/v/e/. Ask the children to first count the phonemes in the word and then to hold up the correct number of fingers.

■ Now say the word again and ask them to write it on their whiteboards and underline the graphemes that represents the phoneme /ie/.

■ Ask the children to tell you the graphemes for the phoneme /ie/. Encourage them to refer to the Phoneme–grapheme chart to support spelling.

STAGE THREE: LESSON PLANS

LESSON 68 'o-e'

1 REVIEW (5 mins)

Hear it

■ Review the long vowel phonemes taught so far by saying the vowel rap in a lively fun way with the children.

■ Help the children to practise hearing the sounds by saying a range of words, some of which contain the phoneme /ie/, grapheme 'i-e' and some that do not, for example: 'glow', 'Mike', 'boat', 'file', 'mice', 'pony'. Ask them to put their hands up every time they hear the phoneme /ie/.

Say it

■ Say several words containing the long vowel phonemes slowly in 'robot talk', for example: /b/i/k/e/ and /l/i/k/e/. Ask the children to blend the phonemes into words and tell their partners.

■ Now ask the children to speak in 'robot talk'. Say a word, for example, 'hive', and ask them to segment it using 'robot talk' first to their partner and then all together.

Read it

■ Write the following words on the board or easel and show the children: 'file', 'crime', 'time'.

■ Ask the children to read the words out loud to their partner. Encourage them to blend the phonemes.

Write it

■ Say a word containing the phoneme /ie/ with the grapheme 'i-e', for example, 'mice'. Ask the children to repeat it and then segment it into phonemes using 'robot talk'. Ask the children to first count the phonemes in the word and then to hold up the correct number of fingers. Ask them to write the answer on their individual whiteboards.

2 PHONEME /oe/ GRAPHEME 'o-e'
(10 mins)

Hear it

■ Explain to the children that they are going to learn more of the rap.

■ Introduce the phoneme /oe/, grapheme 'o-e' by saying several words that contain it for example, 'bone', 'lone', 'phone', 'tone'. Explain that this is the phoneme /oe/ and they have already learned three ways to spell it: 'oa', 'ow' and 'o' but they are now learning another way to spell it.

Say it

■ Say the phoneme /oe/, grapheme 'o-e' emphasising correct articulation and then show the children the corresponding phoneme picture card and mnemonic phrase 'Stone on a bone'. Ask the children to repeat it several times with you.

■ Say the letter names of the new grapheme: 'O-E' (say 'O skip a letter E') and introduce the action (hop several times, pointing to your leg).

■ Now say the full rap for this grapheme and ask the children to do the action: 'o-e' 'o-e' Stone on a bone O-E.

■ Using several words containing the phoneme /oe/, grapheme 'o-e', say these slowly in 'robot talk' for example: /s/t/o/n/e/, /b/o/n/e/, /t/o/n/e/ and ask the children to blend the phonemes into words and tell their partners.

■ Now ask the children to speak in 'robot talk'. Say a word for example, 'phone', and ask them to segment it using 'robot talk' to their partner.

Read it

■ Write words that contain the phoneme /oe/, grapheme 'o-e', on the easel or board, for example: 'bone', 'stone', 'lone' and ask the children to read out the phonemes by blending them together with their partner. Ensure that the children can identify the grapheme 'o-e' and talk about the phoneme being split by another letter and that this is a split-digraph.

■ Display the picture card of the grapheme 'o-e' on the wall under the phoneme /oe/ (the fourth column) to build up the Phoneme-grapheme chart for the long vowel phonemes. Ask the children to tell you the graphemes for the phoneme /oe/ and repeat the mnemonic phrase for 'o-e'.

Write it

■ Say a word containing the phoneme /oe/, grapheme 'o-e'. Ask the children to repeat it and then segment it into phonemes using 'robot talk', for example: 'lone'. Ask the children to first count the phonemes in the word and then to hold up the correct number of fingers.

■ Now say the word again and ask them to write it on their whiteboards and underline the grapheme that represents the phoneme /oe/.

LESSON 69 'u-e'

1 REVIEW *(5 mins)*

Hear it
■ Review the long vowel phonemes taught so far by saying the vowel rap in a lively fun way.
■ Help the children to practise hearing the sounds by saying a range of words, some of which contain the phoneme /oe/, grapheme 'o-e' and some that do not. Ask them to put their hands up every time they hear the phoneme /oe/.

Say it
■ Say several words containing the long vowel phonemes slowly in 'robot talk', for example /b/o/n/e/ and /t/o/n/e/. Ask the children to blend the phonemes into words.
■ Now ask the children to speak in 'robot talk'. Say a word for example: 'code' and ask them to segment it using 'robot talk'.

Read it
■ Write the following words on the board or easel and show the children: 'stone', 'bone', 'phone'.
■ Ask the children to read the words out loud to their partner. Encourage them to blend the phonemes.

Write it
■ Say a word containing the phoneme /oe/ with the grapheme 'o-e'. Ask the children to repeat it and then segment it using 'robot talk'. Ask the children to count the phonemes and to hold up the correct number of fingers, then write it on their whiteboard.

2 PHONEME /ue/ GRAPHEME 'u-e'
(10 mins)

Hear it
■ Explain to the children that they are going to learn more of the rap.
■ Introduce the new grapheme by saying several words that contain it for example, 'tune', 'dune', 'duke'. Explain that this the phoneme /ue/ and they have already learned three ways to spell it: 'oo', 'ue' and 'ew' but they are now learning another spelling.

Say it
■ Say the phoneme /ue/, grapheme 'u-e' emphasising correct articulation, and then show the children the corresponding phoneme picture card and mnemonic phrase, 'Cute tune'. Repeat it several times.
■ Say the letter names of the new grapheme: 'U-E' (say 'U skip a letter E') and introduce the action (pretend to play a tune on a recorder).
■ Now say the full rap for this grapheme and ask the children to do the action: 'u-e' 'u-e' Cute tune U-E.
■ Using several words containing the phoneme /ue/, grapheme 'u-e', say these slowly in 'robot talk' (for example: /c/u/t/e/, /f/l/u/t/e/, /t/u/n/e/) and ask the children to blend the phonemes into words and tell their partners.
■ Now ask the children to speak in 'robot talk'. Say a word, for example, 'cube', and ask them to segment it using 'robot talk' to their partner.

Read it
■ Write words that contain the phoneme /ue/, grapheme 'u-e' on the easel or board (for example: 'tune', 'dune', 'cube' and 'fuse') and ask the children to read out the phonemes by blending them together with their partner. Ensure that the children can identify the grapheme 'u-e' and talk about the phoneme being split by another letter and that this is a split-digraph.
■ Display the picture card of the grapheme 'u-e' on the wall under the phoneme /ue/ (the sixth column) to build up the Phoneme-grapheme chart for the long vowel phonemes. Ask the children to tell you the graphemes for the phoneme /ue/ and repeat the mnemonic phrase for 'u-e'.

Write it
■ Say a word containing the phoneme /ue/, grapheme 'u-e'. Ask the children to repeat it and then segment it into phonemes using 'robot talk', for example: 'tube'.
■ Now say the word again and ask them to write it on their whiteboards and underline the grapheme that represents the phoneme /ue/.
■ Ask the children to tell you the graphemes for the phoneme /ue/.

> ### LESSON 70
> ### REVISE PHONEMES TAUGHT
> ■ Follow the format from Revision Lessons 39/ 40 on page 120 to revise all phonemes and corresponding graphemes taught in the week.

STAGE THREE: LESSON PLANS

LESSON 71 'ow'

1 REVIEW (5 mins)

Hear it

■ Review the long vowel phonemes taught so far by saying the vowel rap in a lively fun way with the children.

■ Help the children to practise hearing the sounds by choosing one of the long vowel sounds taught so far. Say a range of words, some which contain the phoneme and some which do not. Ask the children to put up their hand when they hear the appropriate phoneme.

Say it

■ Say several words containing the phonemes taught so far slowly in 'robot talk', for example: /s/a/k/e/, /f/i/n/e/, /l/o/n/e/, /c/u/b/e/. Ask the children to blend the phonemes into words and tell their partners.

■ Now ask the children to speak in 'robot talk'. Say a word, for example, 'dune', and ask them to segment it using 'robot talk' first to their partner and then all together.

Read it

■ Write the following words on the board or easel and show the children: 'fake', 'file', 'code', 'duke'.

■ Ask the children to read the words out loud to their partner. Encourage them to blend the phonemes together.

Write it

■ Say a word containing the phoneme /ue/ with the grapheme 'u–e', for example: 'tune'. Ask the children to repeat it and then segment it into phonemes using 'robot talk'. Ask the children to count the phonemes in the word and to hold up the correct number of fingers. Then write it on their whiteboard.

2 NEW PHONEME /ow/ GRAPHEME 'ow'
(10 mins)

Hear it

■ Explain to the children that they are going to learn more of the rap.

■ Introduce the new grapheme 'ow' by saying several words that contain it for example 'now', 'row'.

Say it

■ Say the phoneme /ow/, grapheme 'ow', emphasising correct articulation, and then show the children the corresponding phoneme picture card and mnemonic phrase, 'Not now brown cow'. Ask the children to repeat it several times with you.

■ Say the letter names of the new grapheme: 'OW' and introduce the action (hold up finger as if telling off a cow).

■ Now say the full rap for this grapheme and ask the children to do the action: 'ow' 'ow' Not now brown cow OW.

■ Using several words containing the phoneme /ow/, grapheme 'ow', say these slowly in 'robot talk' for example: /n/ow/, /h/ow/ and /c/ow/ and ask the children to blend the phonemes into words and tell their partners.

■ Now ask the children to speak in 'robot talk'. Say a word, for example, 'now', and ask them to segment it using 'robot talk' to their partner.

Read it

■ Write words that contain the phoneme /ow/, grapheme 'ow', on the easel or board (for example: 'sow', 'cow', 'now' and 'brown') and ask the children to read out the phonemes by blending them together with their partner. Ensure that the children can identify the grapheme 'ow'.

■ Display the picture card of the grapheme 'ow' on the wall beginning a new column to build up the Phoneme-grapheme chart for the long vowel phonemes. Ask the children to tell you the grapheme for the phoneme /ow/ and repeat the mnemonic phrase for 'ow'.

Write it

■ Say a word containing the phoneme /ow/, grapheme 'ow'. Ask the children to repeat it and then segment it into phonemes using 'robot talk', for example: 'now' – /n/ow/. Ask the children to first count the phonemes in the word and then to hold up the correct number of fingers.

■ Now say the word again and ask them to write it on their whiteboards and underline the grapheme that represents the phoneme /ow/.

■ Ask the children to tell you the grapheme for the phoneme /ow/. Encourage them to refer to the Phoneme-grapheme chart to support spelling.

LESSON 72 'ou'

1 REVIEW (5 mins)
Hear it
■ Review the long vowel phonemes taught so far by saying the vowel rap in a lively fun way with the children.

■ Help the children to practise hearing the sounds by reading a range of words some of which contain the phoneme /ow/, grapheme 'ow' and some that do not for example: 'now', 'warn', 'cow', 'ball', 'light', 'row', 'girl', 'horn', 'far', 'brown', 'put', 'sow'. Ask them to put their hands up every time they hear the phoneme /ow/.

Say it
■ Say several words containing the long vowel phonemes slowly in 'robot talk', for example: /c/ow/, /v/ow/, /b/r/ow/n/. Ask the children to blend the phonemes into words and tell their partners.

■ Now ask the children to speak in 'robot talk'. Say a word, for example, 'bow', and ask them to segment it using 'robot talk' first to their partner and then all together.

Read it
■ Write the following words on the board or easel and show the children: 'brown', 'cow', 'now', 'sow', 'vow'.

■ Ask the children to read the words out loud to their partner. Encourage them to blend the phonemes together.

Write it
■ Say a word containing the phoneme /ow/ with the grapheme 'ow', for example: 'vow'. Ask the children to repeat it and then segment it into phonemes using 'robot talk'. Ask the children to count the phonemes in the word and hold up the correct number of fingers then to write the answer on their whiteboard.

2 NEW GRAPHEME 'ou' (10 mins)
Hear it
■ Explain to the children that they are going to learn more of the rap.

■ Introduce the new grapheme 'ou' by saying several words that contain it for example 'shout', 'house', 'mouse', 'loud', 'out'.

Say it
■ Say the phoneme /ow/, grapheme 'ou', emphasising correct articulation, and then show the children the corresponding phoneme picture card and mnemonic phrase, 'Shout out loud'. Ask the children to repeat it several times with you.

■ Say the letter names of the new grapheme: 'OU' and introduce the action (put hands to your face and pretend to shout).

■ Now say the full rap for this grapheme and ask the children to do the action: 'ou' 'ou' Shout out loud OU.

■ Using several words containing the phoneme /ow/, grapheme 'ou', say these slowly in 'robot talk' (for example: /sh/ou/t/, /c/ou/n/t/ and /l/ou/d/) and ask the children to blend the phonemes into words and tell their partners.

■ Now ask the children to speak in 'robot talk'. Say a word, for example, 'loud', and ask them to segment it using 'robot talk' to their partner.

Read it
■ Write words that contain the phoneme /ow/, grapheme 'ou', on the easel or board (for example: 'shout', 'loud', 'out', 'mouse') and ask the children to read out the phonemes by blending them together with their partner. Ensure that the children can identify the grapheme 'ou'.

■ Display the picture card of the grapheme 'ou' on the wall underneath the grapheme 'ow' to build up the Phoneme-grapheme chart for the long vowel phonemes. Ask the children to tell you the graphemes for the phoneme /ow/ and say the mnemonic phrase for 'ou'.

Write it
■ Say a word containing the phoneme /ow/, grapheme 'ou'. Ask the children to repeat it and then segment it into phonemes using 'robot talk', for example: 'shout' – /sh/ou/t/. Ask the children to first count the phonemes in the word and then to hold up the correct number of fingers.

■ Now say the word again and ask them to write it on their whiteboards and underline the grapheme that represents the phoneme /ow/.

■ Ask the children to tell you the graphemes for the phoneme /ow/. Encourage them to refer to the Phoneme-grapheme chart on the wall to support spelling.

LESSON 73 'oi'

1 REVIEW *(5 mins)*

Hear it

■ Review the long vowel phonemes taught so far by saying the vowel rap in a lively fun way with the children.

■ Help the children to practise hearing the sounds by reading a range of words, some of which contain the phoneme /ow/, graphemes 'ow' or 'ou', and some that do not, for example: 'shout', 'warn', now, 'out', 'ball', 'light', 'house', 'far', 'put', 'about'. Ask them to put their hands up every time they hear the phoneme /ow/.

Say it

■ Say several words containing the long vowel phonemes slowly in 'robot talk', for example: /sh/ou/t/, /a/b/ou/t/, /l/ou/d/, /m/ou/th/. Ask the children to blend the phonemes into words and tell their partners.

■ Now ask the children to speak in 'robot talk'. Say a word, for example, 'loud' and ask them to segment it using 'robot talk' first to their partner and then all together.

Read it

■ Write the following words on the board or easel and show the children: 'shout', 'loud', 'mouse'.

■ Ask the children to read the words out loud to their partner. Encourage them to blend the phonemes together.

Write it

■ Say a word containing the phoneme /ow/ with the grapheme 'ou', for example: 'mouth'. Ask the children to repeat it and then segment it into phonemes using 'robot talk'. Ask the children to first count the phonemes in the word by counting on their fingers and then to hold up the correct number of fingers. Ask them to write the answer on their individual whiteboards.

2 NEW PHONEME /oi/ GRAPHEME 'oi'
(10 mins)

Hear it

■ Explain to the children that they are going to learn more of the rap.

■ Introduce the new grapheme 'oi' by saying several words that contain it for example 'coin', 'toil', 'coil', 'join', 'oil'.

Say it

■ Say the phoneme /oi/, grapheme 'oi', emphasising correct articulation, and then show the children the corresponding phoneme picture card and mnemonic phrase, 'Join the coin'. Ask the children to repeat it several times with you.

■ Say the letter names of the new grapheme: 'OI' and introduce the action (pretend to hold a coin between your fingers).

■ Now say the full rap for this grapheme and ask the children to do the action: 'oi' 'oi' Join the coin OI.

■ Say several words containing the phoneme /oi/, grapheme 'oi', slowly in 'robot talk' for example: /c/oi/n/, /s/oi/l/, /b/oi/l/. Ask the children to blend the phonemes into words and tell their partners.

■ Now ask the children to speak in 'robot talk'. Say a word, for example, 'join', and ask them to segment it using 'robot talk' to their partner.

Read it

■ Write words that contain the phoneme /oi/, grapheme 'oi', on the easel or board (for example: 'coin', 'foil', 'coil', 'oil') and ask the children to read out the phonemes by blending them together with their partner. Ensure that the children can identify the grapheme 'oi'.

■ Display the picture card of the grapheme 'oi' on the wall beginning a new column to build up the Phoneme–grapheme chart for the vowel phonemes. Ask the children to tell you the grapheme for the phoneme /oi/ and repeat the mnemonic phrase for 'oi'.

Write it

■ Say a word containing the phoneme /oi/, grapheme 'oi'. Ask the children to repeat it and then segment it into phonemes using 'robot talk', for example: 'coin' – /c/oi/n/. Ask the children to first count the phonemes in the word and then to hold up the correct number of fingers.

■ Now say the word again and ask them to write it on their whiteboards and underline the grapheme that represents the phoneme /oi/.

■ Ask the children to tell you the grapheme for the phoneme /oi/. Encourage them to refer to the Phoneme–grapheme chart to support spelling.

LESSON 74 'oy'

1 REVIEW *(5 mins)*

Hear it

■ Review the long vowel phonemes taught so far by saying the vowel rap in a lively fun way with the children.

■ Help the children to practise hearing the sounds by reading a range of words, some of which contain the phoneme /oi/, grapheme 'oi' and some that do not, for example: 'coin', 'now', 'warn', 'join', 'ball', 'light', 'row', 'foil', 'fur', 'boil'. Ask them to put their hands up every time they hear the phoneme /oi/.

Say it

■ Say several words containing the long vowel phonemes slowly in 'robot talk', for example: /j/oi/n/, /c/oi/l/, /t/oi/l/. Ask the children to blend the phonemes into words and tell their partners.

■ Now ask the children to speak in 'robot talk'. Say a word, for example, 'broil', and ask them to segment it using 'robot talk' first to their partner and then all together.

Read it

■ Write the following words on the board or easel and show the children: 'coin', 'joint', 'point', 'oil', 'boil'.

■ Ask the children to read the words out loud to their partner. Encourage them to blend the phonemes.

Write it

■ Say a word containing the phoneme /oi/ with the grapheme 'oi', for example: 'spoil'. Ask the children to repeat it and then segment it into phonemes using 'robot talk'. Ask the children to count the phonemes in the word and to hold up the correct number of fingers. Then to write it on their whiteboard.

2 NEW GRAPHEME 'oy' *(10 mins)*

Hear it

■ Explain to the children that they are going to learn more of the rap.

■ Introduce the new grapheme 'oy' by saying several words that contain it, for example 'toy', 'boy', 'joy'.

Say it

■ Say the phoneme /oi/, grapheme 'oy' emphasising correct articulation, and then show the children the corresponding phoneme picture card and mnemonic phrase 'Roy's a boy'. Repeat it several times.

■ Say the letter names of the new grapheme: 'OY' and introduce the action (point to a boy).

■ Now say the full rap for this grapheme and ask the children to do the action: 'oy' 'oy' Roy's a boy OY.

■ Using several words containing the phoneme /oi/, grapheme 'oy', say these slowly in 'robot talk', for example, /t/oy/, /j/oy/, /p/l/oy/ and ask the children to blend the phonemes into words and tell their partners.

■ Now ask the children to speak in 'robot talk'. Say a word, for example, 'ploy', and ask them to segment it using 'robot talk' to their partner.

Read it

■ Write words that contain the phoneme /oi/, grapheme 'oy', on the easel or board and ask the children to read the phonemes by blending them together using 'robot talk' and tell their partner. Ensure that they can identify the grapheme 'oy'.

■ Display the picture card of the grapheme 'oy' on the wall underneath the grapheme 'oi' to build up the Phoneme–grapheme chart for the vowel phonemes. Ask the children to tell you the graphemes for the phoneme /oi/ and say the mnemonic phrase for 'oy'.

Write it

■ Say a word containing the phoneme /oi/, grapheme 'oy'. Ask the children to repeat it and then segment it into phonemes using 'robot talk', for example: 'boy' – /b/oy/. Ask the children to first count the phonemes in the word and then to hold up the correct number of fingers.

■ Now say the word again and ask them to write it on their whiteboards and underline the grapheme that represents the phoneme /oi/.

■ Ask the children to tell you the graphemes for the phoneme /oi/. Encourage them to refer to the Phoneme–grapheme chart to support spelling.

LESSON 75
REVISE PHONEMES TAUGHT

■ Follow the format from Revision Lessons 39/40 on page 120 to revise all phonemes and corresponding graphemes taught in the week.

■ Ensure that you carry out Assessment 2 on page 187 before continuing with Stage 3.

STAGE THREE: LESSON PLANS

LESSON 76 'ur'

① REVIEW *(5 mins)*
Hear it
■ Review the long vowel phonemes taught so far by saying the vowel rap in a lively fun way with the children.

■ Help the children to practise hearing the sounds by choosing one of the long vowel sounds taught so far. Say a range of words, some which contain the phoneme and some which do not. Ask the children to put up their hand when they hear the appropriate phoneme.

Say it
■ Say several words containing the phonemes taught so far slowly in 'robot talk', for example: /j/oy/, /c/oi/l/, h/ou/s/e/ /s/ow/. Ask the children to blend the phonemes into words and tell their partners.

■ Now ask the children to speak in 'robot talk'. Say a word, for example, 'toy', and ask them to segment it using 'robot talk' first to their partner and then all together.

Read it
■ Write the following words on the board or easel and show the children: 'ploy', 'foil', 'doubt' 'row'.

■ Ask the children to read the words out loud to their partner. Encourage them to blend the phonemes.

Write it
■ Say a word containing the phoneme /oi/ with the grapheme 'oy', for example: 'joy'. Ask the children to repeat it and then segment it into phonemes using 'robot talk'. Ask the children to first count the phonemes in the word by counting on their fingers and then to hold up the correct number of fingers. Ask them to write the answer on their individual whiteboards.

② NEW PHONEME /ur/ GRAPHEME 'ur'
(10 mins)
Hear it
■ Explain to the children that they are going to learn more of the rap.

■ Introduce the new phoneme /ur/, grapheme 'ur', by saying several words that contain it 'burn', 'turn', 'curl'.

Say it
■ Say the phoneme /ur/, grapheme 'ur', emphasising correct articulation, and then show the children the corresponding phoneme picture card and mnemonic phrase 'Turn the fur'. Ask the children to repeat it several times with you.

■ Say the letter names of the new grapheme: 'UR' and introduce the action (pretend to stroke some fur).

■ Now say the full rap for this grapheme and ask the children to do the action: 'ur' 'ur' Turn the fur UR.

■ Using several words containing the phoneme /ur/, grapheme 'ur', say these slowly in 'robot talk' (for example: /c/ur/l/, /s/ur/e/, /f/ur/) and ask the children to blend the phonemes into words and tell their partners.

■ Now ask the children to speak in 'robot talk'. Say a word, for example, 'burn', and ask them to segment it using 'robot talk' to their partner.

Read it
■ Write words that contain the phoneme /ur/, grapheme 'ur', on the easel or board (for example: 'turn', 'curl', 'hurl') and ask the children to read out the phonemes by blending them together with their partner. Ensure that the children can identify the grapheme 'ur'.

■ Display the picture card of the grapheme 'ur' on the wall beginning a new column to build up the Phoneme-grapheme chart for the long vowel phonemes. Ask the children to tell you the grapheme for the phoneme /ur/ and repeat the mnemonic phrase for 'ur'.

Write it
■ Say a word containing the phoneme /ur/, grapheme 'ur'. Ask the children to repeat it and then segment it into phonemes using 'robot talk', for example: 'turn' – /t/ur/n/. Ask the children to first count the phonemes in the word and then to hold up the correct number of fingers. Alternatively they can write the answer on their individual whiteboards.

■ Now say the word again and ask them to write it on their whiteboards and underline the grapheme that represents the phoneme /ur/.

■ Ask the children to tell you the grapheme for the phoneme /ur/. Encourage them to refer to the Phoneme-grapheme chart to support spelling.

LESSON 77 'ir'

1 REVIEW *(5 mins)*

Hear it

■ Review the long vowel phonemes taught so far by saying the vowel rap in a lively fun way with the children.

■ Help the children to practise hearing the sounds by reading a range of words, some of which contain the phoneme /ur/, grapheme 'ur' and some that do not, for example: 'turn', 'car', 'burn', 'far', 'few', 'curl', 'rook', 'fur'. Ask them to put their hands up every time they hear the phoneme /ur/.

Say it

■ Say several words containing the long vowel phonemes slowly in 'robot talk', for example: /t/ur/n/, /h/ur/l/, /c/ur/l/. Ask the children to blend the phonemes into words and tell their partners.

■ Now ask the children to speak in 'robot talk'. Say a word (for example: 'burn') and ask them to segment it using 'robot talk' first to their partner and then all together.

Read it

■ Write the following words on the board or easel and show the children: 'burn', 'hurl', 'fur', 'curl'.

■ Ask the children to read the words out loud to their partner. Encourage them to blend the phonemes.

Write it

■ Say a word containing the phoneme /ur/ with the grapheme 'ur', for example: 'turn'. Ask the children to repeat it and then segment it into phonemes using 'robot talk'. Ask the children to first count the phonemes in the word by counting on their fingers and then to hold up the correct number of fingers. Ask them to write the answer on their individual whiteboards.

2 NEW GRAPHEME 'ir' *(10 mins)*

Hear it

■ Explain to the children that they are going to learn more of the rap.

■ Introduce the new grapheme 'ir' by saying several words that contain it for example: 'girl', 'shirt', 'twirl', 'fir'.

Say it

■ Say the phoneme /ur/, grapheme 'ir', emphasising correct articulation, and then show the children the corresponding phoneme picture card and mnemonic phrase, 'Twirl the girl'. Ask the children to repeat it several times with you.

■ Say the letter names of the new grapheme: 'IR' and introduce the action (twirl round in a circle).

■ Now say the full rap for this grapheme and ask the children to do the action: 'ir' 'ir' Twirl the girl IR.

■ Using several words containing the phoneme /ur/, grapheme 'ir', say these slowly in 'robot talk' for example: /t/w/ir/l/, /g/ir/l/, /sh/ir/t/ and ask the children to blend the phonemes into words and tell their partners.

■ Now ask the children to speak in 'robot talk'. Say a word, for example, 'girl', and ask them to segment it using 'robot talk' to their partner.

Read it

■ Write words that contain the phoneme /ur/, grapheme 'ir', on the easel or board (for example: 'twirl', 'shirt', 'girl') and ask the children to read out the phonemes by blending them together with their partner. Ensure that the children can identify the grapheme 'ir'.

■ Display the picture card of the grapheme 'ir' on the wall underneath the grapheme 'ur' to build up the Phoneme-grapheme chart for the long vowel phonemes. Ask the children to tell you the graphemes for the phoneme /ur/ and repeat the mnemonic phrase for 'ir'.

Write it

■ Say a word containing the phoneme /ur/, grapheme /ir/. Ask the children to repeat it and then segment it into phonemes using 'robot talk', for example: 'twirl' – /t/w/ir/l/. Ask the children to first count the phonemes in the word and then to hold up the correct number of fingers.

■ Now say the word again and ask them to write it on their whiteboards and underline the grapheme that represents the phoneme /ur/.

■ Ask the children to tell you the graphemes for the phoneme /ur/. Encourage them to refer to the Phoneme-grapheme chart on the wall to support spelling.

LESSON 78 'er'

① REVIEW *(5 mins)*
Hear it
■ Review the long vowel phonemes taught so far by saying the vowel rap in a lively fun way with the children.

■ Help the children to practise hearing the sounds by reading a range of words, some of which contain the vowel phoneme /ur/, graphemes 'ur' or 'ir' and some that do not, for example: 'girl', 'twirl', 'fair', 'burn', 'cheer', 'shirt'. Ask them to put their hands up every time they hear the phoneme /ur/.

Say it
■ Say several words containing the long vowel phonemes slowly in 'robot talk', for example: /g/ir/l/, /sh/ir/t/, /f/ir/. Ask the children to blend the phonemes into words and tell their partners.

■ Now ask the children to speak in 'robot talk'. Say a word, for example, 'twirl', and ask them to segment it using 'robot talk' first to their partner and then all together.

Read it
■ Write the following words on the board or easel and show the children: 'twirl', 'girl', 'fir'.

■ Ask the children to read the words out loud to their partner. Encourage them to blend the phonemes together.

Write it
■ Say a word containing the phoneme /ur/ with the grapheme 'ir' for example, 'shirt'. Ask the children to repeat it and then segment it into phonemes using 'robot talk'. Ask the children to first count the phonemes in the word and then to hold up the correct number of fingers. Ask them to write the answer on their individual whiteboards.

② NEW GRAPHEME 'er' *(10 mins)*
Hear it
■ Explain to the children that they are going to learn more of the rap.

■ Introduce the new grapheme 'er' by saying several words that contain it for example 'term', 'fern', 'herb', 'jerk', stern.

Say it
■ Say the phoneme /ur/, grapheme 'er', emphasising correct articulation, and then show the children the corresponding phoneme picture card and mnemonic phrase 'Perm for the term'. Ask the children to repeat it several times with you.

■ Say the letter names of the new grapheme: 'ER' and introduce the action (pat hair and stand up smartly).

■ Now say the full rap for this grapheme and ask the children to do the action: 'er' 'er' Perm for the term ER.

■ Using several words containing the phoneme /ur/, grapheme 'er', say these slowly in 'robot talk' (for example: /t/er/m/, /f/er/n/, /st/er/n/) and ask the children to blend the phonemes into words and tell their partners.

■ Now ask the children to speak in 'robot talk'. Say a word, for example, 'fern', and ask them to segment it using 'robot talk' to their partner.

Read it
■ Write words that contain the phoneme /ur/, grapheme 'er', on the easel or board (for example: 'herb', 'jerk', 'fern') and ask the children to read out the phonemes by blending them together with their partner. Ensure that the children can identify the grapheme 'er'.

■ Display the picture card of the grapheme 'er' on the wall underneath the graphemes 'ur' and 'ir' to build up the Phoneme–grapheme chart for the long vowel phonemes. Ask the children to tell you the graphemes for the phoneme /ur/ and repeat the mnemonic phrase for 'er'.

Write it
■ Say a word containing the phoneme /ur/, grapheme 'er'. Ask the children to repeat it and then segment it into phonemes using 'robot talk', for example: 'term' – /t/er/m/. Ask the children to first count the phonemes in the word and then to hold up the correct number of fingers.

■ Now say the word again and ask them to write it on their whiteboards and underline the grapheme that represents the phoneme /ur/.

■ Ask the children to tell you the graphemes for the phoneme /ur/. Encourage them to refer to the Phoneme–grapheme chart on the wall to support spelling.

LESSON 79 'ear'

1 REVIEW *(5 mins)*

Hear it

■ Review the long vowel phonemes taught so far by saying the vowel rap in a lively fun way with the children.

■ Help the children to practise hearing the sounds by saying a range of words, some of which contain the phoneme /ur/, graphemes 'ur', 'ir', or 'er' and some that do not, for example: 'fern', 'car', 'fir', 'term', 'put', 'herb'. Ask them to put their hands up every time they hear the phoneme /ur/.

Say it

■ Say several words containing the long vowel phonemes slowly in 'robot talk', for example: /h/er/b/, /j/er/k/, /f/er/n/. Ask the children to blend the phonemes into words and tell their partners.

■ Now ask the children to speak in 'robot talk'. Say a word, for example, 'term', and ask them to segment it using 'robot talk' first to their partner and then all together.

Read it

■ Write the following words on the board or easel and show the children: 'term', 'perm', 'herb'.

■ Ask the children to read the words out loud to their partner. Encourage them to blend the phonemes together.

Write it

■ Say a word containing the phoneme /ur/ with the grapheme 'er', for example, 'herb'. Ask the children to repeat it and then segment it into phonemes using 'robot talk'. Ask the children to first count the phonemes in the word and then to hold up the correct number of fingers. Ask them to write the answer on their individual whiteboards.

2 NEW GRAPHEME 'ear' *(10 mins)*

Hear it

■ Explain to the children that they are going to learn more of the rap.

■ Introduce the new grapheme 'ear' by saying several words that contain it for example 'heard', 'early', 'earth', 'search'.

Say it

■ Say the phoneme /ur/, grapheme 'ear' emphasising correct articulation, and then show the children the corresponding phoneme picture card and mnemonic phrase, 'Search the earth'. Repeat it several times.

■ Say the letter names of the new grapheme: 'EAR' and introduce the action (pretend to search and peer in the distance).

■ Now say the full rap for this grapheme and ask the children to do the action: 'ear' 'ear' Search the earth EAR.

■ Using several words containing the phoneme /ur/, grapheme 'ear', say these slowly in 'robot talk' for example: /ear/th/, /s/ear/ch/, /h/ear/d/ and ask the children to blend the phonemes into words and tell their partners.

■ Now ask the children to speak in 'robot talk'. Say a word, for example, 'earth', and ask them to segment it using 'robot talk' to their partner.

Read it

■ Write words that contain the phoneme /ur/, grapheme 'ear', on the easel or board (for example: 'heard', 'early', 'search') and ask the children to read out the phonemes by blending them together with their partner. Ensure that the children can identify the grapheme 'ear' and understand that three letters make the sound (a trigraph).

■ Display the picture card of the grapheme 'ear' on the wall underneath the graphemes 'er', 'ir' and 'ur' to build up the Phoneme–grapheme chart for the vowel phonemes. Ask the children to tell you the graphemes for the phoneme /ur/ and repeat the mnemonic phrase for 'ear'.

Write it

■ Say a word containing the phoneme /ur/, grapheme 'ear'. Ask the children to repeat it and then segment it into phonemes using 'robot talk', for example: 'search' – /s/ear/ch/. Ask the children to first count the phonemes in the word and then to hold up the correct number of fingers.

■ Now say the word again and ask them to write it on their whiteboards and underline the grapheme that represents the phoneme /ur/.

■ Ask the children to tell you the graphemes for the phoneme /ur/. Encourage them to refer to the Phoneme-grapheme chart on the wall to support spelling.

STAGE THREE: LESSON PLANS

LESSON 80 'or'

1 REVIEW (5 mins)

Hear it

■ Review the long vowel phonemes taught so far by saying the vowel rap in a lively fun way.

■ Help the children to practise hearing the sounds by reading a range of words, some of which contain the phoneme /ur/, graphemes 'ur', 'ir', 'er', 'and 'ear', and some that do not, for example: 'fur', 'girl', 'heard', 'car', 'term' 'earth', 'early', 'far'. Ask them to put their hands up every time they hear the phoneme /ur/.

Say it

■ Say several words containing the long vowel phonemes slowly in 'robot talk', for example: /h/ear/d/, /ear/th/, /s/ear/ch/. Ask the children to blend the phonemes into words.

■ Now ask the children to speak in 'robot talk'. Say a word, for example, 'earth', and ask them to segment it using 'robot talk'.

Read it

■ Write the following words on the board or easel and show the children: 'search', 'earth', 'heard'.

■ Ask the children to read the words out loud to their partner. Encourage them to blend the phonemes.

Write it

■ Say a word containing the phoneme /ur/ with the grapheme 'ear', for example: 'earth'. Ask the children to repeat it and then segment it into phonemes using 'robot talk'. Ask the children to count the phonemes in the word and to hold up the correct number of fingers, then to write it on their whiteboards.

2 NEW GRAPHEME 'or' (10 mins)

Hear it

■ Explain to the children that they are going to learn more of the rap.

■ Introduce the new grapheme 'or' by saying several words that contain it for example 'work', 'worm'.

Say it

■ Say the phoneme /ur/, grapheme 'or', emphasising correct articulation and then show the children the corresponding phoneme picture card and mnemonic phrase, 'Work, work, work'. Repeat it several times.

■ Say the letter names of the new grapheme: 'OR' and introduce the action (pretend to write fast).

■ Now say the full rap for this grapheme and do the action: 'or' 'or' Work, work, work OR.

■ Using several words containing the phoneme /ur/, grapheme 'or', say these slowly in 'robot talk' for example, /w/or/m/, /w/or/d/ /w/or/s/e/ and ask the children to blend the phonemes into words and tell their partners.

■ Now ask the children to speak in 'robot talk'. Say a word (for example: 'worm') and ask them to segment it using 'robot talk' to their partner.

Read it

■ Write words that contain the phoneme /ur/, grapheme 'or, on the easel or board (for example: 'word', 'work', 'worth') and ask the children to read out the phonemes by blending them together with their partner. Ensure that the children can identify the grapheme 'or'.

■ Display the picture card of the grapheme 'or' on the wall underneath the graphemes 'ear', 'er', 'ir' and 'ur' to build up the Phoneme–grapheme chart.

Write it

■ Say a word containing the phoneme /ur/, grapheme 'or'. Ask the children to repeat it and then segment it into phonemes using 'robot talk'.

■ Now say the word again and ask them to write it on their whiteboards and underline the grapheme that represents the phoneme /ur/.

LESSON 81
REVISE PHONEMES TAUGHT

■ Please note that this week there are five graphemes to be taught which will take up the whole week. Therefore, to fit in this revision lesson to revise all phonemes and corresponding graphemes taught in this week (following the format from Revision Lessons 39/40 on page 120), you may wish to fit in this revision lesson straight after the final lesson of the week. Alternatively, spend the following week revising all the phonemes and corresponding graphemes taught so far, and start with the next phoneme lessons at the beginning of a new week.

STAGE THREE: LESSON PLANS

LESSON 82 'au'

1 REVIEW (5 mins)

Hear it
■ Review the long vowel phonemes taught so far by saying the vowel rap in a lively fun way with the children.

■ Help the children to practise hearing the sounds by choosing one of the long vowel sounds taught so far. Say a range of words, some which contain the phoneme and some which do not. Ask the children to put up their hand when they hear the appropriate phoneme.

Say it
■ Say several words containing the long vowel phonemes taught so far slowly in 'robot talk', for example: /w/or/m/, /h/ear/d/, /b/ur/n/, /f/ir/, /t/er/m/. Ask the children to blend the phonemes into words and tell their partners.

■ Now ask the children to speak in 'robot talk'. Say a word, for example, 'work', and ask them to segment it using 'robot talk' first to their partner and then all together.

Read it
■ Write the following words on the board or easel and show the children: 'word', 'herb', 'early', 'shirt', 'hurl'.

■ Ask the children to read the words out loud to their partner. Encourage them to blend the phonemes.

Write it
■ Say a word containing the phoneme /ur/ with the grapheme 'or', for example 'word'. Ask the children to repeat it and then segment it into phonemes using 'robot talk'. Ask the children to first count the phonemes in the word and then to hold up the correct number of fingers. Ask them to write the answer on their individual whiteboards.

2 NEW PHONEME /au/ GRAPHEME 'au'
(10 mins)

Hear it
■ Explain to the children that they are going to learn more of the rap.

■ Introduce the new phoneme /au/, grapheme 'au', by saying several words that contain it for example 'haul', 'maul', 'sauce', 'pause', 'autumn'.

Say it
■ Say the phoneme /au/, grapheme 'au', emphasising correct articulation, and then show the children the corresponding phoneme picture card and mnemonic phrase, 'Sauce, lots of sauce'. Ask the children to repeat it several times with you.

■ Say the letter names of the new grapheme: 'AU' and introduce the action (pretend to pat the bottom of the sauce bottle).

■ Now say the full rap for this grapheme and ask the children to do the action: 'au' 'au' Sauce, lots of sauce AU.

■ Using several words containing the phoneme /au/, grapheme 'au', say these slowly in 'robot talk' (for example: /s/au/c/e/, /c/au/s/e/, /p/au/s/e/) and ask the children to blend the phonemes into words and tell their partners.

■ Now ask the children to talk in 'robot talk'. Say a word, for example, 'August', and ask them to segment it using 'robot talk' to their partner.

Read it
■ Write words that contain the phoneme /au/, grapheme 'au', on the easel or board (for example: 'autumn', 'Paul', 'maul', 'cause') and ask the children to read out the phonemes by blending them together with their partner. Ensure that the children can identify the grapheme 'au'.

■ Display the picture card of the grapheme 'au' on the wall beginning a new column to build up the Phoneme–grapheme chart for the vowel phonemes. Ask the children to tell you the grapheme for the phoneme /au/ and say the mnemonic phrase for 'au'.

Write it
■ Say a word containing the phoneme /au/, grapheme 'au'. Ask the children to repeat it and then segment it into phonemes using 'robot talk'. Ask the children to first count the phonemes in the word and then to hold up the correct number of fingers.

■ Now say the word again and ask them to write it on their whiteboards and underline the grapheme that represents the phoneme /au/.

■ Ask the children to tell you the graphemes for the phoneme /au/. Encourage them to refer to the Phoneme–grapheme chart to support spelling.

LESSON 83 'or'

1 REVIEW (5 mins)
Hear it
■ Review the long vowel phonemes taught so far by saying the vowel rap in a lively fun way with the children.

■ Help the children to practise hearing the sounds by reading a range of words, some of which contain the phoneme /au/, grapheme 'au' and some that do not, for example: 'sauce', 'clue', 'autumn', 'girl', 'maul', 'burn', 'far', 'haul', 'put', 'August'. Ask them to put their hands up every time they hear the phoneme /au/.

Say it
■ Say several words containing the long vowel phonemes slowly in 'robot talk', for example: /s/au/ce/, /au/t/u/mn/, /m/au/l/. Ask the children to blend the phonemes into words and tell their partners.

■ Now ask the children to talk in 'robot talk'. Say a word, for example, 'haul', and ask them to segment it using 'robot talk' first to their partner and then all together.

Read it
■ Write the following words on the board or easel and show the children: 'August', 'sauce', 'haul', 'launch'.

■ Ask the children to read the words out loud to their partner. Encourage them to blend the phonemes together.

Write it
■ Say a word containing the phoneme /au/ with the grapheme 'au', for example, 'maul'. Ask the children to repeat it and then segment it into phonemes using 'robot talk'. Ask the children to first count the phonemes in the word and then to hold up the correct number of fingers. Ask them to write the answer on their individual whiteboards.

2 NEW GRAPHEME 'or' (10 mins)
Hear it
■ Explain to the children that they are going to learn more of the rap.
■ Introduce the new grapheme 'or' by saying several

words that contain it for example 'horn', 'fork', 'born', 'corn', 'horse'.

Say it
■ Say the phoneme /au/, grapheme 'or', emphasising correct articulation and then show the children the corresponding phoneme picture card and mnemonic phrase, 'The horn is worn'. Ask the children to repeat it several times with you.

■ Say the letter names of the new grapheme: 'OR' and introduce the action (Pretend to look at an animal's horn).

■ Now say the full rap for this grapheme and ask the children to do the action: 'or' 'or' The horn is worn OR.

■ Using several words containing the phoneme /au/, grapheme 'or', say these slowly in 'robot talk' for example: /b/or/n/, /c/or/n/, /h/or/n/ and ask the children to blend the phonemes into words and tell their partners.

■ Now ask the children to speak in 'robot talk'. Say a word, for example, 'born', and ask them to segment it using 'robot talk' to their partner.

Read it
■ Write words that contain the phoneme /au/, grapheme 'or', on the easel or board (for example: 'horn', 'fork', 'horse') and ask the children to read out the phonemes by blending them together with their partner. Ensure that the children can identify the grapheme 'or'.

■ Display the picture card of the grapheme 'or' on the wall underneath the grapheme 'au' to build up the Phoneme–grapheme chart for the vowel phonemes. Ask the children to tell you the graphemes for the phoneme /au/ and say the mnemonic phrase for 'or'.

Write it
■ Say a word containing the phoneme /au/, grapheme 'or'. Ask the children to repeat it and then segment into phonemes using 'robot talk', for example: 'horn' – /h/or/n/. Ask the children to first count the phonemes in the word and then to hold up the correct number of fingers.

■ Now say the word again and ask them to write it on their whiteboards and underline the grapheme that represents the phoneme /au/.

■ Ask the children to tell you the graphemes for the phoneme /au/. Encourage them to refer to the Phoneme–grapheme chart to support spelling.

LESSON 84 'oor'

1 REVIEW *(5 mins)*
Hear it
■ Review the long vowel phonemes taught so far by saying the vowel rap in a lively fun way with the children.
■ Help the children to practise hearing the sounds by saying a range of words, some of which contain the phoneme /au/ graphemes 'au' and 'or', and some which do not, for example: 'born', 'time', 'light', 'girl', 'horn', 'far', 'corn'. Ask them to put their hands up every time they hear the phoneme /au/.

Say it
■ Say several words containing the long vowel phonemes slowly in 'robot talk', for example: /s/t/or/m/, /b/or/n/, /h/or/se/. Ask the children to blend the phonemes into words and tell their partners.
■ Now ask the children to speak in 'robot talk'. Say a word, for example, 'fork', and ask them to segment it using 'robot talk' first to their partner and then all together.

Read it
■ Write the following words on the board or easel and show the children: 'corn', 'fork'.
■ Ask the children to read the words out loud to their partner. Encourage them to blend the phonemes together.

Write it
■ Say a word containing the phoneme /au/ with the grapheme 'or', for example: 'storm'. Ask the children to repeat it and then segment it into phonemes using 'robot talk'. Ask the children to first count the phonemes in the word and then to hold up the correct number of fingers. Ask them to write the answer on their individual whiteboards.

2 NEW GRAPHEME 'oor' *(10 mins)*
Hear it
■ Explain to the children that they are going to learn more of the rap.
■ Introduce the new grapheme 'oor' by saying several words that contain it for example 'moor', 'door', 'floor', 'outdoor'.

Say it
■ Say the phoneme /au/, grapheme 'oor', emphasising correct articulation and then show the children the corresponding phoneme picture card and mnemonic phrase, 'Door on the moor'. Ask the children to repeat it several times with you.
■ Say the letter names of the new grapheme: 'OOR' and introduce the action (pretend to open a door).
■ Now say the full rap for this grapheme and ask the children to do the action: 'oor' 'oor' Door on the moor OOR.
■ Using several words containing the phoneme /au/, grapheme 'oor', say these slowly in 'robot talk' (for example: /d/oor/, /m/oor/, /f/l/oor/) and ask the children to blend the phonemes into words and tell their partners.
■ Now ask the children to speak in 'robot talk'. Say a word, for example, 'moor', and ask them to segment it using 'robot talk' to their partner.

Read it
■ Write words that contain the phoneme /au/, grapheme 'oor', on the easel or board (for example: 'floor', 'door', 'moor') and ask the children to read out the phonemes by blending them together with their partner. Ensure that the children can identify the grapheme 'oor' and understand that it is written with three letters which is called a trigraph.
■ Display the picture card of the grapheme 'oor' on the wall underneath the graphemes 'or' and 'au', to build up the Phoneme-grapheme chart for the vowel phonemes. Ask the children to tell you the graphemes for the phoneme /au/ and repeat the mnemonic phrase for 'oor'.

Write it
■ Say a word containing the phoneme /au/, grapheme 'oor'. Ask the children to repeat it and then segment it into phonemes using 'robot talk', for example: 'door' – /d/oor/. Ask the children to first count the phonemes in the word and then to hold up the correct number of fingers.
■ Now say the word again and ask them to write it on their whiteboards and underline the grapheme that represents the phoneme /au/.
■ Ask the children to tell you the graphemes for the phoneme /au/. Encourage them to refer to the Phoneme-grapheme chart on the wall to support spelling.

LESSON 85 'ar'

1 REVIEW *(5 mins)*

Hear it

■ Review the long vowel phonemes taught so far by saying the vowel rap in a lively fun way with the children.

■ Help the children to practise hearing the sounds by reading a range of words, some of which contain the phoneme /au/, graphemes 'au', 'or' and 'oor', and some that do not, for example: 'door', 'light', 'girl', 'floor', 'put', 'moor'. Ask them to put their hands up every time they hear the phoneme /au/.

Say it

■ Say several words containing the long vowel phoneme slowly in 'robot talk', for example: /f/l/oor/, /d/oor/, /m/oor/. Ask the children to blend the phonemes into words and tell their partners.

■ Now ask the children to speak in 'robot talk'. Say a word (for example, 'door') and ask them to segment it using 'robot talk' first to their partner and then all together.

Read it

■ Write the following words on the board or easel and show the children: 'floor', 'moor', 'door'.

■ Ask the children to read the words out loud to their partner. Encourage them to blend the phonemes.

Write it

■ Say a word containing the phoneme /au/, grapheme 'oor', for example: 'floor'. Ask the children to repeat it and then segment it into phonemes using 'robot talk'. Ask the children to count the phonemes in the word and to hold up the correct number of fingers. Then write the answer on their individual whiteboards.

2 NEW GRAPHEME 'ar' *(10 mins)*

Hear it

■ Explain to the children that they are going to learn more of the rap.

■ Introduce the new grapheme by saying several words that contain it, for example: 'war', 'warn'.

Say it

■ Say the phoneme /au/, grapheme 'ar', emphasising correct articulation, and then show the children the corresponding phoneme picture card and mnemonic, 'Warn the ward'. Repeat it several times.

■ Say the letter names of the new grapheme: 'AR' and introduce the action (place your hands to your mouth as if shouting to warn people).

■ Now say the full rap for this grapheme and ask the children to do the action: 'ar' 'ar' Warn the ward AR.

■ Using several words containing the phoneme /au/, grapheme 'ar', say these slowly in 'robot talk' (for example: /w/ar/n/, /w/ar/) and ask the children to blend the phonemes into words and tell their partners.

■ Now ask the children to speak in 'robot talk'. Say a word, for example, 'war', and ask them to segment it using 'robot talk' to their partner.

Read it

■ Write words that contain the phoneme /au/, grapheme 'ar', on the easel or board and ask the children to read out the phonemes by blending them together with their partner. Ensure that the children can identify the grapheme 'ar'.

■ Display the picture card of the grapheme 'ar' on the wall underneath the graphemes 'oor', 'or' and 'au' to build up the Phoneme-grapheme chart for the vowel phonemes. Ask the children to tell you the graphemes for the phoneme /au/ and repeat the mnemonic phrase for 'ar'.

Write it

■ Say a word containing the phoneme /au/, grapheme 'ar'. Ask the children to repeat it and then segment into phonemes using 'robot talk', for example: 'ward'. Ask the children to first count the phonemes in the word and then to hold up the correct number of fingers.

■ Now say the word again and ask them to write it on their whiteboards and underline the grapheme that represents the phoneme /au/.

■ Ask the children to tell you the graphemes for the phoneme /au/. Encourage them to refer to the Phoneme-grapheme chart to support spelling.

> **LESSON 86**
> **REVISE PHONEMES TAUGHT**
> ■ Follow the format from Revision Lessons 39/40 on page 120 to revise all phonemes and corresponding graphemes taught in the week.

LESSON 87 'aw'

1 REVIEW (5 mins)

Hear it

■ Review the long vowel phonemes taught so far by saying the vowel rap in a lively fun way with the children.

■ Help the children to practise hearing the sounds by choosing one of the long vowel sounds taught so far. Say a range of words, some which contain the phoneme and some which do not. Ask the children to put up their hand when they hear the appropriate phoneme.

Say it

■ Using several words containing the phonemes taught, say these slowly in 'robot talk', for example: /w/ar/, /h/au/l/, /f/or/k/, /f/l/oor/. Ask the children to blend the phonemes into words and tell their partners.

■ Now ask the children to speak in 'robot talk'. Say a word, for example: 'warn' and ask them to segment it using 'robot talk' first to their partner and then all together.

Read it

■ Write the following words on the board or easel and show the children: 'ward', 'moor', 'corn' and 'August'.

■ Ask the children to read the words out loud to their partner. Encourage them to blend the phonemes together.

Write it

■ Say a word containing the phoneme /au/ with the grapheme 'ar', for example: 'war'. Ask the children to repeat it and then segment it into phonemes using 'robot talk'. Ask the children to first count the phonemes in the word and then to hold up the correct number of fingers. Ask them to write the answer on their individual whiteboards.

2 NEW GRAPHEME 'aw' (10 mins)

Hear it

■ Explain to the children that they are going to learn more of the rap.

■ Introduce the new grapheme 'aw' by saying several words that contain it for example 'claw', 'draw', 'paw', 'dawn', 'lawn', 'yawn', 'saw'.

Say it

■ Say the phoneme /au/, grapheme 'aw', emphasising correct articulation, and then show the children the corresponding phoneme picture card and mnemonic phrase, 'Draw the claw'. Ask the children to repeat it several times with you.

■ Say the letter names of the new grapheme: 'AW' and introduce the action (hold up fingers and bend like a claw).

■ Now say the full rap for this grapheme and ask the children to do the action: 'aw' 'aw' Draw the claw AW.

■ Using several words containing the phoneme /au/, grapheme 'aw', say these slowly in 'robot talk' (for example: /p/aw/, /s/aw/) and ask the children to blend the phonemes into words and tell their partners.

■ Now ask the children to speak in 'robot talk'. Say a word, for example, 'yawn', and ask them to segment it using 'robot talk' to their partner.

Read it

■ Write words that contain the phoneme /au/, grapheme 'aw', on the easel or board (for example: 'dawn', 'draw', 'saw', 'paw') and ask the children to read out the phonemes by blending them together with their partner. Ensure that the children can identify the grapheme 'aw'.

■ Display the picture card of the grapheme 'aw' on the wall underneath the graphemes 'ar', 'oor', 'or' and 'au' to build up the Phoneme–grapheme chart for the vowel phonemes. Ask the children to tell you the graphemes for the phoneme /au/ and repeat the mnemonic phrase for 'aw'.

Write it

■ Say a word containing the phoneme /au/, grapheme 'aw'. Ask the children to repeat it and then segment into phonemes using 'robot talk', for example: 'draw' – /d/r/aw/. Ask the children to first count the phonemes in the word and then to hold up the correct number of fingers.

■ Now say the word again and ask them to write it on their whiteboards and underline the grapheme that represents the phoneme /au/.

■ Ask the children to tell you the graphemes for the phoneme /au/. Encourage them to refer to the Phoneme–grapheme chart to support spelling.

LESSON 88 'a'

1 REVIEW (5 mins)
Hear it
■ Review the long vowel phonemes taught so far by saying the vowel rap in a lively fun way with the children.

■ Help the children to practise hearing the sounds by reading a range of words, some of which contain the phoneme /au/, grapheme 'aw' and some that do not, for example: 'draw', 'time', 'claw', 'light', 'girl', 'far', 'put'. Ask them to put their hands up every time they hear the phoneme /au/.

Say it
■ Say several words containing the long vowel phonemes slowly in 'robot talk', for example: /c/l/aw/, /y/aw/n/, /r/aw/. Ask the children to blend the phonemes into words and tell their partners.

■ Now ask the children to speak in 'robot talk'. Say a word, for example, 'dawn', and ask them to segment it using 'robot talk' first to their partner and then all together.

Read it
■ Write the following words on the board or easel and show the children: 'paw', 'claw', 'draw', 'lawn'.

■ Ask the children to read the words out loud to their partner. Encourage them to blend the phonemes together.

Write it
■ Say a word containing the phonemes /au/ with the grapheme 'aw', for example: 'paw'. Ask the children to repeat it and then segment it into phonemes using 'robot talk'. Ask the children to first count the phonemes in the word and then to hold up the correct number of fingers. Ask them to write the answer on their individual whiteboards.

2 NEW GRAPHEME 'a' (10 mins)
Hear it
■ Explain to the children that they are going to learn more of the rap.

■ Introduce the new grapheme 'a' by saying several words that contain it, for example: 'ball', 'call', 'bald', 'fall'.

Say it
■ Say the phoneme /au/, grapheme 'a' emphasising correct articulation, and then show the children the corresponding phoneme picture card and mnemonic phrase, 'Call the ball'. Ask the children to repeat it several times with you.

■ Say the letter name of the new grapheme: 'A' and introduce the action (pretend to hold up a ball).

■ Now say the full rap for this grapheme and ask the children to do the action: 'a' 'a' Call the ball A.

■ Using several words containing the phoneme /au/, grapheme 'a', say these slowly in 'robot talk' (for example: /b/a/l/d/) and ask the children to blend the phonemes into words and tell their partners.

■ Now ask the children to speak in 'robot talk'. Say a word, for example, 'fall', and ask them to segment it using 'robot talk' to their partner.

Read it
■ Write words that contain the phoneme /au/, grapheme 'a', on the easel or board (for example: 'fall', 'call', 'ball', 'bald') and ask the children to read out the phonemes by blending them together with their partner. Ensure that the children can identify the grapheme 'a'.

■ Display the picture card of the grapheme 'a' on the wall underneath the graphemes 'aw', 'ar', 'oor', 'or' and 'au' to build up the Phoneme–grapheme chart for the vowel phonemes. Ask the children to tell you the graphemes for the phoneme /au/ and repeat the mnemonic phrase for 'a'.

Write it
■ Say a word containing the phoneme /au/, grapheme 'a'. Ask the children to repeat it and then segment it into phonemes using 'robot talk', for example: 'ball' – /b/a/ll/. Ask the children to first count the phonemes in the word and then to hold up the correct number of fingers.

■ Now say the word again and ask them to write it on their whiteboards and underline the grapheme that represents the phoneme /au/.

■ Ask the children to tell you the graphemes for the phoneme /au/. Encourage them to refer to the Phoneme–grapheme chart on the wall to support spelling.

LESSON 89 'ar'

1 REVIEW *(5 mins)*

Hear it

■ Review the long vowel phonemes taught so far by saying the vowel rap in a lively fun way with the children.

■ Help the children to practise hearing the sounds by saying a range of words, some of which contain the phoneme /au/, graphemes 'a' and 'aw', and some that do not, for example: 'put', 'draw', 'stew', 'call', 'ball', 'true'. Ask them to put their hands up every time they hear the phoneme /au/.

Say it

■ Say several words containing the long vowel phonemes slowly in 'robot talk', for example: /b/a/ll/. Ask the children to blend the phonemes into words and tell their partners.

■ Now ask the children to speak in 'robot talk'. Say a word, for example, 'fall' and ask them to segment it using 'robot talk' first to their partner and then all together.

Read it

■ Write the following words on the board or easel and show the children: 'call', 'ball', 'fall'.

■ Ask the children to read the words out loud to their partner. Encourage them to blend the phonemes.

Write it

■ Say a word containing the phoneme /au/ with the grapheme 'a', for example: 'fall'. Ask the children to repeat it and segment it using 'robot talk'. Ask them to count the phonemes and to hold up the correct number of fingers. Then write it on the whiteboard.

2 NEW PHONEME /ar/ GRAPHEME 'ar'

(10 mins)

Hear it

■ Explain to the children that they are going to learn more of the rap.

■ Introduce the new phoneme /ar/, grapheme 'ar', by saying several words that contain it.

Say it

■ Say the phoneme /ar/, grapheme 'ar', emphasising correct articulation, and then show the children the corresponding phoneme picture card and mnemonic phrase, 'Park the car'. Repeat several times.

■ Say the letter names of the new grapheme: 'AR' and introduce the action (pretend to drive a car with your hands on the wheel).

■ Now say the full rap for this grapheme and ask the children to do the action: 'ar' 'ar' Park the car AR.

■ Using several words containing the phoneme /ar/, grapheme 'ar', say these slowly in 'robot talk' and ask the children to blend the phonemes into words and tell their partners.

■ Now ask the children to speak in 'robot talk'. Say a word, for example, 'park', and ask them to segment it using 'robot talk' to their partner.

Read it

■ Write words that contain the phoneme /ar/, grapheme 'ar', on the easel or board and ask the children to read out the phonemes by blending them together with their partner. Ensure that the children can identify the grapheme 'ar'.

■ Display the picture card of the grapheme 'ar' on the wall beginning a new column to build up the Phoneme–grapheme chart for the vowel phonemes. Ask the children to tell you the grapheme for the phoneme /ar/ and say the mnemonic phrase for 'ar'.

Write it

■ Say a word containing the phoneme /ar/, grapheme 'ar'. Ask the children to repeat it and then segment into phonemes using 'robot talk', for example: 'farm' – /f/ar/m/. Ask the children to first count the phonemes in the word and then to hold up the correct number of fingers.

■ Now say the word and ask them to write it on their whiteboards and underline the grapheme that represents the phoneme /ar/.

■ Ask the children to tell you the grapheme for the phoneme /ar/. Encourage them to refer to the Phoneme–grapheme chart to support spelling.

LESSON 90/91
REVISE PHONEMES TAUGHT

■ Follow the format from Revision Lessons 39/40 on page 120 to revise all phonemes and corresponding graphemes taught in the week.

■ Ensure that you Assessment 3 on page 187, before continuing with Stage 3.

LESSON 92 'air'

1 REVIEW *(5 mins)*

Hear it

■ Review the long vowel phonemes taught so far by saying the vowel rap in a lively fun way with the children.

■ Help the children to practise hearing the sounds by choosing one of the long vowel sounds taught so far. Say a range of words, some which contain the phoneme and some which do not. Ask the children to put up their hand when they hear the appropriate phoneme.

Say it

■ Say several words containing the long vowel phonemes taught so far slowly in 'robot talk', for example: /d/r/aw/, /c/a/ll/, /d/ar/k/. Ask the children to blend the phonemes into words and tell their partners.

■ Now ask the children to speak in 'robot talk'. Say a word, for example, 'far', and ask them to segment it using 'robot talk' first to their partner and then all together.

Read it

■ Write the following words on the board or easel and show the children: 'fall', 'paw', 'far'.

■ Ask the children to read the words out loud to their partner. Encourage them to blend the phonemes together.

Write it

■ Say a word containing the phoneme /ar/ with the grapheme 'ar', for example: 'park'. Ask the children to repeat it and then segment it into phonemes using 'robot talk'. Ask the children to first count the phonemes in the word and then to hold up the correct number of fingers. Ask them to write the answer on their individual whiteboards.

2 NEW PHONEME /air/ GRAPHEME 'air'
(10 mins)

Hear it

■ Explain to the children that they are going to learn more of the rap.

■ Introduce the phoneme /air/ with grapheme 'air' by saying several words that contain it for example 'fair', 'lair', 'chair', 'hair', 'stair'.

Say it

■ Say the phoneme /air/, grapheme 'air', emphasising correct articulation, and then show the children the corresponding phoneme picture card and mnemonic phrase, 'Fair hair'. Ask the children to repeat it several times with you.

■ Say the letter names of the new grapheme: 'AIR' and introduce the action (pretend to brush hair).

■ Now say the full rap for this grapheme and ask the children to do the action: 'air' 'air' Fair hair AIR.

■ Using several words containing the phoneme /air/, grapheme 'air', say these slowly in 'robot talk' (for example: /p/air/r/, /l/air/r/) and ask the children to blend the phonemes into words and tell their partners.

■ Now ask the children to speak in 'robot talk'. Say a word, for example, 'chair', and ask them to segment it using 'robot talk' to their partner.

Read it

■ Write words that contain the phoneme /air/, grapheme 'air', on the easel or board (for example: 'fair', 'stair', 'pair', 'lair') and ask the children to read out the phonemes by blending them together with their partner. Ensure that the children can identify the grapheme 'air' and understand that we write it with three letters which is called a trigraph.

■ Display the picture card of the grapheme 'air' on the wall beginning a new column to build up the Phoneme–grapheme chart for the vowel phonemes. Ask the children to tell you the grapheme for the phoneme /air/ and say the mnemonic phrase for 'air'.

Write it

■ Say a word containing the phoneme /air/, grapheme 'air'. Ask the children to repeat it and then segment into phonemes using 'robot talk', for example: 'stair'. Ask the children to first count the phonemes in the word and then to hold up the correct number of fingers.

■ Now say the word again and ask them to write it on their whiteboards and underline the grapheme that represents the phoneme /air/.

■ Ask the children to tell you the grapheme for the phoneme /air/. Encourage them to refer to the Phoneme–grapheme chart on the wall to support spelling.

LESSON 93 'ear'

1 REVIEW *(5 mins)*

Hear it

■ Review the long vowel phonemes taught so far by saying the vowel rap in a lively fun way with the children.

■ Help the children to practise hearing the sounds by saying a range of words, some of which contain the phoneme /air/, grapheme 'air' and some that do not for example: 'fair', 'now', 'chair', 'join', 'lair', 'light', 'foil', 'pair', 'boil', 'stair'. Ask them to put their hands up every time they hear the phoneme /air/.

Say it

■ Say several words containing the long vowel phonemes slowly in 'robot talk', for example: /s/t/air/, /p/air/, /l/air/. Ask the children to blend the phonemes into words and tell their partners.

■ Now ask the children to speak in 'robot talk'. Say a word, for example, 'fair', and ask them to segment it using 'robot talk' first to their partner and then all together.

Read it

■ Write the following words on the board or easel and show the children: 'pair', 'hair', 'fair', 'chair', 'stair'.

■ Ask the children to read the words out loud to their partner. Encourage them to blend the phonemes.

Write it

■ Say a word containing the phoneme /air/ with the grapheme 'air', for example: 'pair'. Ask the children to repeat it and then segment it into phonemes using 'robot talk'. Ask the children to count the phonemes in the word and to hold up the correct number of fingers. Then write the answer on their whiteboard.

2 NEW GRAPHEME 'ear' *(10 mins)*

Hear it

■ Explain to the children that they are going to learn more of the rap.

■ Introduce the new grapheme by saying several words that contain it, for example: 'bear', 'pear', 'tear'.

Say it

■ Say the phoneme /air/, grapheme 'ear', emphasising correct articulation, and then show the children the corresponding phoneme picture card and mnemonic phrase, 'Bear in a pear'. Ask the children to repeat it several times with you.

■ Say the letter names of the new grapheme: 'EAR' and introduce the action (point and look amazed).

■ Now say the full rap for this grapheme and ask the children to do the action: 'ear' 'ear' Bear in a pear EAR.

■ Using several words containing the phoneme /air/, grapheme 'ear', say these slowly in 'robot talk' (for example: /w/ear/, /p/ear/, /t/ear/) and ask the children to blend the phonemes into words and tell their partners.

■ Now ask the children to speak in 'robot talk'. Say a word, for example, 'tear', and ask them to segment it using 'robot talk' to their partner.

Read it

■ Write words that contain the phoneme /air/, grapheme 'ear', on the easel or board (for example: 'bear', 'pear', 'tear', 'wear') and ask the children to read out the phonemes by blending them together with their partner. Ensure that the children can identify the grapheme 'ear' and understand that we write it with three letters which is called a trigraph.

■ Display the picture card of the grapheme 'ear' on the wall underneath the grapheme 'air' to build up the Phoneme-grapheme chart for the vowel phonemes. Ask the children to say the graphemes for the phoneme /air/ and say the mnemonic phrase for 'ear'.

Write it

■ Say a word containing the phoneme /air/, grapheme 'ear'. Ask the children to repeat it and then segment into phonemes using 'robot talk', for example: 'pear' – /p/ear/. Ask the children to first count the phonemes in the word and then to hold up the correct number of fingers.

■ Now say the word again and ask them to write it on their whiteboards and underline the grapheme that represents the phoneme /air/.

■ Ask the children to tell you the graphemes for the phoneme /air/. Encourage them to refer to the Phoneme-grapheme chart on the wall to support spelling.

LESSON 94 'are'

1 REVIEW *(5 mins)*

Hear it

■ Review the long vowel phonemes taught so far by saying the vowel rap in a lively fun way with the children.

■ Help the children to practise hearing the sounds by saying a range of words, some of which contain the phoneme /air/, graphemes 'air' and 'ear', and some that do not, for example: 'bear', 'light', 'fair', 'wear', 'boil', 'tear'. Ask them to put their hands up every time they hear the phoneme /air/.

Say it

■ Say several words containing the long vowel phonemes slowly in 'robot talk', for example: /b/ear/, /p/ear/, /t/ear/. Ask the children to blend the phonemes into words and tell their partners.

■ Now ask the children to speak in 'robot talk'. Say a word, for example, 'wear', and ask them to segment it using 'robot talk' first to their partner and then all together.

Read it

■ Write the following words on the board or easel and show the children: 'wear', 'tear', 'bear', 'pear'.

■ Ask the children to read the words out loud to their partner. Encourage them to blend the phonemes.

Write it

■ Say a word containing the phoneme /air/ with the grapheme 'ear', for example, 'wear'. Ask the children to repeat it and then segment it using 'robot talk'. Ask the children to count the phonemes in the word and to hold up the correct number of fingers. Then write the answer on their whiteboard.

2 NEW GRAPHEME 'are' *(10 minutes)*

Hear it

■ Explain to the children that they are going to learn more of the rap.

■ Introduce the new grapheme by saying several words that contain it, for example: 'share', 'dare'.

Say it

■ Say the phoneme /air/, grapheme 'are', emphasising correct articulation, and then show the children the corresponding phoneme picture card and mnemonic phrase, 'Fare share'. Repeat it several times.

■ Say the letter names of the new grapheme: 'ARE' and introduce the action (pretend to give some money).

■ Now say the full rap for this grapheme and ask the children to do the action: 'are' 'are' Fair share ARE.

■ Using several words containing the phoneme /air/, grapheme 'are', say these slowly in 'robot talk' (for example: /sh/are/, /f/are/, /c/are/) and ask the children to blend the phonemes into words and tell their partners.

■ Now ask the children to speak in 'robot talk'. Say a word, for example, 'share', and ask them to segment it using 'robot talk' to their partner.

Read it

■ Write words that contain the phoneme /air/, grapheme 'are', on the easel or board (for example: 'share', 'dare', 'fare') and ask the children to read out the phonemes by blending them together with their partner. Ensure that the children can identify the grapheme 'are' and understand that we write it with three letters (a trigraph).

■ Display the picture card of the grapheme 'are' on the wall underneath the graphemes 'ear' and 'air' to build up the Phoneme-grapheme chart for the vowel phonemes. Ask the children to tell you the graphemes for the phoneme /air/ and repeat the mnemonic phrase for 'are'.

Write it

■ Say a word containing the phoneme /air/, grapheme 'are'. Ask the children to repeat it and then segment into phonemes using 'robot talk', for example: 'dare'. Ask the children to count the phonemes in the word and to hold up the correct number of fingers.

■ Now say the word again and ask them to write it on their whiteboards and underline the grapheme that represents the phoneme /air/.

■ Ask the children to tell you the graphemes for the phoneme /air/.

> ## LESSON 95/96
> ### REVISE PHONEMES TAUGHT
> ■ Follow the format from Revision Lessons 39/ 40 on page 120 to revise all phonemes and corresponding graphemes taught in the week.

LESSON 97 'ear'

1 REVIEW (5 mins)

Hear it
■ Review the long vowel phonemes taught so far by saying the vowel rap in a lively fun way with the children.
■ Help the children to practise hearing the sounds by choosing one of the long vowel sounds taught so far. Say a range of words, some which contain the phoneme and some which do not. Ask the children to put up their hand when they hear the appropriate phoneme.

Say it
■ Say several words containing the phonemes taught so far slowly in 'robot talk', for example: /sh/are/, /p/ear/, /ch/air/. Ask the children to blend the phonemes into words and tell their partners.
■ Now ask the children to speak in 'robot talk'. Say a word, for example, 'share', and ask them to segment it using 'robot talk' first to their partner and then all together.

Read it
■ Write the following words on the board or easel and show the children: 'stair', 'wear', 'fare'.
■ Ask the children to read the words out loud to their partner. Encourage them to blend the phonemes together.

Write it
■ Say a word containing the phoneme /air/ with the grapheme 'are', for example: 'square'. Ask the children to repeat it and then segment it into phonemes using 'robot talk'. Ask the children to count the phonemes in the word and to hold up the correct number of fingers. Then write the answer on their whiteboard.

2 NEW PHONEME /ear/ GRAPHEME 'ear' (10 mins)

Hear it
■ Explain to the children that they are going to learn more of the rap.
■ Introduce the new grapheme 'ear' by saying several words that contain it for example 'fear', 'ear', 'dear', 'rear'.

Say it
■ Say the phoneme /ear/, grapheme 'ear', emphasising correct articulation, and then show the children the corresponding phoneme picture card and mnemonic phrase, 'Hear with your ear'. Ask the children to repeat it several times with you.
■ Say the letter names of the new grapheme: 'EAR' and introduce the action (pull on ear lobe).
■ Now say the full rap for this grapheme and ask the children to do the action: 'ear' 'ear' Hear with your ear EAR.
■ Using several words containing the phoneme /ear/, grapheme 'ear', say these slowly in 'robot talk' (for example: /f/ear/, /h/ear/, /t/ear/) and ask the children to blend the phonemes into words and tell their partners.
■ Now ask the children to speak in 'robot talk'. Say a word, for example, 'fear', and ask them to segment it using 'robot talk' to their partner.

Read it
■ Write words that contain the phoneme /ear/, grapheme 'ear', on the easel or board (for example: 'rear', 'fear', 'dear') and ask the children to read out the phonemes by blending them together with their partner. Ensure that the children can identify the grapheme 'ear' and understand that we write it with three letters which is called a trigraph.
■ Display the picture card of the grapheme 'ear' on the wall beginning a new column to build up the Phoneme–grapheme chart for the vowel phonemes. Ask the children to say the grapheme for the phoneme /ear/ and repeat the mnemonic phrase for 'ear'.

Write it
■ Say a word containing the phoneme 'ear', grapheme 'ear'. Ask the children to repeat it and then segment it into phonemes using 'robot talk', for example: 'fear'. Ask the children to first count the phonemes in the word and then to hold up the correct number of fingers.
■ Now say the word again and ask them to write it on their whiteboards and underline the grapheme that represents the phoneme /ear/.
■ Ask the children to tell you the grapheme for the phoneme /ear/. Encourage them to refer to the Phoneme–grapheme chart on the wall to support spelling.

LESSON 98 'ere'

1 REVIEW *(5 mins)*

Hear it

■ Review the long vowel phonemes taught so far by saying the vowel rap in a lively fun way with the children.

■ Help the children to practise hearing the sounds by saying a range of words, some of which contain the phoneme /ear/, grapheme 'ear' and some that do not, for example: 'fear', 'cow', 'fair', 'dear', 'chair', 'rear', 'bear', 'light', 'ear', 'boil'. Ask them to put their hands up every time they hear the phoneme /ear/.

Say it

■ Say several words containing the long vowel phonemes slowly in 'robot talk', for example: /r/ear/, /d/ear/, /f/ear/. Ask the children to blend the phonemes into words and tell their partners.

■ Now ask the children to speak in 'robot talk'. Say a word, for example, 'tear', and ask them to segment it using 'robot talk' first to their partner and then all together.

Read it

■ Write the following words on the board or easel and show the children: 'fear', 'rear', 'dear'.

■ Ask the children to read the words out loud to their partner. Encourage them to blend the phonemes together.

Write it

■ Say a word containing the phoneme /ear/ with the grapheme 'ear', for example: 'fear'. Ask the children to repeat it and then segment it into phonemes using 'robot talk'. Ask the children to first count the phonemes in the word and then to hold up the correct number of fingers. Ask them to write the answer on their individual whiteboards.

2 NEW GRAPHEME 'ere' *(10 mins)*

Hear it

■ Explain to the children that they are going to learn more of the rap.

■ Introduce the new grapheme 'ere' by saying several words that contain it, for example: 'here', 'sphere', 'mere'.

Say it

■ Say the phoneme /ear/, grapheme 'ere', emphasising correct articulation, and then show the children the corresponding phoneme picture card and mnemonic phrase, 'Here, here'. Ask the children to repeat it several times with you.

■ Say the letter names of the new grapheme: 'ERE' and introduce the action (beckon with your finger).

■ Now say the full rap for this grapheme and ask the children to do the action: 'ere' 'ere' Here, here ERE.

■ Using several words containing the phoneme /ear/, grapheme 'ere', say these slowly in 'robot talk' (for example: /h/ere/, /m/ere/) and ask the children to blend the phonemes into words and tell their partners.

■ Now ask the children to speak in 'robot talk'. Say a word, for example, 'sphere', and ask them to segment it using 'robot talk' to their partner.

Read it

■ Write words that contain the phoneme /ear/, grapheme 'ere', on the easel or board (for example: 'here', 'sphere', 'mere') and ask the children to read out the phonemes by blending them together with their partner. Ensure that the children can identify the grapheme 'ere' and understand that we write it with three letters which is called a trigraph.

■ Display the picture card of the grapheme 'ere' on the wall underneath the grapheme 'ear'. Ask the children to tell you the graphemes for the phoneme /ear/ and repeat the mnemonic phrase for 'ere'.

Write it

■ Say a word containing the phoneme /ear/, grapheme 'ere'. Ask the children to repeat it and then segment into phonemes using 'robot talk', for example: 'here' – /h/ere/. Ask the children to first count the phonemes in the word and then to hold up the correct number of fingers.

■ Now say the word again and ask them to write it on their whiteboards and underline the grapheme that represents the phoneme /ear/.

■ Ask the children to tell you the graphemes for the phoneme /ear/. Encourage them to refer to the Phoneme–grapheme chart on the wall to support spelling.

LESSON 99 'eer'

1 REVIEW (5 mins)
Hear it
■ Review the long vowel phonemes taught so far by saying the vowel rap in a lively fun way with the children.

■ Help the children to practise hearing the sounds by saying a range of words, some of which contain the phoneme /ear/, graphemes 'ear' and 'ere', and some that do not, for example: 'cow', 'fair', 'hear', 'chair', 'light', 'mere', 'boil'. Ask them to put their hands up every time they hear the phoneme /ear/.

Say it
■ Say several words containing the long vowel phonemes slowly in 'robot talk', for example: /m/ere/, /h/ere/. Ask the children to blend the phonemes into words and tell their partners.

■ Now ask the children to speak in 'robot talk'. Say a word, for example, 'here', and ask them to segment it using 'robot talk' first to their partner and then all together.

Read it
■ Write the following words on the board or easel and show the children: 'here', 'sphere', 'mere'.

■ Ask the children to read the words out loud to their partner. Encourage them to blend the phonemes.

Write it
■ Say a word containing the phoneme /ear/ with the grapheme 'ere', for example, 'mere'. Ask the children to repeat it and then segment it into phonemes using 'robot talk'. Ask the children to count the phonemes and to hold up the correct number of fingers. Then write the answer on their whiteboard.

2 NEW GRAPHEME 'eer' (10 mins)
Hear it
■ Explain to the children that they are going to learn more of the rap.

■ Introduce the new grapheme by saying several words that contain it for example 'deer', 'cheer'.

Say it
■ Say the phoneme /ear/, grapheme 'eer', emphasising correct articulation, and then show the children the corresponding phoneme picture card and mnemonic phrase, 'Cheer the deer'. Ask the children to repeat it several times with you.

■ Say the letter names of the new grapheme: 'EER' and introduce the action (clap several times).

■ Now say the full rap for this grapheme and ask the children to do the action: 'eer' 'eer' Cheer the deer EER.

■ Using several words containing the phoneme /ear/, grapheme 'eer', say these slowly in 'robot talk' (for example: /d/eer/, /p/eer/, /j/eer/) and ask the children to blend the phonemes into words and tell their partners.

■ Now ask the children to speak in 'robot talk'. Say a word, for example, 'peer', and ask them to segment it using 'robot talk' to their partner.

Read it
■ Write words that contain the phoneme /ear/, grapheme 'eer', on the easel or board, for example: 'deer', 'cheer', 'jeer' and ask the children to read out the phonemes by blending them together with their partner. Ensure that the children can identify the grapheme 'eer' and understand that we write it with three letters which is called a trigraph.

■ Display the picture card of the grapheme 'eer' on the wall underneath the graphemes 'ere' and 'ear'. Ask the children to tell you the graphemes for the phoneme /ear/ and repeat the mnemonic phrase for 'eer'.

Write it
■ Say a word containing the phoneme /ear/, grapheme 'eer'. Ask the children to repeat it and then segment it using 'robot talk', for example: 'cheer'. Ask the children to count the phonemes in the word and hold up the correct number of fingers.

■ Now say the word again and ask them to write it on their whiteboards and underline the grapheme that represents the phoneme /ear/.

■ Ask the children to tell you the graphemes for the phoneme /ear/.

LESSON 100/101
REVISE PHONEMES TAUGHT
■ Follow the format from Revision Lessons 39/40 on page 120 to revise all phonemes and corresponding graphemes taught in the week.

LESSON 102 'ure'

1 REVIEW (5 mins)

Hear it

■ Review the long vowel phonemes taught so far by saying the vowel rap in a lively fun way with the children.

■ Help the children to practise hearing the sounds by choosing one of the long vowel sounds taught so far. Say a range of words, some which contain the phoneme and some which do not. Ask the children to put up their hand when they hear the appropriate phoneme.

Say it

■ Say several words containing the phonemes taught so far slowly in 'robot talk', for example: /ch/eer/, /h/ere/, /d/ear/. Ask the children to blend the phonemes into words and tell their partners.

■ Now ask the children to speak in 'robot talk'. Say a word, for example, 'peer', and ask them to segment it using 'robot talk' first to their partner and then all together.

Read it

■ Write the following words on the board or easel and show the children: 'cheer', 'here', 'fear'.

■ Ask the children to read the words out loud to their partner. Encourage them to blend the phonemes.

Write it

■ Say a word containing the phoneme /ear/ with the grapheme 'eer', for example: 'steer'. Ask the children to repeat it and then segment it into phonemes using 'robot talk'. Ask the children to first count the phonemes in the word and then to hold up the correct number of fingers. Ask them to write the answer on their individual whiteboards.

2 NEW PHONEME /ure/ GRAPHEME 'ure' (10 mins)

Hear it

■ Explain to the children that they are going to learn more of the rap.

■ Introduce the new grapheme 'ure' by saying several words that contain it for example sure, pure, lure, cure.

Say it

■ Say the phoneme /ure/, grapheme 'ure', emphasising correct articulation, and then show the children the corresponding phoneme picture card and mnemonic phrase, 'Sure, sure'. Ask the children to repeat it several times with you.

■ Say the letter names of the new grapheme: 'URE' and introduce the action (nod your head several times).

■ Now say the full rap for this grapheme and ask the children to do the action: 'ure' 'ure' Sure, sure URE.

■ Using several words containing the phoneme /ure/, grapheme 'ure', say these slowly in 'robot talk' (for example: /c/ure/, /l/ure/, /p/ure/) and ask the children to blend the phonemes into words and tell their partners.

■ Now ask the children to speak in 'robot talk'. Say a word, for example, 'cure', and ask them to segment it using 'robot talk' to their partner.

Read it

■ Write words that contain the phoneme /ure/, grapheme 'ure', on the easel or board (for example: 'pure', 'lure', 'sure') and ask the children to read out the phonemes by blending them together with their partner. Ensure that the children can identify the grapheme 'ure' and understand that we write it with three letters which is called a trigraph.

■ Display the picture card of the grapheme 'ure' on the wall beginning a new column. Ask the children to tell you the grapheme for the phoneme /ure/ and repeat the mnemonic phrase for 'ure'.

Write it

■ Say a word containing the phoneme /ure/, grapheme 'ure'. Ask the children to repeat it and then segment into phonemes using 'robot talk', for example: 'pure'. Ask the children to first count the phonemes in the word and then to hold up the correct number of fingers.

■ Now say the word again and ask them to write it on their whiteboards and underline the grapheme that represents the phoneme /ure/.

■ Ask the children to tell you the grapheme for the phoneme /ure/. Encourage them to refer to the Phoneme-grapheme chart on the wall to support spelling.

LESSON 103 'our'

1 REVIEW *(5 mins)*

Hear it

■ Review the long vowel phonemes taught so far by saying the vowel rap in a lively fun way with the children.

■ Help the children to practise hearing the sounds by saying a range of words, some of which contain the phoneme /ure/, grapheme 'ure' and some that do not, for example: 'sure', 'now', 'pure', 'here', 'chair', 'cure', 'light', 'deer', 'lure'. Ask them to put their hands up every time they hear the phoneme /ure/.

Say it

■ Say several words containing the long vowel phonemes slowly in 'robot talk', for example: /p/ure/, /l/ure/, /c/ure/. Ask the children to blend the phonemes into words and tell their partners.

■ Now ask the children to speak in 'robot talk'. Say a word, for example, 'sure', and ask them to segment it using 'robot talk' first to their partner and then all together.

Read it

■ Write the following words on the board or easel and show the children: 'pure', 'cure', 'lure', 'sure'.

■ Ask the children to read the words out loud to their partner. Encourage them to blend the phonemes together.

Write it

■ Say a word containing the phoneme /ure/ with the grapheme 'ure', for example: 'sure'. Ask the children to repeat it and then segment it into phonemes using 'robot talk'. Ask the children to first count the phonemes in the word and then to hold up the correct number of fingers. Ask them to write the answer on their individual whiteboards.

2 NEW GRAPHEME 'our' *(10 mins)*

Hear it

■ Explain to the children that they are going to learn more of the rap.

■ Introduce the new grapheme by saying several words that contain it for example tour, velour, detour.

Say it

■ Say the phoneme /ure/, grapheme 'our', emphasising correct articulation, and then show the children the corresponding phoneme picture card and mnemonic phrase, 'Tour and detour'. Ask the children to repeat it several times with you.

■ Say the letter names of the new grapheme: 'OUR' and introduce the action (walk in a circle).

■ Now say the full rap for this grapheme and ask the children to do the action: 'our' 'our' Tour and detour OUR.

■ Using several words containing the phoneme /ure/, grapheme 'our', say these slowly in 'robot talk' (for example: /t/our/, /f/our/, /p/our/) and ask the children to blend the phonemes into words and tell their partners.

■ Now ask the children to speak in 'robot talk'. Say a word, for example, 'tour', and ask them to segment it using 'robot talk' to their partner.

Read it

■ Write words that contain the phoneme /ure/, grapheme 'our', on the easel or board (for example: 'tour', 'detour', 'velour') and ask the children to read out the phonemes by blending them together with their partner. Ensure that the children can identify the grapheme 'our' and understand that we write it with three letters which is called a trigraph.

■ Display the picture card of the grapheme 'our' on the wall underneath the grapheme 'ure' to build up the Phoneme–grapheme chart. Ask the children to tell you the graphemes for the phoneme /ure/ and repeat the mnemonic phrase for 'our'.

Write it

■ Say a word containing the phoneme /ure/, grapheme 'our'. Ask them to repeat it and then segment it into phonemes using 'robot talk', for example: 'detour'. Ask the children to first count the phonemes in the word and then to hold up the correct number of fingers.

■ Now say the word again and ask them to write it on their whiteboards and underline the grapheme that represents the phoneme /ure/.

■ Ask the children to tell you the graphemes for the phoneme /ure/. Encourage them to refer to the Phoneme–grapheme chart on the wall to support spelling.

LESSON 104 'er'

❶ REVIEW (5 mins)
Hear it
■ Review the long vowel phonemes taught so far by saying the vowel rap in a lively fun way with the children.

■ Help the children to practise hearing the sounds by saying a range of words, some of which contain the phoneme /ure/, graphemes 'ure' and 'our', and some that do not, for example: 'tour', 'coin', 'pure', 'chair', 'detour'. Ask them to put their hands up every time they hear the phoneme /ure/.

Say it
■ Say several words containing the long vowel phonemes slowly in 'robot talk', for example: /t/our/, /v/e/l/our/, /d/e/t/our/. Ask the children to blend the phonemes into words and tell their partners.

■ Now ask the children to speak in 'robot talk'. Say a word, for example, 'tour', and ask them to segment it using 'robot talk'.

Read it
■ Write the following words on the board or easel and show the children: 'tour', 'velour', 'detour'.

■ Ask the children to read the words out loud to their partner. Encourage them to blend the phonemes.

Write it
■ Say a word containing the phoneme /ure/ with the grapheme 'our', for example, 'tour'. Ask the children to repeat it and then segment into phonemes using robot talk. Then write it on their whiteboard.

❷ NEW PHONEME /er/ GRAPHEME 'er'
(10 mins)
Hear it
■ Explain to the children that they are going to learn the last part of the rap.

■ Introduce the new grapheme by saying several words that contain it: 'sister', 'teacher', 'cover'. Explain that this phoneme is often at the end of words.

Say it
■ Say the phoneme /er/, grapheme 'er', emphasising correct articulation, and then show the children the corresponding phoneme picture card and mnemonic phrase, 'Teacher, doctor, sister too'.

■ Say the letter names of the new grapheme: 'ER' and introduce the action (point to different people).

■ Now say the full rap for this grapheme and ask the children to do the action: 'er' 'er' Teacher, doctor, sister too ER.

■ Using several words containing the phoneme /er/, grapheme 'er', say these slowly in 'robot talk' and ask the children to blend the phonemes into words.

■ Now ask the children to speak in 'robot talk' to their partner. Say a word, for example, 'sister' and ask them to segment it using 'robot talk' to their partner.

Read it
■ Write words that contain the phoneme 'er', grapheme 'er', on the easel or board and ask the children to read out the phonemes by blending them together with their partner. Ensure that the children can identify the grapheme 'er'.

■ Display the picture card of the grapheme 'er' on the wall beginning a new column to build up the Phoneme–grapheme chart for the vowel phonemes.

Write it
■ Say a word containing the phoneme /er/, grapheme 'er'. Ask the children to repeat it and then segment it into phonemes using 'robot talk'.

■ Ask the children to tell you the grapheme for the phoneme /er/. Encourage them to refer to the Phoneme–grapheme chart on the wall to support spelling.

■ Explain that this phoneme can be spelled in many ways: 'er' in sister; 'or' in doctor; 'ar' in collar

■ As alternatives spellings occur, you may also want to explain that we spell this phoneme as 'e' in wooden and 'u' in fungus. We also find it difficult to hear and distinguish as it is in unstressed syllables.

LESSON 105/106
REVISE PHONEMES TAUGHT
■ Follow the format from Revision Lessons 39/40 on page 120 to revise all phonemes and corresponding graphemes taught in the week.

■ Ensure that you carry out Assessment 4 on page 187 after completing Stage 3. Provide more revision and reinforcement lessons for children who are not secure with the phonemes and graphemes taught in Stage 3.

Baby Tiger's cold coat

Words which the children will require support to read:
one, too, said, won't, look

"But I still feel cold," she cried.

2

This is Baby Tiger. See what a bright coat she has?

1

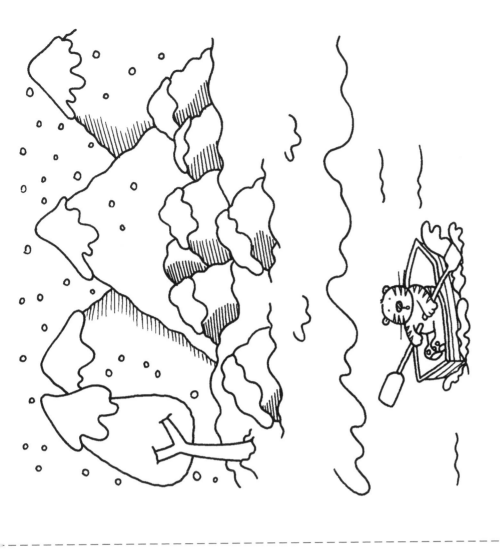

Baby Tiger had to row and row.
It made her hot to row, until...

4

One day, she had an idea.
"I know, I shall go off in the boat and look
for the right coat."

3

But the boat floated back.

9

...she had a coat of snow.
Baby Tiger was too cold to row.

5

"Then I won't feel cold."

8

"I will lie in the sun till my old coat is dry," said Baby Tiger.

7

Woof's bone cake

Words which the children will require support to read:
woof, said

"I should like to put my bone in a cake," he said.

2

Woof the dog had a bone.

1

STAGE THREE: PHOTOCOPIABLE MINIBOOKS ■■▪

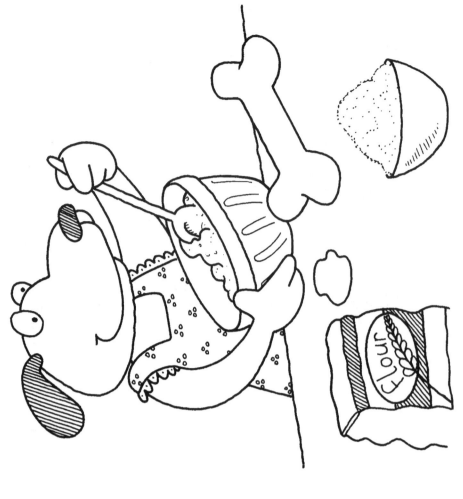

"It would take a long time," he said.

4

Cake

preparation time 45 minutes

eggs

flour

sugar

butter

cooking time 1 hour 10 minutes

Woof got the cook-book to see if he could make a bone cake.

3

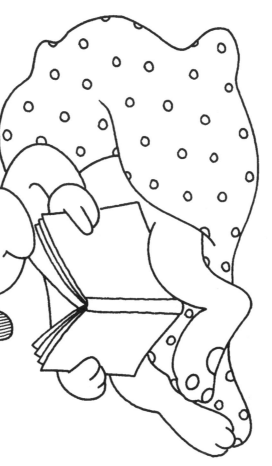

True, it did take a long time to cook!

6

Woof made the cake a nice cube shape.

5

"That was nice," said Woof.

8

But it took no time at all to eat it.

7

The early bird

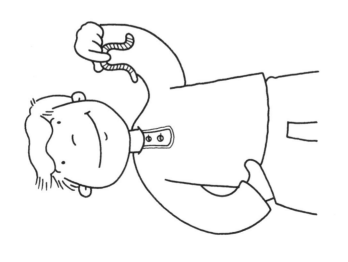

Words which the children will require support to read:
was, watched, said

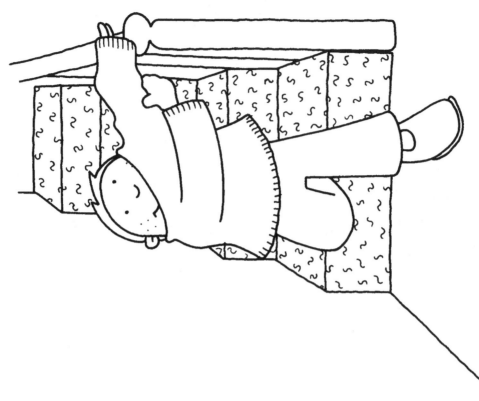

It was still dark when the boy ran out of the house.

2

Paul was going fishing. Lorna was going to join him.

1

The girl, still in her night-shirt, watched Paul from the door.

4

"It's the early bird that catches the first worm," he called to Lorna.

3

■SCHOLASTIC
www.scholastic.co.uk

Lorna got a torch and saw poor Paul on the floor. The boy got up.

6

"It's too early to search for worms," she called. Then she heard a fall and a shout in the

5

"Yes," said Paul, "but didn't I tell *you*... it's the early *boy* that catches the first worm!"

8

"I did warn you," said Lorna. "It's lucky you landed on the lawn."

7

Tom's bear

Words which the children will require support to read:
Mary, said, fix, magic

"Cheer up, Tom, dear," said his sister, Mary.

2

PHONICS: A COMPLETE SYNTHETIC PROGRAMME FOR AGES 4+

■ SCHOLASTIC
www.scholastic.co.uk

Tom's bear had a hole in his ear.

1

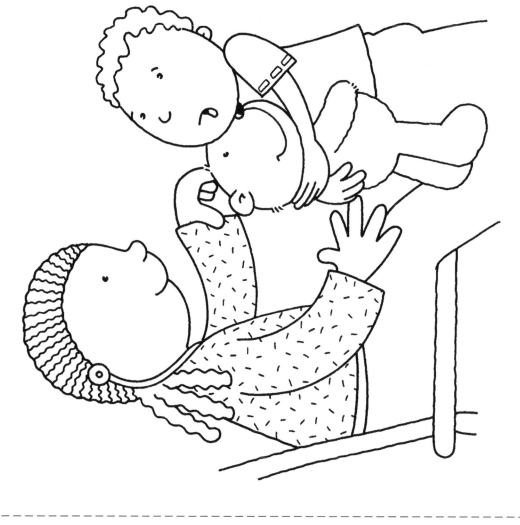

"Are you sure?" said Tom.

4

"I will play Doctor. I'm sure I can fix the hole," said Mary, as she sat on the chair.

3

"All fair wear and tear, young bear!" Mary told Tom's bear.
"I dare say we can cure you."

6

"Never fear! – bring your bear here," said his sister.

5

"Pure magic!" said Tom. "Thank you, Doctor!"

8

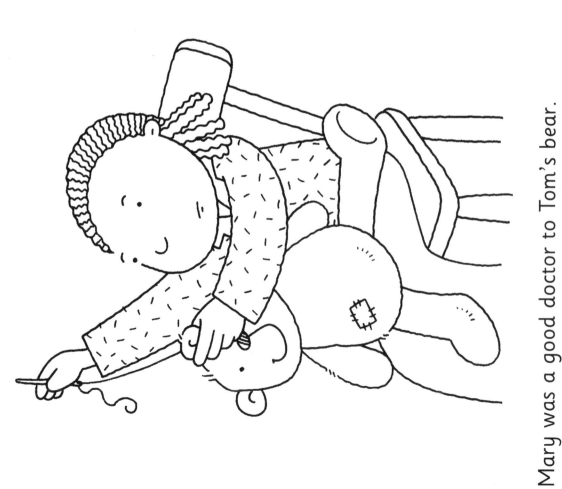

Mary was a good doctor to Tom's bear.
Soon the hole was a mere line in the bear's fur.

7

STAGE THREE:
ASSESSMENT

ASSESSMENTS ❶ to ❹

The following instructions apply to each of the four assessment photocopiables on pages 188, 189, 190 and 191.

The assessments should be carried out according to the following time scales:

> **Assessment 1:** following end of week 12
> **Assessment 2:** following end of week 16
> **Assessment 3:** following end of week 19
> **Assessment 4:** following end of week 22

The instructions below refer to Assessments 1, 2, 3 and 4. Each assessment follows the same format and the children are asked to carry out the same activities each time. These are:

A Identifying phonemes
B Blending
C Segementing phonemes and writing graphemes.

The only elements that change are the phonemes and graphemes which are being reinforced, and the words being used to determine the level that the children are at. By repeating the same format for the Assessment activities, you can ensure that the children's phonic knowledge is being reinforced, and therefore determine whether they are ready to move on to the next week.

Ⓐ IDENTIFYING PHONEMES
What to do
■ Read the words in table 1A for Assessment 1 (page 188), table 2A for Assessment 2 (page 189), table 3A for Assessment 3 (page 190) and table 4A for Assessment 4 (page 191) to the children. Ask them to tell you which phoneme they can hear repeated.
■ Note the phonemes the children have difficulty identifying next to the words in the table and write the total number of phonemes identified.

Ⓑ BLENDING
What to do
■ Read the words in table 1B for Assessment 1 (page 188), table 2B for Assessment 2 (page 189), table 3B for Assessment 3 (page 190) and table 4B for Assessment 4 (page 191), to check the children are able to blend the phonemes. Explain that some of the words are nonsense words.
■ Note any errors next to the words in the table and write the total number of words blended.

Ⓒ SEGMENTING PHONEMES AND WRITING GRAPHEMES
What to do
■ Read the words in table 1C for Assessment 1 (page 188), table 2C for Assessment 2 (page 189), table 3C for Assessment 3 (page 190) and table 4C for Assessment 4 (page 191) to the children and ask them to write the words down (segmenting phonemes and writing corresponding graphemes).
■ Record the total number of words read and correctly written.

> Record the child's progress for sections A to C in the corresponding tables for Assessments 1, 2, 3, or 4.

Child's name: Date:

ASSESSMENT **1** (following end of Week 12)

TABLE **1 A** IDENTIFYING PHONEMES

may	play	day
see	tree	bee
tie	pie	lie
boat	goat	float
Total number of phonemes identified (possible 4)		

TABLE **1 B** BLENDING

fay	dail	acrin	jee
feach	le	runny	hie
dight	fly	hi	coat
row	sold		
Total number of words blended and read (possible 14)			

TABLE **1 C** SEGMENTING PHONEMES AND WRITING GRAPHEMES

day	fail	acorn	fee
beach	he	bony	lie
right	cry	hi	coat
row	cold		
Total number of words correctly written (possible 14)			

Phonemes to be reinforced:
■ Ensure that the children are secure with these phonemes before proceeding with the programme.

Child's name:	Date:

ASSESSMENT ❷ (following end of Week 16)

TABLE ❷Ⓐ IDENTIFYING PHONEMES

moon	soon	school
book	cook	rook
make	rake	sake
time	file	hive
bone	lone	mode
cow	row	now
shout	mouse	doubt
coin	join	toil
boy	toy	joy
Total number of phonemes identified (possible 9):		

TABLE ❷Ⓑ BLENDING

soon	clue	bune
sook	could	put
blew	blake	bine
rone	lune	cow
mouse	joil	noy
Total number of words blended and read (possible 15)		

TABLE ❷Ⓒ SEGMENTING PHONEMES AND WRITING GRAPHEMES

hoop	true	dew	fuse
cook	should	put	take
hive	lone	now	shout
toil	joy		
Total number of words correctly written (possible 14)			

Phonemes to be reinforced:
- Ensure that children are secure with these phonemes before proceeding with the programme.

Child's name:	Date:

ASSESSMENT ❸ (following end of Week 19)

TABLE ❸ Ⓐ IDENTIFYING PHONEMES

burn	curl	hurl
shirt	fir	girl
term	fern	herb
earth	early	search
word	work	worm
haul	maul	August
door	floor	moor
warn	ward	wart
fork	corn	horn
claw	draw	paw
call	ball	fall
car	far	park
Total number of phonemes identified (possible 12)		

TABLE ❸ Ⓑ BLENDING

burl	fir	fern	earth
work	sauce	sork	moor
warn	baw	tall	dar
Total number of words blended and read (possible 12)			

TABLE ❸ Ⓒ SEGMENTING PHONEMES AND WRITING GRAPHEMES

burn	shirt	fern	heard
haul	fork	door	claw
ward	ball	dark	work
Total number of words correctly written (possible 12)			

Phonemes to be reinforced:
■ Ensure that children are secure with these phonemes before proceeding with the programme.

Child's name:	Date:

ASSESSMENT 4 (following end of Week 22)

TABLE 4 A IDENTIFYING PHONEMES

hair	fair	chair
bear	pear	wear
share	dare	fare
fear	ear	rear
sphere	mere	here
cheer	steer	peer
sure	pure	lure
tour	velour	detour
sister	teacher	preacher (omit if not taught)
Total number of phonemes identified (possible 9)		

TABLE 4 B BLENDING

jair	tear	mare	sear	
mere	steer	lure	tour	cover (omit if not taught)
Total number of words blended and read (possible 9)				

TABLE 4 C SEGMENTING PHONEMES AND WRITING GRAPHEMES

lair	tear	fare	rear	
here	peer	pure	tour	sister (omit if not taught)
Total number of words correctly written (possible 9)				

STAGES ONE TO THREE:
APPENDIX

STAGE TWO
ANSWERS TO SEGMENTATION AND BLENDING (SEE PAGE 36-37)

Word	No. of phonemes	Split the word into phonemes	Word	No. of phonemes	Split the word into phonemes
that	3	/th/a/t/	dress	4	/d/r/e/ss/
ship	3	/sh/i/p/	scrap	5	/s/c/r/a/p/
thing	3	/th/i/ng/	flop	4	/f/l/o/p/
splash	5	/s/p/l/a/sh/	stand	5	/s/t/a/n/d/
day	2	/d/ay/	make	3	/m/a/k/e
train	4	/t/r/ai/n/	green	4	/g/r/ee/n/
spoon	4	/s/p/oo/n/	smoke	4	/s/m/o/k/e
girl	3	/g/ir/l/	grass	4	/g/r/a/ss/
burn	3	/b/ur/n/	join	3	/j/oi/n/
three	3	/th/r/ee/	bear	2	/b/ear/
sound	4	/s/ou/n/d/	horse	3	/h/or/se/
spoil	4	/s/p/oi/l/	know	2	/kn/ow/

STAGE THREE
ANSWERS TO PHONEME QUIZ (SEE PAGE 102)

1. sail, mail, fail **2.** /igh/ **3.** 'ow', 'ou' **4.** bone
5. 'ur', 'ir', 'er' **6.** 'e', 'y' **7.** 'ar', 'e', 'u', 'or', 'er'
8. tie, right, shy or time, cide **9.** make, dime, lone, tune **10.** 'y'

STAGE THREE
ANSWERS TO COUNTING PHONEMES ACCURATELY (SEE PAGE 102)

Word	Divide into phonemes	Number of phonemes
brain	/b/r/ai/n/	4
tree	/t/r/ee/	3
crime	/c/r/i/m/e/	4
float	/f/l/oa/t/	4
wait	/w/ai/t/	3
groan	/g/r/oa/n/	4
stew	/s/t/ew/	3
shark	/sh/ar/k/	3
stern	/s/t/er/n/	4
horse	/h/or/se/	3
shout	/sh/ou/t/	3
bear	/b/ear/	2
square	/s/q/u/are/	4
green	/g/r/ee/n/	4
teacher	/t/ea/ch/er/	4

TERMINOLOGY
A full glossary of terms is included below.
It is important to be clear of the following terms:

Alliteration A sequence of words beginning with the same sound.
Blend A combination of letters where individual letters retain their sounds.
Blending To draw individual sounds together to pronounce a word, for example: '/c/l/a/p/' blended together reads 'clap'.
Digraph Two letters which combine to make a new sound.
Grapheme A letter or combinations of letters that represent a phoneme.
Consonant blends The consonants retain their original sounds but are blended together as in 'slip'.
Long vowel sounds The long vowel phonemes and their corresponding graphemes as in 'feel' or 'cold'.
Mnemonic A device for remembering something, such as '/ee/ee/ Feel the tree'.
Phoneme The smallest single identifiable sound, for example: the letters 'ch' representing one sound.
Rhyme Words that sound the same but do not necessarily share the same spelling.
Segmenting Splitting up a word into its individual phonemes in order to spell it, that is: the word 'pat' has three phonemes – '/p/a/t/'.
Split digraph Two letters, making one sound, for example: 'a–e' as in 'cake'.
Syllable A unit of pronunciation having one vowel sound. This can be taught by identifying 'beats' in a word. Putting a hand flat underneath your chin and then saying a word can help, as every time the hand moves, it represents another syllable.
Trigraph Three letters which combine to make a new sound.

FURTHER READING
Adams, MJ (1990) *Beginning to Read: Thinking and Learning about Print.* Cambridge, MA: MIT Press
Brooks, G (2003) *Sound Sense: the phonics element of the National Literacy Strategy.* Report to the DfES, July 2003
DfES, (2006) Rose, J *The Independent Review of the Teaching of Early Reading: Final Report* Ref: 0201-2006DOC-EN
Ehri, L C, Nunes, SR, Stahl, AS and Willows, DA (2001) *Systematic phonics instruction helps children learn to read: evidence from the National Reading Panel's meta-analysis* Review of Educational Research, 71, 3, 393-447
Watson, J Johnston, R (2005) *The Effects Of Synthetic Phonics Teaching On Reading and Spelling Attainment: A Seven Year Longitudinal Study.* Report to The Scottish Executive (www.scotland.gov.uk)